Frauke Hofmeister und Dietmar Böhnke (Hrsg.)

Kulturkontakte
Cultures in Contact

Essays für Joachim Schwend

Joachim Schwend im Kontakt mit steinalten Zeugnissen irischer Kultur

Frauke Hofmeister und Dietmar Böhnke (Hrsg.)

Kulturkontakte
Cultures in Contact

Essays für Joachim Schwend

Edition
Hamouda

1. Auflage
Alle Rechte vorbehalten
Umschlagbild und Sektionstitel: Hans-Walter Schmidt-Hannisa
Covergestaltung: Kati Voigt und Julia Walch
Druck: PBtisk s. r. o., Příbram
© Edition Hamouda, Leipzig, Juli 2014
ISBN 978-3-940075-92-5
www.hamouda.de

Tabula Gratulatoria

Katrin Berndt, Bremen
Dietmar Böhnke, Leipzig
Reinhild und Gunter Böhnke, Leipzig
Alexander Brock, Halle-Wittenberg
Stefani Brusberg-Kiermeier, Hildesheim
Isabelle Buchstaller, Leipzig
Anne Cäsar, Leipzig
Ian Campbell, Edinburgh
Heide Cech, Germersheim
Sabine Coelsch-Foisner, Salzburg
Hilary Dannenberg, Trier
Christel Drescher, Bellheim
Maria Fleischhack, Leipzig
Crister S. Garrett, Leipzig
Dagmar Hirschberg, München
Frauke Hofmeister, Leipzig
Jürgen Kramer, Dortmund
Thomas Kühn, Dresden
Paul Kußmaul, Germersheim
Stefan Lampadius, Leipzig
Fergal Lenehan, Jena
Frank Liedtke, Leipzig
Gabriele Linke, Rostock
Wolfgang Lörscher, Leipzig
Katharina und Michael Magnus, Donnbronn
Sophia Manns-Süßbrich, Leipzig
Silvia Mergenthal, Konstanz
Rudolf Mikus, Germersheim
Katharina und Johannes von Miller, Bad Wiessee
Paul Monks, Landau-Mörzheim
Klaus Peter Müller, Mainz
David Nisters, Leipzig
Anette Pankratz, Bochum
Clausdirk Pollner, Leipzig
Klaus Pörtl, Germersheim
Sylvia Reuter, Leipzig
Jürgen Ronthaler, Leipzig
Stephanie Roscher und Friedrich Schmidt-Roscher, Haßloch/Pfalz
Ingrid von Rosenberg und Gerd Stratmann, Berlin
Danuta Rytel-Schwarz und Wolfgang F. Schwarz, Leipzig
Anna Saunders, Bangor, Wales
Barbara Schaffeld, Lilienthal
Norbert Schaffeld, Bremen
Elmar Schenkel, Leipzig
Norbert Schlüter, Leipzig
Ulrich Johannes Schneider, Leipzig
Doris Schönefeld, Leipzig
Marie Schönherr, Leipzig
Beate Schwend, Essingen
Jürgen Schwend, Riedlingen/Donau
Beate Seidel, Leipzig
Kathleen Starck, Landau
Clarissa Steger, Leipzig
Richard Stinshoff, Oldenburg
Karl-Heinz Stoll, Germersheim
Klaus Stolz, Chemnitz
Christian Todenhagen, Chico, CA
Alfonso de Toro, Leipzig
Peter J. Tosic, Leipzig
Kati Voigt, Leipzig
Hermann Völkel, Germersheim
Julia Walch, Bad Soden
Stefan Welz, Leipzig

Department of German, University College Cork, Ireland
German Department, National University of Ireland, Galway
Institut für Anglistik, Universität Leipzig
Institute for American Studies, Universität Leipzig
Seminar für Englische Philologie der Universität Göttingen
Universitätsbibliothek Leipzig
Zentrum für Lehrerbildung und Schulforschung, Universität Leipzig

Inhaltsverzeichnis – Table of Contents

Dietmar Böhnke und **Frauke Hofmeister**
Einleitung: Kulturen, Kontakte, Charaktere
… *and Congratulatory Complications*   8

Dietmar Böhnke
Scots and Saxons – Notes on an Unfinished Project, or:
Conspicuous *VerSchwendung*   19

Grenzüberschreitungen – Crossing Borders

Paul Kußmaul
„Sind die aber komisch!" Kulturkontakt im Alltag   35

Claire O'Reilly
As Time Goes By:
Some Thoughts on the Year Abroad as a Vehicle of *Kulturkontakt*   46

Elmar Schenkel
Velozipedische Kulturwissenschaft.
Über Roland Girtlers Radtour nach Italien   62

Gabriele Linke
Aufbruch zu neuen Welten: Fahrräder und andere Verkehrsmittel
in schottischen autobiographischen Texten   70

Gert Hofmann
„Dass alle heiligen Orte der Erde zusammen sind um einen Ort …"
Hölderlins Frankreichreise und die Geburt einer neuen Poetik   84

Kathleen Starck
Die Regionen, der Professor und ich   94

Mediale Kulturkontakte – Cultural Encounters in the Media and the Arts

Ian Campbell
Understanding and Misunderstanding Scottish Fiction   105

Jürgen Ronthaler
Royal Representation and Self-Representation: Analysing Images
of British Royalty in Photographs and Other Media   117

Fergal Lenehan
"I am aware you don't speak German – yet".
Depicting Germans on Irish Television   133

Rita Singer
„Vielen Dank im Voraus, meidet die Menschen und bleibt gesund", oder:
Die hohe Kunst der universitären E-Mail-Korrespondenz   145

Hans-Walter Schmidt-Hannisa
Irish Zen   155

Diachrone Kulturkontakte – The Past and the Present

Jürgen Kramer
Von den Möglichkeiten und Grenzen kultureller Einflüsse –
Am Beispiel des Brandes von London 1666 und seinen
städtebaulichen Folgen   167

Anna Saunders
Memorialising the 'Heldenstadt der DDR'   181

David Nisters
Open Texts and Reanimated Authors:
Roland Barthes and Medieval Manuscript Culture   194

Christian Todenhagen
What on Earth Was I Thinking?
Linguistics' Role in Re-viewing the Past Reluctantly   206

Sabine Coelsch-Foisner
Erinnerung an eine Flusswanderung, oder:
Gedanken zum „Museal Turn"   212

Transferleistungen – Transfer and Translation

Crister Garrett
Britain's Place in the Transatlantic Space: Cultural Studies,
International Politics, and Narrative Choices   219

Klaus Stolz
The Americanisation of British Democracy?   233

Clausdirk Pollner
"The Twits? They're Just Eejits!"
Matthew Fitt Translates Roald Dahl into Scots   245

Thomas Kühn
„Popular Culture" –
Kulturkontakt und die Übersetzung eines Terminus   250

Anne Koenen
Dachshund Revisited, or: Excesses of Consumerism   266

Dietmar Böhnke und Frauke Hofmeister (Leipzig)*
Einleitung: Kulturen, Kontakte, Charaktere
... and Congratulatory Complications

So what's this book about, then? It's a Festschrift *in disguise, isn't it?*

Eine wie auch immer geartete Festschrift für Joachim Schwend ist eindeutig eine heikle Sache, selbst in dem Jahr, in dem er zu unser aller Verwunderung bereits das *retiring age* erreicht. Wahre Bescheidenheit, Verweigerung des Professoren-Kults, vielleicht sogar konsumkritische und ökologische Anmerkungen zur Produktion eines weiteren materiellen Gutes mögen dem entgegenstehen. Und doch: Gerade derjenige, der es ablehnt, so herausgehoben zu werden, hat eine Würdigung verdient, finden wir. Aber möglichst eine, bei der er nicht auf einen Sockel gestellt wird, sondern gewissermaßen in „gemütlicher Runde" kollegial gefeiert wird. Wie wäre es also mit einer unprätentiösen Sammlung unterschiedlichster und vor allem kurzer Beiträge von jüngeren und nicht mehr ganz so jungen Weggefährten, die man vielleicht auch noch vor dem Zubettgehen (also nach den Deutschlandfunk-Nachrichten) oder bei einer schönen

---

* Frauke Hofmeister ist wissenschaftliche Mitarbeiterin an der Philologischen Fakultät der Universität Leipzig, was sie zu einem großen Teil Joachim Schwend zu verdanken hat. 2005 erklärte dieser sich bereit, die Betreuung der Dissertation einer ihm quasi völlig unbekannten frischgebackenen Diplom-Kulturwirtin von der Universität Passau zu übernehmen. Diese Arbeit mit dem Titel *Making English Regions. The Construction of Regional Images in the North East, the West Midlands and the South West of England* konnte sie zunächst im Rahmen des Promotionsstudienganges „Regionalisierung und Transnationalisierung" und dann auch als Mitarbeiterin in den Kulturstudien Großbritanniens erfolgreich abschließen. Tief beeindruckt war und ist sie davon, wie viel Vertrauen Joachim Schwend ihr und anderen in persönlicher und beruflicher Hinsicht von Anfang an entgegengebracht hat. Auch die Tatsache, dass er während ihrer Promotionsphase zweimal „Doktor-Opa" wurde, hat seinen Glauben an einen erfolgreichen Abschluss nicht erschüttern können. Frauke Hofmeister hat diverse wissenschaftliche Beiträge veröffentlicht, u.a. zur Regionalisierung Englands, zur Lehre in den Cultural Studies und zu Denkmälern als Medien der Erinnerungskultur. [Zur Biografie Dietmar Böhnke vgl. nächster Beitrag.]

Tasse Tee lesen mag? Ein kleines aber feines Buch, das wissenschaftlichen Anspruch mit Lesbarkeit vereint, gewürzt mit Herzlichkeit und Humor, und das außerdem verschiedenste alte und neue Interessen des Geehrten abdeckt oder sogar miteinander verbindet? So etwas könnte doch auch Jochen (wie er von den meisten Kollegen, Familie und Freunden genannt wird) gefallen – und mit ihm auch anderen Lesern, mögen sie Joachim Schwend nun kennen oder nicht. Vielleicht sollte man es eher als „Fastschrift" bezeichnen, gewissermaßen als Dekonstruktion des Genres von innen. Immerhin hat Joachim selbst an verschiedenen Festschriften mitgewirkt und kann sich somit kaum beschweren…

Well, I suppose it's a very German thing, this Festschrift *business. We don't even have a word for it in English. Why not simply give it a catchy title and put "Essays for Joachim" on the cover – what counts, after all, is having so many of your friends and colleagues assembled in one book. And in any case, to paraphrase George Orwell: By the time you are sixty-five, you get the book you deserve.*

Verdient hat Joachim Schwend aber mit Sicherheit ein Buch, dessen Thema eine Relevanz für ihn als Mensch, als Lehrenden und Forschenden besitzt. Dass es etwas mit Kultur – oder besser: mit Kulturen! – zu tun haben muss, versteht sich eigentlich von selbst. Schließlich ist er nicht umsonst Professor für Kulturstudien Großbritanniens in Leipzig geworden. Und selbst wenn er nie müde wird, die Problematik dieses Begriffs zu betonen, wie diverse Studentengenerationen bestätigen können, so ist er doch auch ein echter „Kulturmensch", ein Liebhaber der Literatur und des Reisens. Nun ist natürlich die Kultur, zumal im Plural und in ihrer kulturstudientypischen Ausprägung als *whole ways of life* (um den von Joachim sehr verehrten Raymond Williams zu bemühen), kaum in dieser Form zu behandeln, selbst wenn wir Zeit bis zum 100. Geburtstag hätten.

Hier hilft jedoch ein Blick in Joachims „Leben und Werk", wie es im Festschrift-Jargon heißen würde. Bereits zu Beginn seines Lebens in Schwäbisch Hall und Backnang spielt ein preußisch-schwäbischer Kulturkontakt eine entscheidende Rolle. Der von ihm immer wieder betonte Kontakt zwischen Kultur und Natur lässt sich mindestens bis zu seiner Zeit als Pfadfinder zurückverfolgen, welche nicht nur die Grundlagen für seine Liebe zur Natur und zu Tieren (v.a. Hunden) legte, sondern ihm später auch bei diversen Auslandsaufenthalten und gelegentlichen weidmännischen und holzfällerischen Aufgaben zugutekam. Wann genau er den ersten Kontakt mit der Fahrradkultur machte, ist nicht überliefert, aber er wird auch in diese Frühphase fallen.

All dies führte gewissermaßen zwangsläufig zu einem Studium (an der Universität Mainz in Germersheim), welches sich mit Kontakten zwischen verschiedenen Kulturen und den interkulturellen Vermittlungsversuchen in Form von Übersetzen und Dolmetschen beschäftigte – die Wahl der englischen und russischen Kultur und Sprache als Fächer steht symbolisch für Joachims ungewöhnliches Interesse an den zu dieser Zeit konträr entgegengesetzten Kulturen von Ost und West, das später sicher auch zu seiner Entscheidung beitrug, in den deutschen Osten zu gehen. In die Studienzeit fällt auch sein erster längerer Auslandsaufenthalt in London (sozusagen als praktischer Kulturkontakt), welcher ihn offensichtlich so faszinierte, dass er später noch zweimal längere Zeit auf den „Inseln" verbrachte, in den 1980er Jahren in Dublin und zu Beginn der 1990er in Edinburgh – womit auch schon die regionalen Schwerpunkte seiner Forschung benannt wären: England, Schottland und Irland. Nachdem er sich zunächst dem innerenglischen Kulturkontakt zwischen Literatur und Literaturkritik gewidmet hatte (Dissertation zu John Wain 1983, vgl. Schwend 1984), wendete er sich bald den anglo-schottischen und anglo-irischen Themen zu, immer noch mit einem literarischen Schwerpunkt aber schon zunehmend in die gesellschaftlichen und kulturellen Kontexte ausgreifend (Habilitation zur Rolle der Kirche in der schottischen Literatur 1992, vgl. Schwend 1996). Eine wichtige Rolle in dieser Zeit spielte sicherlich das unter seinem Doktorvater Horst W. Drescher gegründete *Scottish Studies Centre* in Germersheim, an dessen Arbeit Joachim viele Jahre maßgeblich beteiligt war und durch das er viele Kontakte nach Schottland knüpfte. Besonders wichtig waren ihm immer auch die studentischen und institutionellen Kontakte mit Großbritannien und Irland, u.a. über das Erasmus-Programm, für die er sich bis heute sehr einsetzt.

Der größte Umschwung in Joachims (Arbeits-)Leben nahm seinen Anfang in Leipzig, noch bevor er seinen Fuß in diese Stadt gesetzt hat. Die hiesigen Montagsdemonstrationen im Jahr 1989 lösten Veränderungen in der DDR aus, die schließlich zum Fall der Mauer und zur Wiedervereinigung führten und somit Joachims Wechsel nach Leipzig 1992 (noch als wissenschaftlicher Mitarbeiter) überhaupt erst möglich machten. Auch hier spielten persönliche Ost-West-Kontakte, u.a. zu Prof. Wolfgang Thiele von der Leipziger Anglistik, eine entscheidende Rolle. Dieser Wechsel brachte jedoch nicht nur einen Ortswechsel, sondern neben diversen privaten Veränderungen auch eine entscheidende fachliche Neuorientierung mit sich, hin zu den Cultural Studies und Fragen von regionalen Identitäten und politischen Systemen im europäischen Kontext, Erinnerungs- und Konsumkulturen sowie Migration und Diaspora – alles wiederum Themen, die Kulturkontakte voraussetzen oder sie zum Untersuchungsgegenstand machen. Zusätzlich dazu ergaben sich diverse neue konkrete Kontakte, v.a. nach Irland (Cork, Galway etc.), aber auch nach Wales (Bangor).

Es kann somit nur das eine Thema für diesen Band geben, nämlich „Kulturkontakte" – und dies wird aus diversen Perspektiven und von verschiedenen Wegbegleitern Joachims beleuchtet, die sich auf den oben geschilderten Werdegang beziehen. Gefeiert werden soll also dieser „Kulturkontakt", der der Leipziger Anglistik einen Kollegen und der Kulturstudienabteilung ab 2000 einen („spätberufenen") Professor bescherte, wie man ihn sich kompetenter, kollegialer, hilfsbereiter, bescheidener und arbeitseifriger (selbst wenn es um ungeliebte Studiendekansarbeiten ging) kaum denken kann – aber Vorsicht, hinter diesem „kalvinistischen" Joachim Jekyll verbirgt sich der ironisch-bissige und hintersinnige, *spoon-feeding*-hassende, in Vorlesungen gern zum *Dachshund Turn* abschweifende Royalist Franz Eberhard Hyde!

Well, Jochen & Hyde is going a bit too far, don't you think? Rather, what all this reminds me of is David Lodge's novel Changing Places, *one of Joachim's favourite reads, I believe. Let's just hope he didn't have to play that embarrassing game about the most important work of literature (or cultural theory?) that you've never read – but then, there aren't too many of those in his case. So you're saying his life and work is all about contacts and exchanges, and intercultural relationships; I'm sure you can find some fancy teutonic phrase or concept to make it sound just a little more* wissenschaftlich...

Tatsächlich pflegt und predigt Joachim Schwend in guter Cultural Studies-Manier ein eher pragmatisches Verhältnis zu theoretischen Diskussionen (vgl. Schwend 2003: 302), sodass wir uns auch hier nicht allzu lange mit Definitionen und Typologien beschäftigen möchten. Meist wird der Begriff „Kulturkontakt" für Begegnungen zwischen dem „Eigenen" und dem „Fremden" verwendet, zunächst vor allem in der Kolonialgeschichte (Bitterli 1976), dann auch zunehmend im Zusammenhang mit Migration oder auch Berührungen unterschiedlicher (Sub-)Kulturen innerhalb einer Gesellschaft. Im Englischen taucht in diesen Zusammenhängen gerne der Begriff *cultural encounters* auf. Galt das Augenmerk lange dem Konfliktpotential durch das Zusammentreffen verschiedener Kulturen, wurden diese spätestens seit den 1990er Jahren vor allem als Entwicklungsmotor angesehen (vgl. z.B. Hoerder 2002), und die Untersuchung von gegenseitigen Einflüssen dieser *cultures in contact* und ihrer Hybridisierungen in sogenannten *contact zones* ist in den Vordergrund gerückt. Damit wird auch berücksichtigt, dass eine Kultur natürlich kein stabiles und homogenes Gebilde, und dass der Einzelne immer Teil mehrerer, sich zum Teil überlagernder (Sub-)Kulturen ist.

I knew you could do it – that's just like the 'cloudy metaphysicians' we've always known you to be, Professor Heavysternes and Teufelsdröckhs all of you. To me, it's much more down-to-earth, like in Joachim's understanding of the ultimate aim of his teaching: "[t]he quintessence of Cultural Studies can be seen in the wish to acquire a sound knowledge of one's own culture and of a foreign culture so that in a dialogic process comparisons can be made and that cross-cultural communication is nurtured and not precluded." (Schwend 2001: 29) and "Cultural Studies can teach us to see by means of creativity and inspiration, to build bridges between cultures and to achieve understanding beyond frontiers." (ibid.: 32).

Die Beiträge in diesem Band für den „Brückenbauer" Joachim Schwend greifen die „klassische" Bedeutung von „Kulturkontakt" zwar in mancherlei Hinsicht auf, erstrecken sich aber gleichzeitig auf weit vielfältigere Arten von Kontakten. Ein Großteil der Artikel wurde dabei zunächst von sehr persönlichen Kontakten zwischen den Autoren und dem Menschen und Wissenschaftler Joachim Schwend inspiriert. Da wir auch aus eigener Erfahrung die grundlegende Bedeutung dieser zwischenmenschlichen Ebene – die ja auch eine Art Kulturkontakt darstellt – für jeglichen fachlichen und wissenschaftlichen Austausch sehr zu schätzen wissen, ermutigten wir alle Beiträger, ihren Artikeln ein persönliches Vorwort voranzustellen oder sogar einen rein persönlichen Beitrag zu verfassen – letztere befinden sich farblich abgesetzt am Ende der Sektionen. Gleichzeitig zeigen alle Beiträge in der Wahl ihrer Gegenstände, auf welch vielfältigen Ebenen Kulturkontakte analysiert und erlebt werden können. In jedem Falle aber findet sich ein Bezug zu Joachim Schwends eigenen Interessen oder Forschungsschwerpunkten.

Nice work – at least you are not hiding the fact that like any other Festschrift *this one is also largely characterised by the sheer variety of contributions concerning topics, purposes and style. So what then is your grand narrative to create an imagined* Kulturkontakt *community, so to speak?*

Trotz der Vielfalt der Beiträge lassen sich gemeinsame Linien und Schwerpunkte erkennen. Ganz generell wird die oben bereits erwähnte Einstellung deutlich, dass Kontakte zwischen Kulturen immer einen *third space* eröffnen (um ein auch von Joachim immer wieder gern verwendetes Schlagwort zu gebrauchen), in dem sich Identitäten begegnen, mischen und verwirren, aber auch Neues entstehen kann – und dass dies grundlegend positiv konnotiert und als Chance begriffen wird. Konkreter widmen sich die Artikel unterschiedlichen aber miteinander korrespondierenden Themenbereichen, die sich hier in vier größeren Sektionen wiederfinden. Die erste Sektion wendet sich der wohl offensichtlichsten Form des Kulturkontaktes zu: dem Reisen. Denn dabei überschreiten Individuen sichtbare und auch unsichtbare Grenzen. Paul Kußmaul beschäftigt sich in seinem Beitrag mit den Missverständnissen, die sich dabei auf verschiedensten Ebenen ergeben können. Claire O'Reilly wertet die Erfahrungen und nachträglichen Bewertungen irischer Austauschstudierender in Deutschland aus. Elmar Schenkel folgt dem radelnden Kulturwissenschaftler Roland Girtler nach Italien. Nicht ganz zufällig spielt das Fahrrad auch in Gabriele Linkes Beitrag eine zentrale Rolle: neben anderen Verkehrsmitteln erlaubt es den Schotten unterschiedlichsten Alters und Standes, deren Autobiografien sie untersucht, geografische wie soziale Grenzen zu überschreiten. In allen diesen Fällen bewirkt das Reisen auch eine Veränderung des Reisenden – in besonderer Weise gilt dies auch für die Frankreichreise Friedrich Hölderlins, die Gert Hofmann in seinem Beitrag fokussiert. Die Sektion wird abgeschlossen von Kathleen Starcks sehr persönlicher Reflexion ihrer eigenen Reisen und Grenzüberschreitungen, die teilweise von Joachim Schwend inspiriert und indirekt begleitet wurden.

All right, we all know that travelling and crossing borders brings different cultures into contact and doesn't leave the traveller unchanged – not least from personal experience. Duns Scotus could have told you as much centuries ago, or H.V. Morton, say (I am not going to start with David Lodge again). We do see the world differently away from home – even without Homi…

In der zweiten Sektion geht es um mediale Kulturkontakte im weitesten Sinn – Berührungen verschiedener Kulturen in Literatur, Fernsehen, Photographie und neuen Medien. Ian Campbell diskutiert die Ambivalenz des (Miss)Verstehens in und von schottischen Texten u.a. von J.M. Barrie, John Galt und Walter Scott, und zeigt, wie das Betrachten des vermeintlich Bekannten mit neuen Augen zu überraschenden Einsichten führen kann. Jürgen Ronthaler analysiert das Spannungsfeld von Tradition und Innovation in der (Selbst-)Darstellung der britischen Royals v.a. in Taufbildern – aus aktuellem Anlass, aber mit historischen Vergleichen. Fergal Lenehan widmet sich der oft satirischen Repräsentation der Deutschen im irischen Fernsehen. Auch in der E-Mail-Kommunikation prallen zuweilen verschiedene Kulturen aufeinander, wie Rita Singer – wiederum persönlich inspiriert vom Geehrten dieses Bandes, einem Meister der skurril-hintersinnigen Korrespondenz – exemplarisch und augenzwinkernd darlegt. Der Fotoessay „Irish Zen" von Hans-Walter Schmidt-Hannisa (von dem auch das Cover-Foto dieses Bandes und die Sektionsbilder stammen) lässt wiederum ganz eigene Reflexionen zum Thema Natur/Kulturkontakte zu. Gemeinsam ist diesen Beiträgen die Betonung der medialen Vermittlung von Kultur(en) und der Relevanz von sich ständig wandelnden *signifying practices* (um noch einmal Raymond Williams zu bemühen).

Something with ‚media' always sells, of course, especially these days. And we know that every decoding is another encoding. Who said that again – the late Stuart Hall? Or was it Morris Zapp? I do like the photos, by the way.

Ging es bisher vor allem um die Berührungen mit und zwischen gleichzeitig existierenden Kulturen, richtet die dritte Sektion das Augenmerk auf Begegnungen zwischen Vergangenheit und Gegenwart (*the past is* schließlich auch *a foreign country…*). Jürgen Kramer zeigt in seinem Beitrag zur Stadtentwicklung Londons nach dem Brand von 1666, dass sich das heutige architektonische Ensemble der Metropole zwar teilweise aus kontinentalen Vorbildern speist, eine weitgehende Angleichung an diese aber ausblieb. Anna Saunders widmet sich dem durchaus ambivalenten Umgang der Stadt Leipzig mit der eigenen „Heldengeschichte". David Nisters setzt Roland Barthes' poststrukturalistische Ideen in Beziehung zu mittelalterlichen Vorstellungen von Autorschaft und Text. Die nachträgliche Sinngebung eigener Taten und Versäumnisse aus linguistisch-philosophischer Sicht ist das Thema des Beitrags von Christian Todenhagen. Abgeschlossen wird die Sektion wiederum von sehr persönlichen Reflexionen des eigenen und gesellschaftlichen Umgangs mit Vergangenheit, Gegenwart und Zukunft von Sabine Coelsch-Foisner. Geschichte und Vergangenheit werden hier im Sinne der Cultural Studies als (gegenwärtige) kulturelle Konstruktion gedeutet, die immer nach ihrem jeweiligen Kontext und den beteiligten Produzenten befragt werden sollte.

Well, that's what I call culture: medieval manuscripts, splendid architecture, museums and monuments. As Karl Valentin so aptly put it: even our future used to be better in the past. But to be honest: the past often is a foreign country to me – the good thing about getting older is that you forget so much that wasn't really worth remembering in the first place.

In der vierten Sektion stehen schließlich Transferleistungen unterschiedlicher Art im Mittelpunkt. Zunächst geht es um die Beziehungen zwischen den USA und Großbritannien. Crister S. Garrett stellt heraus, wie und mit welchen Konsequenzen das eigene internationale Rollenverständnis der Briten von der Einbettung in unterschiedliche Erzählungen geprägt ist. Klaus Stolz' Analyse der vermeintlichen Amerikanisierung der britischen Demokratie zeigt, dass Kulturkontakte keinesfalls in Angleichung enden müssen. Zwei weitere Beiträge widmen sich dann sprachlichen Transferleistungen: Clausdirk Pollner betrachtet eine Literaturübersetzung vom Englischen ins Schottische, während Thomas Kühn sich mit den Schwierigkeiten der Übersetzung von „popular culture" ins Deutsche auseinandersetzt. All diesen Ausführungen liegt die Erkenntnis zugrunde, dass Transferleistungen allenthalben gefragt und vonnöten, oft aber komplex, provisorisch und kompromisshaft sind. Den Abschluss der Sektion und des Bandes bildet Anne Koenens Aufruf (Joachim vermutlich aus dem Herzen gesprochen und von seinem tierischen *alter ego* inspiriert), die Prinzipien der Konsumgesellschaft nicht auf alle Lebensbereiche zu übertragen, und die Kulturkontakte zwischen Mensch und Tier nicht als Einbahnstraße zu betrachten. Vielleicht sind Hunde ja doch die besseren Menschen…

Are you suggesting Joachim is going to turn into a dachshund on retiring? (Well, he wouldn't mind, I suppose…) I think this is taking both the translation and transfer metaphors and the Jekyll & Hyde theme one step too far. In any case, some kind of transformation is in the air, so it's probably just as well to end on this note of uncertainty and provisionality coupled with opportunity.

Da wir sowohl dieses Buch als auch Joachims Lehr- und Forschungstätigkeit (unter dem Motto „in der Welt unterwegs – der Region verpflichtet") als durchaus unabgeschlossenes Projekt betrachten, wollen wir den Band mit einem Beitrag beginnen, der ebenfalls ein *unfinished project* beschreibt, das sich mit einem von Joachim Schwends Kernthemen, den regionalen Identitäten im europäischen Kontext, beschäftigt und in diesem Zusammenhang nicht nur die Bandbreite und die Hauptströmungen in seinen Schriften aufzeigt, sondern ihm möglicherweise auch Anregungen für die Verwendung all der Zeit gibt, die dem „Jubilar" (einmal dürfen wir dieses Wort verwenden…) mit dem Eintritt in seine *Golden Years* bald zur Verfügung stehen wird.

So bleibt uns an dieser Stelle nur noch das Vergnügen, all denen zu danken, die zum Gelingen dieses Bandes beigetragen haben. Dazu gehören natürlich in erster Linie die Autoren, die mit ihren anregenden und unterhaltsamen Beiträgen das Buch überhaupt erst ermöglichten. Zum Teil griffen sie sogar Joachims Arbeitsethos auf und reichten ihre Beiträge deutlich vor der vereinbarten Deadline ein. Alle warteten geduldig auf unsere Anmerkungen und setzten sie dann zügig um – herzlichen Dank für die Mitwirkung, Geduld und Kooperation! Das Institut für Anglistik der Universität Leipzig stellt nicht nur einige der Verfasser, sondern ist auch maßgeblich an der Finanzierung dieses Bandes beteiligt. Die muttersprachliche Kontrolle der meisten englischen Beiträge in Rekordzeit verdanken wir Fiona Hynes, und Kati Voigt gestaltete mit Kreativität und Knowhow den Einband (mit dankenswerter Unterstützung von Julia Walch). Ganz herzlich danken wir Fayçal Hamouda für seine Bereitschaft, diesen Band in sein Verlagsprogramm aufzunehmen, und für die geduldige Begleitung dieses Projektes. Besonderer Dank gilt auch all denjenigen Kollegen und Weggefährten von Joachim Schwend, die sich zwar nicht mit einem Beitrag im Band wiederfinden, die das Projekt jedoch im Geiste ebenfalls begleiteten, wie auch die lange Liste der Gratulanten am Anfang dieses Buches deutlich macht (und eine Entschuldigung denen, die wir evtl. ganz vergessen haben – dies war sicher keine Absicht). Dem disziplinierten Stillschweigen aller dieser Beteiligten und dem unauffälligen Agieren unserer hilfsbereiten Informanten, die so manche unserer Wissenslücken bezüglich Joachims „Leben und Werk" schließen konnten, ist es zu verdanken, dass dieser Band auch eine echte Überraschung sein dürfte.

Lieber Jochen, wir hoffen sehr, mit dieser „Fastschrift" deinen Geschmack getroffen zu haben, und wünschen dir alles erdenklich Gute für den kommenden Lebensabschnitt, egal ob du ihn als *sheep farmer* in Irland, als Dauergast in der Universitätsbibliothek oder als radelnder Feldforscher verbringen möchtest.

Well, let's not get sentimental (wipes a tear from her/his left eye)*:*
Cheers, Joachim, here's to you! (strictly no alcohol, of course)

Quellen

Bitterli, Urs (1976), *Die „Wilden" und die „Zivilisierten": Grundzüge einer Geistes- und Kulturgeschichte der europäisch-überseeischen Begegnung*, München: Beck.

Hoerder, Dirk (2002), *Cultures in Contact: World Migrations in the Second Millennium*, Durham, NC: Duke University Press.

Schwend, Joachim (1984), *John Wain. Schriftsteller und Kritiker* (Anglistische Forschungen 173), Heidelberg: Winter.

Schwend, Joachim (1996), *Kirk, Gesellschaft und Literatur: Die Kirche im Kontext der literarischen Tradition Schottlands* (Scottish Studies 20), Frankfurt/Main: Peter Lang.

Schwend, Joachim *et al.* (2001), „Cultural Studies and National Academia: A panel discussion between scholars from the U.S., Japan and Germany", in Steffi Richter & Annette Schad-Seifert, Hrsg., *Cultural Studies and Japan*, Leipzig: Leipziger Universitätsverlag, 21-39.

Schwend, Joachim (2003), „'Culture is Ordinary' (Raymond Williams). Kultur und Kulturstudien – Entwicklungen und Tendenzen", in Christa Grimm, Ilse Nagelschmidt & Ludwig Stockinger, Hrsg., *Theorie und Praxis der Kulturstudien* (Literatur und Kultur. Leipziger Texte – Reihe A: Dialoge und Kolloquien 3), 285-305.

Dietmar Böhnke (Leipzig)*
Scots and Saxons – Notes on an Unfinished Project, or: Conspicuous *VerSchwendung*

At this point in time, I have known Joachim Schwend for exactly half of my life. I was his student at Leipzig in the 1990s and profited enormously from the cultural transfer to Saxony of his expertise on all things Scottish. He supervised my MA thesis on the contemporary Scottish author James Kelman with his characteristic competence, generosity and good humour, and was one of the inspirations behind and readers of my PhD on another Scot, Alasdair Gray. My start as a university lecturer came when I substituted one half of him, so to speak, during his time as stand-in professor in Germersheim from 1999. When he came back to Leipzig as Professor of British Cultural Studies the following year, I was allowed to continue as his colleague and a little later won that rarest of prizes in the German academic lottery: a full and permanent post as lecturer – not least thanks to his help and support. He was also instrumental in my successfully applying for a five-month period as Visiting Research Fellow at the Institute for Advanced Studies in the Humanities at the University of Edinburgh in 2005, a position he himself had held in 1990, and his own Doktorvater Horst W. Drescher (the late doyen of Scottish Studies in Germany) before him. It is only fitting, therefore, that the following thoughts are based on my research project during that stay (though they remain tentative). Warmest thanks, dear Jochen, for your help, support and friendship over so many years – I very much hope this will also remain an unfinished project for a long time to come.

---

* Dietmar Böhnke is Senior Lecturer in British Cultural Studies at the University of Leipzig. His research interests include the Victorian Age and its contemporary rewritings; Scottish literature and culture; and the British media, especially film. He has published various articles on these topics, as well as two books on contemporary Scottish authors: *Kelman Writes Back: Literary Politics in the Work of a Contemporary Scottish Writer* (Berlin 1999), and *Shades of Gray: Science Fiction, History and the Problem of Postmodernism in the Work of Alasdair Gray* (Berlin 2004). Most recently, he has co-edited *Victorian Highways, Victorian Byways: New Approaches to Nineteenth-Century British Literature and Culture* (Berlin 2010). He is a member of the editorial board of *Neo-Victorian Studies*.

False Starts

Next to Swabians and the Irish (about whom I cannot write with too much expertise), the most important groups of people in Joachim Schwend's life are arguably the Scots and Saxons (who I know much more about). In a book on cultures in contact dedicated to him, therefore, an investigation of these two identities makes for a fitting contribution. But how to go about it? One obvious way to start is to look for direct contacts between the cultures in question. This does not turn out to be a very promising course, however, as I quickly noticed. While there is a lot of evidence for Anglo-German crosscurrents in literature, culture and history (cf. Kielinger 1997; Görner 2012), and occasionally either the Scottish or the Saxon context appears (as in Walter Scott's influence on German literature and culture or Bach, Mendelssohn and Wagner's on English music; cf. Schenkel 2010; Welz & Dellemann 2010), there are simply not enough significant direct contacts between the Scottish and Saxon cultures to make such a study worthwhile, I feel. An alternative approach could be to compare the two regions in a European context: medium-sized territories with 4-5m inhabitants, formerly independent kingdoms, now semi-autonomous entities with their own parliaments, rich in historical and cultural heritage, heartlands of industrialisation and working-class movements, deindustrialised yet future-oriented ('Silicon Glen' vs. 'Silicon Saxony'), and so forth. While this perspective seems promising, there are problems here, too: Scotland harbours a pronounced political nationalism, with the Scottish National Party in power and about to take a vote on independence in September 2014, it is unambiguously seen as a nation in its own right and has a clear antagonist in England; while Saxony has no ambitions for secession, no political nationalism and only a tenuous claim to nationhood, and 'othering' works mostly through its integration in the bigger region of Eastern Germany (as against the West).

These were my preliminary thoughts when I started a research project on Scottish and Saxon identities in 2005. I did not really get very far with it in Edinburgh that year, but I learnt that "Sassenach" is commonly used as a derogatory Scottish term for Southerners or Englishmen and that at the end of the fifteenth century, the Scottish poet Blind Harry, author of the famous epic *The Wallace*, called "Saxons, Scotland's very pest" and "enemies profest" of the "brave true ancient Scots" (Hamilton 1998: 1) – both of which did not particularly help. I was clearly in a bit of a dilemma here. What I needed was a guiding spirit, a framework to bring my various interests in comparing the regions (literature, history, politics, media) into sharper focus. Back in Leipzig, I kept thinking about the topic and the issues involved intermittently, but never found the time to return to it wholeheartedly. When the occasion of Joachim Schwend's 65th birthday beckoned and we decided on a publication with the 'cultures in contact' theme, I immediately saw the golden opportunity to revive the project. And while the time taken up with editorial work did not allow for a full academic paper on the topic, it offered me the occasion – and the great pleasure – of (re)discovering the range of Jochen's publications on a variety of topics, which remains a rather well-kept secret even to his closest colleagues (a token of his exceptional modesty). In the course of this, somewhat miraculously, there arose the vision of this guiding spirit – let us call him a *multikultureller Dolmetsch* (cf. Schwend 1997) – suggesting various perspectives and approaches for such a study, and whispering resonant fragments and quotations in my ear from time to time. Above all, he suggested taking the very emphases of those publications as structural aids to the investigation by looking at the four main issues of identities, history, politics and representations, and focussing on their interrelations in both cultures. Thus, the aim would be less a direct comparison than a parallel analysis inspired by some of the core themes of Cultural Studies as practiced by Joachim Schwend. At the same time, this approach allows me survey the majority of his publications and to present those themes and some of his recurring catchphrases to the readers of this volume – if not always in a deadly serious way. So in what follows, I will very briefly outline the parameters of such a study of Saxon and Scottish identities in a European context with the help of this inspiration. Who knows, maybe Jochen himself will be interested in actually realising this endeavour together with me in the future – this may be read as an invitation.

Enigmatic Identities – Region, Nation, Europe

"What ish my nation? Qu'est-ce qu'une nation?", whispered the voice in my ear, and the answer came immediately: "It is an imagined community, a brand to be consumed, a glocalised salad bowl, loosening its moorings in a Europe of Regions." Identification processes are clearly complex, mostly in transition and often enigmatic. So in this sense, the initial quote from Blind Harry is quite pertinent, after all, since it highlights the ambiguity and slipperiness of terms and concepts for regional and/or national entities and identities, and their evolution and change over time. The "Saxon" in the quote is obviously not the same as the one in the present German federal state of Saxony with which I am mainly concerned, but there is a historical link between the two. The project therefore needs to start from such an emphasis on the constructed nature of national and regional identities, on the central role played by cultural representations or 'signifying practices' in the process of 'imagining communities'. It needs to take the complex interplay of different levels of identity in Europe into account. (cf. Schwend 2009c: 213) This is the background against which a study of particular (regional) identities and their comparison can be undertaken. This is also where the literary and cultural critic can contribute to the debate on pressing and topical problems of our 'glocalising' world. Whereas there exist many studies on Europeanisation in general and on the impact it has on particular national/regional identities (such as Joachim Schwend's own writings on Scotland, Ireland, East Germany and Saxony – cf. 1996b; 2000c; 2001; 2006; 2007a; 2009a+c), as well as of those identities in isolation, comparative research on more than one European region is rarer, particularly so where the historical and literary/cultural dimensions are concerned. Again, Joachim Schwend has worked in this area, highlighting interrelations between English and Scottish (1992b), English and German (2000a; 2010) and Scottish and Irish (2003) discourses, especially in the field of literature. He has also been at pains to stress the legacy of the Enlightenment tradition and its values in and for Europe (with reference to William Penn or Edmund Burke, for example), thus pointing to the central significance of history (and politics) in this context. Therefore, before I return to the representation of identities in literature and other media as one of the most interesting aspects of the topic at the end of this article, let us start with those other central issues suggested by the guiding spirit.

Hidden Histories

I can hear the voice again, whispering about "invented traditions and cultural memory, manifested in monuments, rituals and *lieux de mémoire*, perpetuated and consumed through media discourses and the heritage industry. It's all about the past in the present, about getting your history wrong." (cf. e.g. Schwend 2003: 167; 2013) Almost all theories on collective identities stress the role of a common perception of the past, of cultural memory. In the case of regional identities this is certainly of central importance. However, frequently the regional (hi)story is overlaid by larger national histories and often relegated to little more than a footnote. This has been challenged recently in the broader context of postmodern and postcolonial attacks on dominant 'History' and its deconstruction by subversive 'histories' from below (e.g. from the perspective of women, the working class or ethnic minorities). In the British Isles, this has resulted in a renewed interest in so-called 'Four Nations' perspectives on formerly Anglo-centric British history, including a rediscovery and astonishing revival of Scottish history. In Germany, recent decades have seen acrimonious debates among historians both on its more distant past (Bismarck, Nazi era) and on recent developments (GDR history, *Ostalgie* etc.), but also a marked resurgence of *Regionalgeschichte*. Such recuperative historical endeavour is clearly visible in Joachim Schwend's oeuvre, who has worked historically almost from the start: his interests range from the medieval and Renaissance period (e.g. Schwend 1984; 1989; 1992a; 1996a; 2001) through the nineteenth century (e.g. Schwend 1985; 1996a; 2009b; 2010) to the present, in which he significantly finds the sediments of the past at every turn (e.g. Schwend 1996b; 2000c; 2001; 2002; 2006; 2007a+b; 2013). Significantly, this is always linked either to (literary) representations or to political and ideological structures influencing identity constructions.

Following this lead, there are several potentially fascinating comparisons to be made between Scotland and Saxony in this regard. Besides the issues mentioned at the beginning, one could think of the Scottish Enlightenment and the *Sächsische Aufklärung*, Glasgow and Leipzig as cities of trade and industry, the ancient universities etc. Some recent anniversaries of significant regional historical events may serve to illustrate the potential benefits in rediscovering some of those 'hidden' developments (sometimes actually in plain view) and their (ab)uses in and for the present, exactly in such a parallel or comparative analysis. The obvious Scottish example in 2014 would be the 700th anniversary of the Battle of Bannockburn (in which the Scots defeated the superior English troops), deliberately chosen by the Scottish National Party as the occasion for the Referendum on Independence this year. Already the Referendum on Scottish Devolution in 1997 had been set for the 700th anniversary of William Wallace's victory over Edward I's forces at the Battle of Stirling Bridge, even though it is to be doubted whether its success can be emulated this time around. The significance of the Wars of Independence for the Scottish national imagination is undeniable, in any case. (cf. Schwend 1992a; 2000c; 2001) And who can blame them, when large parts of their history are populated by 'glorious failures' (think Flodden, Mary Stuart, Bonnie Prince Charlie and Culloden). Something one could also say of Saxony with some justification. It is interesting to see how smaller regional powers with dominant neighbours (England and Prussia in these cases) often become caught in the bigger European power struggles and find themselves on the wrong side of history, so to speak. A case in point for Saxony would be the Napoleonic Wars (in which it sided with France for the most part), symbolised in the disastrous Battle of Leipzig or *Völkerschlacht* of 1813. Again, the bicentenary of this event, together with the centenary of the erection of the gigantic monument to the Battle, the *Völkerschlachtdenkmal*, in 2013 offers the opportunity to analyse the uses of history in and for the present, and in conjunction with regional identity formation. It is certainly difficult to celebrate this bloodiest battle on European soil before the First World War as a positive marker of regional and national identity, especially because the nationalist sentiment so clearly expressed in the monument led directly to the disasters of German twentieth-century history. It is not surprising, therefore, that there was a controversial debate on these celebrations, and that somewhat ambivalently, a large-scale re-enactment of the battle coexisted with a 'European Peace Festival'. It is unarguable, however, that such historical milestones are significant elements in the 'invented traditions' of regions and nations, so that a comparison of the way such battles are commemorated (Culloden and the bombing of Dresden in World War II would be further examples) can give us an insight into the different and maybe sometimes parallel structures of feeling and identity in Scotland and Saxony. Another case in point would be the highly contentious history and memorialisation of the recent political changes in both Scotland and Saxony (on the latter cf. Anna Saunders's contribution in this volume), which leads directly to my next point.

Politics and Power
"It's all about power and how it is distributed in societies," I can hear the spirit whispering conspiratorially, "Hobbes, Locke and Burke discussed it, Gramsci, Orwell and Foucault were fascinated by it, Raymond Williams and Stuart Hall wrote about it continually. But it is also multifaceted, affected by (interregional) transformation processes, and significantly linked to money and consumption." Cultural Studies was originally an eminently political project (and has remained so for many of its practitioners). Therefore, when investigating regional identities in a European context from such a perspective, one of the first questions to be asked is who are the (political) actors involved and what are the power structures underlying those identities. As Ernest Gellner and Eric Hobsbawm, among other theorists on collective identities, have claimed, such identities are always purposeful constructions driven by particular political and ideological agendas. Joachim Schwend has worked on various aspects of these socio-political themes, including the question of federal vs. devolved systems of government (cf. Schwend 2000b; 2001), the role of consumption and branding in (regional) identification processes (2004; 2007b; 2009b+c) and transformations in political and social systems due to globalisation and Europeanisation (2002; 2007c; 2009a+c). What emerges from this research, despite the emphasis on the largely anonymous forces of globalisation and consumer cultures, is a belief in common

(European, humanist or Enlightenment) values and a fundamental reliance on individual agency (on this aspect, see also the contribution by Crister Garrett in this volume). At the same time, the continued focus on historical and literary developments and precedents is obvious and clearly significant.

In this context, Saxony and Scotland offer particularly interesting examples since political power structures have experienced periodic upheavals and have often been dominated by larger (supra)national forces. In the past three decades, for example, both societies have seen major transitions, a new political structure has been (re)instated and a whole new political class developed. It can be argued that regional identities were centrally involved and affected in these transitions, so that the (re)invention of Scottish and Saxon identities as a result of these political and economic processes offers itself for investigation. One of the parallels to be noted here, I think, is the involvement of primarily non-political actors from the civil sector, as seen in the role of the Constitutional Convention in Scotland and the church groups and *Bürgerbewegung* in Saxony in the 1980s and 90s. The church context may prove a particularly fascinating case study, taken its importance for both regions historically, as one of the surviving national institutions after the 1707 Act of Union in Scotland, and as a significant marker of identity in the Saxon heartland of the European Reformation. Again, Joachim Schwend has contributed to this religious theme repeatedly in his research. (cf. Schwend 1984; 1990; 1991; 1996a) Moreover, it is clear that in both regions literature and the arts have had a particularly close relationship with politics and identity. Thus, it is commonly argued that the recent political changes in Scotland were preceded by a wide-ranging cultural renaissance since at least the 1980s, and several important members of oppositional groups during the *Wende* in Saxony came from literary and artistic backgrounds. In fact, the particularly Saxon identity (as opposed to GDR or East German identity) was mostly upheld by literature (such as the works of the late Erich Loest) and the arts (music, painting, even *Mundart* culture). This broadly speaking 'cultural' element to the political changes in both Scotland and Saxony cannot be overestimated, as several commentators on these developments agree, so that it seems logical to arrive finally at the centrally important question of how these identities are constructed and represented in culture and the media.

Regions Represented

Suddenly, the ghostly voice is starting to quote from Alasdair Gray's *magnum opus Lanark* (for 'city' one may read 'region'):

> "Glasgow is a magnificent city," said McAlpin. "Why do we hardly ever notice that?" "Because nobody imagines living here," said Thaw. McAlpin lit a cigarette and said, "If you want to explain that I'll certainly listen."—"Then think of Florence, Paris, London, New York. Nobody visiting them for the first time is a stranger because he's already visited them in paintings, novels, history books and films. But if a city hasn't been used by an artist not even the inhabitants live there imaginatively." (Gray 1982: 241)

"Literature and Nation belong together", it says, "the imagined community is formed on the page, through representation, and then conspicuously consumed by the body politic. It is a sign and a brand, continuously shifting its meaning and developing mythical structures on the second semiological level." Next to the political meaning of the 'representation' of regions outlined above, it is the representation of the region in literature, arts and media that has always interested me most, and has been in the centre of Cultural Studies' approach to the topic, significantly including popular culture and the actual consumption of such representations. This is also Joachim Schwend's main emphasis in most of his publications on the theme, be it on Scottish (cf. e.g. Schwend 1989, 1992b, 2000c, 2001), Irish (1995, 1996b, 2007a) or (East) German (2009a+c) identities. Increasingly, he has moved from analysing the representation of (mainly Scottish and Irish) identity in literature to investigating the complex identification processes in (transitional) societies at large, especially with reference to economic and consumer choices – such as in Ireland and Eastern Germany. One aspect of this is advertising and the tourist industry and their use and reinforcing of national and regional stereotypes. Once again, there is a clear sense here that culture, politics, history and identity are closely interlinked and must be seen together.

Against this background, one could start the investigation by looking at the representation of Scotland and Saxony in tourist brochures and on websites such as www.visitscotland.org or www.sachsen-tourismus.de. It will surprise no one that in an age of global branding of regions and 'glocalisation' (one of Joachim Schwend's catchwords) these representations show more similarities than differences: for Edinburgh and Glasgow read Dresden and Leipzig, for the Scottish Highlands read *Sächsische Schweiz* or *Erzgebirge*, for Scott, Burns and Stevenson read Bach, Schumann and Wagner, for Edinburgh Castle read Frauenkirche Dresden etc. – culture and history are clearly 'selling points' (more or less unique) for both regions. However, there are also significant differences, which it would be important to trace and explain further, in order to arrive at a more differentiated view of the respective identity building process. Most interestingly, perhaps, both regions have a long and eminent tradition in the arts, as witnessed by the names mentioned above, among many others. However, whereas in Scotland this is often seen as a national tradition, it is rare to hear people talk of Bach as a 'Saxon' composer. Why is that so? Maybe it is partly to do with the competing local and supra-regional identities: people talk of *Mitteldeutschland* as a cultural region (something of a misnomer, from a contemporary point of view, including Thuringia and Saxony-Anhalt), and we have a *Leipziger Schule* in painting but not a *Sächsische Schule*. This goes some way to give an idea of the complexities that need to be taken into account. In this context, it would be interesting to analyse and compare depictions of regional identities in writers like James Kelman (Glasgow) and Clemens Meyer (Leipzig), both of whom depict an urban 'underclass' sympathetically and with real insight and have become significant, prize-winning 'national' (i.e. 'British' and 'German') authors. For the historical (and political) theme, one could compare Erich Loest (*Reichsgericht*) and James Robertson (*And the Land Lay Still*), maybe, and on the more popular side Sabine Ebert (*1813 - Kriegsfeuer*) and John Prebble (*Culloden*). What do the imagined communities constructed in these representations look like, and how do they change over time? What are the political and ideological structures in which they acquire meaning? What about similar constructions in long-running TV series representing the big cities in both regions, such as *River City* and *In aller Freundschaft*, or *Taggart* and *SoKo Leipzig*? In any of these cases, an argument could be constructed highlighting the survival of sub-national or stateless identities through such mediatised imaginings, but the complexity and specificity of Saxon and Scottish 'represented regions' precisely in their interplay of historical, political and cultural identities would be the ultimate aim of such an analysis.

A Cautious Conclusion

The rest was (as yet) silence... To such an unfinished project, there can only be an open conclusion. And maybe that is the point. Robert Crawford once spoke of the simultaneous necessity to internationalise and "dedefine" both Scotland and Scottish Studies (cf. Crawford 2003). And Joachim Schwend himself has argued forcefully that "different levels of identity can be preserved in a European framework of common values." (Schwend 2009c: 213) This is the context in which this endeavour may be situated, I hope, and he himself could perhaps be more than just the guiding spirit of it – by taking an active part in it and thus both ending and realising its ultimate *VerSchwendung*. Such a study would certainly profit from his expertise and at the same time help to qualify the often one-sided views on specific European regional identities. At a time when Scotland is about to vote on independence and many regions in the whole of Europe (and maybe the continent as such) seem to be in dire straits, we could do worse than investigate two or more regional identities in Europe (what about Wales, maybe, or (Northern) Ireland, or Swabia?) in such a comparative, deconstructive and yet productive way. This may as well remain an unfinished project for some time to come.

Sources

Crawford, Robert (2003), "Dedefining Scotland", in Susan Bassnett, ed., *Studying British Cultures* (Second Edition), London – New York: Routledge, 87-100.

Görner, Rüdiger (2012), *Dover im Harz. Studien zu britisch-deutschen Kulturbeziehungen*, Heidelberg: Winter.

Gray, Alasdair (1982), *Lanark: A Life in Four Books* (First Edition 1981), London: Granada.

Hamilton of Gilbertfield, William (1998), *Blind Harry's Wallace* (First Edition 1722), Edinburgh: Luath Press.

Kielinger, Thomas (1997), *Die Kreuzung und der Kreisverkehr: Deutsche und Briten im Zentrum der europäischen Geschichte*, Bonn – London: Presse- und Informationsamt der Bundesregierung; Britisches Außen- und Commonwealth-Ministerium.

Schenkel, Elmar, ed. (2010), *Englisches Leipzig. Eine Spurensuche von A bis Z*, Leipzig: Edition Hamouda.

Schwend, Joachim (1984), "Religion and Religiosity in *The Bruce*", in Dietrich Strauss & Horst W. Drescher, eds., *Scottish Language and Literature, Medieval and Renaissance* (Scottish Studies 4), Frankfurt/Main: Peter Lang, 207-215.

Schwend, Joachim (1985), "Sir Walter Scott: Aufgeklärte Helden in *Waverley*, *Old Mortality*, *Rob Roy* und *Redgauntlet*", in Horst W. Drescher & Joachim Schwend, eds., *Studies in Scottish Fiction: Nineteenth Century* (Scottish Studies 3), Frankfurt/Main: Peter Lang, 91-100.

Schwend, Joachim (1989), "Nationalism in Scottish Medieval and Renaissance Literature", in Horst W. Drescher & Hermann Völkel, eds., *Nationalism in Literature – Literarischer Nationalismus: Literature, Language and National Identity* (Scottish Studies 8), Frankfurt/Main: Peter Lang, 29-42.

Schwend, Joachim (1990), "Calvin Walker – Still Going Strong. The Scottish Kirk in Early 20th-Century Scottish Fiction", in Joachim Schwend & Horst W. Drescher, eds., *Studies in Scottish Fiction: Twentieth Century* (Scottish Studies 10), Frankfurt/Main: Peter Lang, 335-345.

Schwend, Joachim (1991), "Kalvinismus in der literarischen Tradition Schottlands bis zu Alasdair Gray", in Armin Geraths & Peter Zenzinger, eds., *Text und Kontext in der modernen englischsprachigen Literatur*, Frankfurt/Main: Peter Lang, 191-208.

Schwend, Joachim (1992a), "Demokratie und Rationalismus in David Lyndsays *Ane Pleasant Satyre of the Thrie Estaitis*", in Joachim Schwend, Susanne Hagemann & Hermann Völkel, eds., *Literatur im Kontext – Literature in Context. Festschrift für Horst W. Drescher* (Scottish Studies 14), Frankfurt/Main: Peter Lang, 3-17.

Schwend, Joachim (1992b), "'In Bed with an Elephant?' The Anglo-Scottish Experience as Reflected in 20th-century Scottish Literature", in Rüdiger Ahrens & Heinz Antor, eds., *Text, Culture, Reception: Cross-Cultural Aspects of English Studies*, Heidelberg: Winter, 271-293.

Schwend, Joachim (1995), "A Europe of Regions? Regionalism and National Identity in Contemporary Anglo-Irish Fiction", in Wolfgang Riehle & Hugo Keiper, eds., *Anglistentag 1994 Graz: Proceedings*, Tübingen: Max Niemeyer, 43-57.

Schwend, Joachim (1996a), *Kirk, Gesellschaft und Literatur: Die Kirche im Kontext der literarischen Tradition Schottlands* (Scottish Studies 20), Frankfurt/Main: Peter Lang.

Schwend, Joachim (1996b), "The Nation-State or a Europe of Regions? Some Utopian Ideas about the End of a Paradigm and Possibilities for a New Approach in Ireland", in Horst W. Drescher & Susanne Hagemann, eds., *Scotland to Slovenia: European Identities and Transcultural Communication* (Scottish Studies International 21), Frankfurt/Main: Peter Lang, 113-139.

Schwend, Joachim (1997), "Kultur, Kulturwissenschaft und Translation", in Horst W. Drescher, ed., *Transfer: Übersetzen – Dolmetschen – Interkulturalität* (FASK 23), Frankfurt/Main: Peter Lang, 263-278.

Schwend, Joachim (2000a), "David Lodge, *Out of the Shelter*. Rites of Passage into Paradise?", in Susanne Stark, ed., *The Novel in Anglo-German Context: Cultural Cross-Currents and Affinities*, Amsterdam – Atlanta: Rodopi, 317-331.

Schwend, Joachim (2000b), "A United Federal Kingdom? The Nation State and Federalism", *English Language Teaching News*, 41 (June), 33-43.

Schwend, Joachim (2000c), "Scottishness: The Representation of a Frame of Mind", *Journal for the Study of British Cultures*, 7/1, 29-38.

Schwend, Joachim (2001), "'Freedom Is a Noble Thing': Scottish Independence Rhetorics and the Referendum of 11 September 1997", in Wolfgang Thiele, Albrecht Neubert & Christian Todenhagen, eds., *Text – Varieties – Translation*, Tübingen: Stauffenburg, 117-130.

Schwend, Joachim (2002), "Das Vereinigte Königreich im Wandel – Globalisierung und Europäische Integration. Eine kulturwissenschaftliche Textbewertung", in Christian Todenhagen, ed., *Text – Text Structure – Text Type: Festschrift für Wolfgang Thiele*, Tübingen: Stauffenburg, 207-220.

Schwend, Joachim (2003), "The Irish Connection – Cultural Links between Ireland and Scotland", in Bernard Sellin, ed., *Écosse des Highlands Mythes et réalité* (TRIADE 8), Brest: Centre de Recherches Bretonne et Celtique, 167-184.

Schwend, Joachim & Dietmar Böhnke, eds. (2004), *Journal for the Study of British Cultures*, 11/2: "Consumption and Consumer Cultures".

Schwend, Joachim (2006), "'Watch This!' Regional Pride: Scotland – A Nation in Its Own Right", in Werner Delanoy & Laurenz Volkmann, eds., *Cultural Studies in the EFL Classroom*, Heidelberg: Winter, 75-84.

Schwend, Joachim (2007a), "Ireland and Irishness. Myths and Myth-Making, or Constructing an Imagined Community", in Wolfgang Thiele & Christian Todenhagen, eds., *Nominalization, Nomination and Naming*, Tübingen: Stauffenburg, 83-98.

Schwend, Joachim (2007b), "'Pecunia non olet': Money and Consumer Cultures", in Fiona Cox & Hans-Walter Schmidt-Hannisa, eds., *Money and Culture*, Frankfurt/Main: Peter Lang, 353-368.

Schwend, Joachim (2007c), "Im globalen Dorf – der Region verbunden", in Susanne Hagemann & Andreas F. Kelletat, eds., *Amici Amico. Ein Bündel Texte für Karl-Heinz Stoll zum Geburtstag*, Berlin: SAXA Verlag, 72-76.

Schwend, Joachim (2009a), "Identification and Identity Developments in East Germany since the Fall of the Berlin Wall. Interregional and Intercultural Transformation Processes", in Niamh O'Mahony & Claire O'Reilly, eds., *Societies in Transition: Ireland, Germany and Irish-German Relations in Business and Society since 1989*, Baden-Baden: Nomos, 121-140.

Schwend, Joachim (2009b), "The End of the Curious Old Shop – Woman as the Self-Confident Consumer", in Sabine Coelsch-Foisner & Dorothea Flothow, eds., *High Culture and / versus Popular Culture*, Heidelberg: Winter, 169-186.

Schwend, Joachim (2009c), "Silicon Saxony: New Life in an Old Country", in Laura Rorato & Anna Saunders, eds., *The Essence and the Margin: National Identities and Collective Memories in Contemporary European Culture*, Amsterdam – New York: Rodopi, 199-215.

Schwend, Joachim (2010), "Friedrich Max Müller. Zwischen Orientalismus und Völkerverständigung", in Stefan Welz & Fabian Dellemann, eds., *Anglosachsen. Leipzig und die englischsprachige Kultur*, Frankfurt/Main: Peter Lang, 73-88.

Schwend, Joachim (2013), "Cultures of Memory – Sites of Memory", in Marie Hologa, Christian Lenz, Cyprian Piskurek & Stefan Schlensag, eds., *Cases of Intervention: The Great Variety of British Cultural Studies*, Newcastle: Cambridge Scholars Publishing, 63-82.

Welz, Stefan & Fabian Dellemann, eds. (2010), *Anglosachsen. Leipzig und die englischsprachige Kultur*, Frankfurt/Main: Peter Lang.

Paul Kußmaul (Germersheim)*
„Sind die aber komisch!" Kulturkontakt im Alltag

Als Jochen Schwend und ich in den 1980er Jahren noch Kollegen in Germersheim waren, prüften wir gelegentlich zusammen im mündlichen Teil der Diplomprüfung: er Landeskunde (heute heißt das Kulturwissenschaft), ich Übersetzungswissenschaft. Ich war immer sehr beeindruckt von seiner gründlichen Kenntnis der englischen und irischen Geschichte und habe als zuhörender Prüfer einiges gelernt. Inzwischen befasst sich Jochen Schwend u.a. mit aktuellen Themen der Alltagskultur, z.B. mit Konsum, Status und Lebensstil als kulturübergreifenden Phänomenen in westlichen Gesellschaften (z.B. Schwend 2007, Schwend 2009). Für mich als Übersetzungswissenschaftler sind dagegen kulturspezifische, aber ebenfalls alltägliche, Verhaltensweisen ein als wichtig erkanntes Gebiet geworden. Unsere Gebiete ergänzen sich: sie sind sowohl relevant für Kulturmittler, z.B. für Lehrer, Übersetzer und Dolmetscher, als auch für Menschen, die beruflich in unterschiedlichen Kulturen unterwegs sind. Dazu möchte ich ein paar Gedanken zu Papier bringen, die durch persönliche Erlebnisse angeregt wurden.

Körpersprache
Als ich in Indien war, ging ich in den ersten Tagen zu einem Taxistand und fragte den Fahrer, ob er frei sei. Er schüttelte den Kopf. Ich wandte mich also an den zweiten Fahrer in der Reihe; auch der schüttelte den Kopf. Ich fragte den nächsten: die gleiche Reaktion. So ging es weiter, bis der erste mir nachlief und sagte: „Sir, why don't you get in?" Das Verhalten kam mir seltsam vor, aber bei der Fülle der Eindrücke, die auf einen Europäer in Indien einprasseln, machte ich mir keine weiteren Gedanken. Erst als ich im Haus

---

* Paul Kußmaul, Ph.D. (Bristol), war am Fachbereich Angewandte Sprach- und Kulturwissenschaft (FASK) der Universität Mainz in Germersheim in der Übersetzerausbildung tätig. Er publizierte zahlreiche Aufsätze und Bücher zum Thema Übersetzen; in letzter Zeit *Verstehen und Übersetzen* (Narr 2007) und *Übersetzen — nicht leicht gemacht* (Saxa 2009). Für den DAAD nahm er Kurzzeitdozenturen an Universitäten in Jordanien, Indien, Indonesien, Thailand, China, Argentinien und in der Türkei wahr. 1992-1995 war er im Gründungsvorstand der *European Society for Translation Studies* (EST). Seit 2005 ist er pensioniert.

eines deutschen Kollegen zusammen mit einem indischen Gast zum Essen eingeladen war, erkannte ich, dass irgendetwas nicht stimmen konnte. Immer, wenn ich etwas sagte, schüttelte der indische Gast den Kopf – ein Zeichen der Verwunderung oder vielleicht auch der Missbilligung, wie ich dachte. Aber ich hatte doch gar nichts Verwunderliches oder Unangemessenes gesagt. Später am Tag sprach ich darüber mit meinem deutschen Kollegen, der schon seit fünf Jahren in Indien lebte, und er erklärte mir, dass Kopfschütteln in Indien „ja" bedeute und Kopfnicken „nein", und dass Kopfschütteln auch ein Zeichen des höflichen Zuhörens sei, ganz ähnlich wie in Deutschland das Kopfnicken.

Kommunikativ gesehen hatte das Problem für mich darin gelegen, dass diese Zeichen in Deutschland und Indien die gleiche Form haben, aber ihre Bedeutungen verschieden sind. An diesem Beispiel wird etwas Typisches sichtbar: Wir interpretieren ein Zeichen im Bezugsrahmen unserer eigenen Kultur, was in diesem Fall zu einer Fehlinterpretation führte. Und wir nehmen die Zeichen nicht einmal genau wahr. Mein Kollege machte mich darauf aufmerksam, dass es sich eigentlich nicht um ein Kopfschütteln handle, sondern um eine Kombination aus Drehen und Wiegen des Kopfes. Diese Feinheiten hatte ich nicht bemerkt.

Körpersprachliche Zeichen sind in ihrer Menge begrenzt; es gibt nicht so viele davon wie Wörter in einer Sprache. Das hat zur Folge, dass in verschiedenen Kulturen die gleichen oder ähnliche Zeichen benützt werden, aber mit jeweils unterschiedlichen Bedeutungen. Wenn wir ein unbekanntes Zeichen sehen, ist die Gefahr von Missverständnissen geringer, denn wir ordnen ihm nicht gleich eine vermeintlich wohlvertraute Bedeutung zu. Beim indischen Namaste als Begrüßungsgeste zum Beispiel, bei der die Handinnenflächen vor der Brust zusammengelegt werden, verbunden mit einer leichten Verbeugung, ist die Gefahr der Fehlinterpretation für uns relativ gering. Aber Zeichen, die wir aus unserer eigenen Kultur kennen, werden von uns meist automatisch mit der uns bekannten Bedeutung verknüpft, und die kann falsch sein. Es ist wie bei den ‚falschen Freunden' beim Sprachenlernen. Englisch *sensible* z.B. hat eben nicht die deutsche Entsprechung „sensibel", sondern „vernünftig", obwohl die sprachliche Form vergleichbar ist.

Wer sich interkulturell richtig verhalten will, muss flexibel sein und die Perspektive der eigenen Kultur verlassen können. Dass wir etwas aus der eigenen Perspektive falsch sehen, können wir oft daran merken, dass wir denken: „Sind die aber komisch!" oder „Das ist aber seltsam!" Dann müssten bei uns Warnlampen aufleuchten. Wir müssten dann versuchen, die Dinge aus der Sicht der anderen Kultur zu sehen, oder wir müssten nachfragen, wie etwas gemeint ist, wie ich das im obigen Fall, allerdings mit ziemlicher Verspätung, getan habe. Edward T. Hall, der von meinem Germersheimer Kollegen Heinz Göhring als „Vater der Kulturanthropologie" bezeichnet wurde, weist in seinem einflussreichen Buch *The Silent Language* an vielen Stellen auf das Perspektivenproblem hin (Hall 1990a, ¹1959). In der Übersetzungswissenschaft ist man sich dieser Problematik ebenfalls seit längerem bewusst (vgl. z.B. Hönig & Kußmaul 1982: passim, Witte 1999: 346-347 und Witte 2000: passim).

Man muss nicht nach Indien reisen, um solche Erfahrungen zu machen. Manche Deutsche haben sich sicher schon gewundert, warum Engländer unseren zupackenden Händedruck ziemlich schlaff erwidern und uns beim Abschied die Hand meist völlig drucklos überlassen. Zwar ist in England genauso wie in Deutschland das Händeschütteln ein körpersprachliches Begrüßungsritual, ist also ein Zeichen mit gleicher Bedeutung, aber das Zeichen ist ein bisschen anders, und seine situative Verteilung ist auch nicht die gleiche. Der Händedruck ist schwächer, und er ist bei der Begrüßung, vor allem beim ersten Kennenlernen üblich, aber eher nicht beim Abschied.

Es ist interessant zu sehen, dass sich die Gesten der Begrüßungsrituale verändern. Vor ein paar Jahrzehnten war eine Umarmung als Begrüßung in Deutschland noch nicht die Regel. Zwischen Frauen und zwischen Frauen und Männern ist sie heute, wenn man sich gut kennt, in Kombination mit einem meist nur angedeuteten Küsschen (in England „kissing the air") auf die rechte und die linke Wange üblich. Zwischen Männern scheint eine Umarmung mit gegenseitigem Schulterklopfen, etwas unsicher zwar und zögerlich, üblich zu werden. Auch über solche Veränderungen Bescheid zu wissen ist, denke ich, wichtig für Kulturmittler.

Raum und Abstand
Körpersprachliche Zeichen sind Bewegungen im Raum. Dass sie der Kommunikation dienen können, ist unmittelbar einsichtig. Dass wir aber bereits durch unseren Umgang mit dem Raum kommunizieren, wissen oder merken wir manchmal nicht. Der bereits erwähnte Edward T. Hall hat sich als erster mit diesem Thema beschäftigt und prägte dafür den Begriff „Proxemik" (Hall 1990b, [1]1969). Gemeint sind damit Signale, die Menschen austauschen, wenn sie je nach Situation bestimmte Abstände (Distanzzonen) zueinander einhalten. Die jeweilige Situation ist dabei ein entscheidendes Klassifikationskriterium. So wird z.B. von der *public distance* bei Ansprachen in einem größeren Raum Gebrauch gemacht, von der *personal distance* dagegen beim privaten Gespräch. Letztere ist für die Beobachtung kultureller Unterschiede besonders interessant. In den USA und in Mitteleuropa variiert sie zwischen 50 und 120 cm (vgl. Hall 1990b: 119-120). In seinem populärwissenschaftlichen Buch *Body Language* beschreibt der Schriftsteller Julius Fast (1983) auf der Grundlage von Hall den unterschiedlichen Gebrauch dieser Distanzzone nicht nur in entfernten Kulturen, sondern auch in der westlichen Welt. Amerikaner z.B. umgeben sich mit der persönlichen Distanzzone, wo immer sie gehen und stehen. Wenn ein Bekannter über etwas Privates mit ihnen sprechen will, kommen sie ihm nahe genug, sodass sich die Distanzzonen vereinen können. Für einen Deutschen dagegen kann ein Zimmer im eigenen Haus eine persönliche Distanzzone bilden, und wenn jemand in diesem Zimmer ein persönliches Gespräch führt, ohne ihn einzubeziehen, reagiert er möglicherweise beleidigt (Fast 1983: 40).

Werden die Distanzzonen nicht eingehalten, fühlt man sich unwohl. In Südamerika ist die persönliche Distanzzone generell geringer als in Mitteleuropa. In *Focus Online* vom 26.1.2004 wird von einem skurrilen Vorfall berichtet:

In einem brasilianischen Reitclub hatten derartige Missverständnisse [...] schmerzhafte Folgen: Ein Schreiner musste das Geländer einer Veranda erhöhen, weil immer wieder Nordamerikaner und Nordeuropäer rücklings hinunter gestürzt waren. Ihre südamerikanischen Pferdefreunde hatten den üblichen „nordischen" Gesprächsabstand von einer Armlänge nicht eingehalten, und die Gäste hatten sich unbewusst bedroht gefühlt. Da sie Schritt um Schritt zurückwichen und die Südländer nachrückten, hatte dies fatale Folgen.[1]

Innerhalb der Distanzzonen lassen sich bestimmte körpersprachliche Phänomene beobachten. In Amman in Jordanien ging ich eines Abends mit einem meiner älteren Studenten in einer Hotelbar ein Bier trinken, und während wir uns angeregt unterhielten, klopfte er mir immer wieder aufs Knie. In Deutschland und in vielen westlichen Kulturen ist das ziemlich unüblich, wenn nicht sogar befremdlich. Sicher wären bei den meisten Menschen in meiner Situation jetzt nicht nur Warnlampen aufgeleuchtet, sondern hätten die Alarmglocken geschrillt. Da ich aber damals schon Edward T. Hall gelesen hatte, wusste ich, dass in der arabischen Kultur die persönliche Gesprächsdistanz viel geringer ist als bei uns und z.B. ständiger Blickkontakt und der gute Atem der Gesprächspartner eine wichtige Rolle spielen (vgl. Hall 1990b: 159-162), und so nahm ich einfach einmal an, dass das Berühren des Knies beim lebhaften Gespräch auch dazu gehört. Das gegenseitige Berühren im Gespräch war damit für mich kein separates körpersprachliches Zeichen mit einer besonderen – vielleicht sogar sexuellen – Bedeutung, sondern eine Begleiterscheinung des geringen Gesprächsabstands. Ich passte mich also im Lauf des Abends kulturell an und klopfte meinem Studenten ebenfalls aufs Knie. Der Abend verlief sehr harmonisch und ohne körpersprachliche Missverständnisse, und ich hoffe, dass mein Student das Gefühl hatte, er würde sich mit jemandem aus seiner eigenen Kultur unterhalten.

Die Gesprächsdistanz zwischen Frauen scheint in der arabischen Kultur ähnlich gering zu sein. Während meines Aufenthalts in Amman besuchte mich meine Kollegin Sigrid Kupsch-Losereit mit

---

[1] Vgl. http://www.focus.de/finanzen/karriere/management/koerpersprache/koerpersprache/distanzzonen_aid_ 5455.html (11. April 2014).

ihrem Mann. Wir fuhren an einem Morgen mit dem öffentlichen Bus in die Stadt. Meine Kollegin hatte ein hübsches grünes Sommerkleid an. Im Bus setzte sich eine einheimische Frau neben sie, rückte eng an sie heran und fing an, wohl weil sie den Stoff sehr edel fand, das Kleid und damit natürlich auch meine Kollegin zu betasten. Dies wäre in Deutschland, wissenschaftlich formuliert, eine unzulässige soziale Interaktion. Bei der Interpretation dieser Handlung kommt nun das ins Spiel, was Sigrid Kupsch-Losereit als „Reflexion der eigenen kulturellen Bedingungen" (Kupsch-Losereit 2002: 97) bezeichnet. Nehmen wir einmal an, die Frau wäre ein Mann gewesen, dann hätte man als kulturell naive Deutsche spontan reagiert mit: „Pfoten weg, Sie!". Da es eine Frau war, hätte man sich fragen können: „Ist sie vielleicht lesbisch?" Wer nun aber kulturell kompetent reflektiert, fragt sich eben erst einmal: „Haben uns bekannte Gesten in anderen Kulturen vielleicht eine andere Bedeutung?" Meine Kollegin erwies sich als kulturell sehr kompetent und fing mit der Frau ein freundliches Gespräch auf Englisch an und trug damit zum gegenseitigen kulturellen Verständnis bei. Dass die Frau gar kein Englisch konnte, spielte dabei keine Rolle.

Umgang mit der Zeit
Nicht nur der Raum, sondern auch die Zeit „spricht", wie es Edward T. Hall sehr treffend ausdrückt (Hall 1990a: 137, 158), und sie spricht in verschiedenen Kulturen eine ganz unterschiedliche Sprache. Es ist allgemein bekannt, dass die Zeitspanne für Pünktlichkeit z.B. in Südamerika viel länger ist und damit auch eine andere Bedeutung hat als in den USA und in Nordeuropa. Es ist gut, das zu wissen, wenn man in Lateinamerika eine Verabredung hat. Was bei uns fünf Minuten sind, ist dort oft gut und gerne eine halbe Stunde, und wenn man eine halbe Stunde warten muss, sollte man sich nicht ärgern (vgl. Hall 1990a: 4-5). Was jedoch als pünktlich gilt, ist innerhalb einer Kultur situationsspezifisch. Die Zeitspannen sind z.B. in Lateinamerika für Verabredungen im Privatleben noch vager als im Geschäftsleben. Als ich in Argentinien war, lud mich der deutsche DAAD-Lektor zu einer abendlichen Party bei sich ein, und sagte: „Du kannst ruhig schon um 9 Uhr kommen, aber die meisten Gäste kommen sicher erst zwischen 10 und 12 Uhr." Auch im

westeuropäischen Kulturkreis gibt es in Bezug auf Pünktlichkeit situationsbedingte Unterschiede. In England wird z.B. bei beruflichen Verabredungen genauso wie in Deutschland, wenn man mehr als fünf Minuten zu spät kommt, eine Entschuldigung erwartet. Bei Einladungen zu *wine-and-cheese parties* dagegen, dies ist meine Erfahrung, wird man die Gastgeber, wenn man auf die Minute pünktlich ist, unter Umständen noch bei den Vorbereitungen, wenn nicht gar unter der Dusche antreffen. Es ist höflich, eine Viertelstunde bis eine halbe Stunde später zu kommen.

In Jordanien erlebte ich einen völlig anderen Umgang mit der Zeit. Ich unterrichtete an der Universität Amman und wollte mit dem Leiter der englischen Abteilung ein Treffen in seinem Büro vereinbaren. Ich rief ihn an und fragte, ob ihm der nächste Vormittag recht sei. Als gut planender Deutscher wollte ich eine genaue Uhrzeit mit ihm ausmachen, aber er sagte: „Kommen Sie einfach, egal wann." Als ich ankam, bot er mir die übliche Tasse Kaffee an, und wir begannen mit unserem Gespräch. Dann erschien ein anderer Kollege, erhielt ebenfalls einen Kaffee, und der Abteilungsleiter begann nun ein Gespräch mit ihm, anstatt das Gespräch mit mir fortzusetzen, wie es sich, wie ich dachte, eigentlich gehörte. Nach einer Weile kam wieder ein Kollege, erhielt auch seinen Kaffee, und der Abteilungsleiter wandte sich ihm zu. Im Laufe der nächsten Stunde kamen immer mehr Leute, und es war immer der letzte, mit dem ein Gespräch begonnen wurde. Allmählich wurde ich etwas ungeduldig, aber ich sagte mir, dass hier eben manches anders sei. Als alle Personen ausreichend zu Wort gekommen waren und alles Nötige besprochen hatten – inzwischen waren mehrere Stunden vergangen –, war ich schließlich wieder an der Reihe. Mein jordanischer Kollege, der viel gereist und kulturell sensibel war, hatte wohl meine Ungeduld bemerkt und erklärte mir, dass in Jordanien derjenige, der zuletzt ankommt, als erster dran ist. Einem Westeuropäer mag das als Zeitverschwendung erscheinen, weil dann alle anderen warten müssen – aber was bedeutet im Orient schon Zeit? Die Kulturanthropologie liefert für dieses Verhalten eine Erklärung. Unter dem Begriff *Chronemics* unterscheidet sie zwischen monochroner und polychroner Zeit. Für die monochrone Zeitauffassung gilt die Devise „time is money". Zeit ist wie eine Ware; sie kann gekauft oder verkauft werden. Monochronie ist geprägt durch ein Nacheinander; man erledigt erst das eine, dann das nächste. Zeitpläne und Pünktlichkeit spielen eine wichtige Rolle. Zu den monochronen Kulturen gehören z.b. die USA, Deutschland, England und Skandinavien. Im polychronen Zeitsystem können mehrere Dinge gleichzeitig erledigt werden, und gegenüber Pünktlichkeit und Zeitplänen hat man eine flexible Einstellung. Polychrone Kulturen finden sich z.b. in Lateinamerika, Afrika, Asien und in arabischen Ländern (vgl. Hall 1990a: 137-157). Hätte ich das damals in Jordanien gewusst, wäre ich im Büro meines Abteilungsleiters noch gelassener geblieben. Auch die Parabel, die Jesus von den Arbeitern im Weinberg erzählt und die in der Pointe gipfelt „Also werden die Letzten die Ersten und die Ersten die Letzten sein" (Matthäus 20, 16) hätte mir in meiner Situation eine Verständnishilfe sein können. Schließlich lebte Jesus in einer orientalischen Kultur.

Sprachliche Konventionen und Indirektheit
Nachdem es bisher um Körpersprache, um die Sprache des Raums und um die Sprache der Zeit ging, soll zum Schluss noch von der wirklichen Sprache die Rede sein. Als ich in meinen jungen Jahren DAAD-Lektor an der Universität Bristol in England war, nahm ich einmal an einer Diskussion im Anschluss an einen Vortrag eines deutschen Professors teil. Mein deutscher Lektoren-Kollege und ich fanden den Vortrag sehr anregend, waren aber nicht in allen Punkten einverstanden, und wir äußerten unsere Kritik. Am Tag darauf erzählte mir mein Kollege, eine ältere Dozentin der Abteilung habe ihm gesagt, er sei sehr aggressiv gewesen.

Wir waren beide überrascht und versuchten herauszufinden, was geschehen war. Wir hatten unsere Ansichten und unsere Kritik gegenüber dem Vortragenden frei geäußert, wie wir das von Deutschland her gewohnt waren. Wir versuchten uns zu erinnern, wie sich die englischen Kollegen verhalten hatten und stellten rückblickend fest, dass sie nie direkte Kritik geäußert, sondern meist nur Fragen gestellt hatten wie z.B. „Was halten Sie von der Methode von Kollege X?" oder „Mich würde Ihre Meinung über das neue

Buch von Kollege Y interessieren." Für diejenigen, die auf dem Gebiet Bescheid wussten, waren die Fragen im Grunde kritisch, denn sie implizierten, dass der Professor diese Literatur nicht genügend berücksichtigt hatte. Es wurde ihm jedoch die Chance gegeben, wenn er geschickt genug war, seine Versäumnisse oder gar sein Nichtwissen zu überspielen und sein Gesicht zu wahren. Offenbar gab es, wie wir erkannten, zwei unterschiedliche Arten des akademischen Diskurses: Deutsche scheinen bei ihrer Kritik und beim Äußern unterschiedlicher Meinungen direkter zu sein, wogegen englische Akademiker sich indirekter verhalten, was jedoch nicht heißt, dass sie nicht kritisch sind.

Dies ist eine Anekdote, aber vielleicht ist sie typisch. Der Friedensforscher Johan Galtung hat Prototypen des intellektuellen Diskurses beschrieben, die sehr gut zu meiner Anekdote passen. Laut Galtung beginnen im „sachsonischen" Diskurs (in Großbritannien und den USA) Kommentare zu einem Vortrag normalerweise mit ein paar lobenden Worten, und dann folgt nach einem „aber" eine höflich formulierte Kritik (vgl. Galtung 1985: 157). Im „teutonischen" Diskurs (in Deutschland) und übrigens auch im „gallischen" Diskurs (in Frankreich) dagegen, so Galtung, steuert man „schnurstracks auf den schwächsten Punkt des Vortrags" zu und stellt ihn „ins hellste Rampenlicht" (ibid.:158).

Für Akademiker gehören solche Diskurs-Situationen zum Alltag. Es wäre sicher interessant zu sehen, ob sich Engländer und Deutsche im ganz normalen Alltag auch so verhalten, wie Galtung es für den akademischen Stil beschrieben hat. Vieles weist darauf hin, dass Engländer in allen Situationen eine auf Ironie beruhende Indirektheit pflegen. Auch das typisch englische Understatement beruht ja auf Indirektheit. George Mikes nennt dafür in seinem Bestseller über die Engländer *How to Be an Alien* viele Beispiele, die zweifellos literarisch zugespitzt sind, aber etwas Wahres ausdrücken. Wenn z.B. ein junger Mann seiner Angebeteten eine Liebeserklärung machen will, so Mikes, dann sagt er mit sanfter Stimme: „I don't object to you, you know." Wenn er ganz verrückt nach ihr ist, fügt er vielleicht noch hinzu: „I rather fancy you, in fact." (Mikes 1960:

249). Die Anthropologin Kate Fox spricht in ihrem sehr unterhaltsamen Buch *Watching the English* sogar von einer *understatement rule*, die Engländer quasi mit der Muttermilch aufsaugen und die mit der englischen Abneigung gegen alles Pompöse, allzu Emotionale und allzu Wichtigtuerische zu tun hat, sodass ein schreckliches Erlebnis ganz kühl als „not exactly what I would have chosen", ein atemberaubend schöner Anblick ganz trocken als „quite pretty" oder eine herausragende Leistung schlicht als „not bad" bezeichnet wird (Fox 2005: 66-67).

Um zu merken, was Engländer meinen, ist es sicher gut zu wissen, wie man Understatements und höfliche Indirektheit zu verstehen hat. Nicht alles ist ein Lob, was wie ein Lob klingt. Als ich vor vielen Jahren einem englischen Freund ein deutsches Bauernomelett servierte und fragte, wie es ihm schmecke, meinte er: „It tastes interesting". Das klang für mich positiv, und ich fragte weiter, was ich vielleicht nicht hätte tun sollen; da sagte er: „It needs an iron teutonic stomach to digest."

Quellen

Fast, Julius (1983), *Body Language* (Erstauflage 1971), London and Sydney: Pan Books.

Fox, Kate (2005), *Watching the English. The Hidden Rules of English Behaviour*, London: Hodder.

Galtung, Johan (1985), „Struktur, Kultur und intellektueller Stil. Ein vergleichender Essay über sachsonische, teutonische, gallische und nipponische Wissenschaft", in Alois Wierlacher, Hrsg., *Das Fremde und das Eigene: Prolegomena zu einer interkulturellen Germanistik*, München: Iudicium, 151-193.

Hall, Edward T. (1990a), *The Silent Language* (Erstauflage 1959), New York: Anchor Books.

Hall, Edward T. (1990b), *The Hidden Dimension* (Erstauflage 1969), New York: Anchor Books.

Hönig, Hans & Paul Kußmaul (1982), *Strategie der Übersetzung*, Tübingen: Narr.

Kupsch-Losereit, Sigrid (2002), „Die kulturelle Kompetenz des Translators", *Lebende Sprachen*, 47/3, 97-101.

Mikes, George (1960), *How to Be an Alien* (Erstauflage 1946), London: Andre Deutsch.

Schwend, Joachim (2007), „'Pecunia non olet': Money and Consumer Cultures", in Fiona Cox & Hans-Walter Schmidt-Hannisa, Hrsg., *Money and Culture*, Frankfurt/Main: Peter Lang, 353-368.

Schwend, Joachim (2009), „Identification and Identity Developments in East Germany since the Fall of the Berlin Wall. Interregional and Intercultural Transformation Processes", in Niamh O'Mahoney & Claire O'Reilly, Hrsg., *Societies in Transition: Ireland, Germany and Irish-German Relations in Business and Society since 1989*, Baden-Baden: Nomos, 121-140.

Witte, Heidrun (1999), „Die Rolle der Kulturkompetenz", in Mary Snell-Hornby *et al.*, Hrsg., *Handbuch Translation* (Erstauflage 1998), Tübingen: Stauffenburg, 345-348.

Witte, Heidrun (2000), *Die Kulturkompetenz des Translators. Begriffliche Grundlegung und Didaktisierung* (Studien zur Translation 9), Tübingen: Stauffenburg.

Claire O'Reilly (Cork)*
As Time Goes By: Some Thoughts on the Year Abroad as a Vehicle of *Kulturkontakt*

I first met Joachim Schwend while he was visiting University College Cork on a Teaching Exchange in March 2006. For me, as perhaps for any interlocutor, his quietly-spoken, unassuming ways ensured immediate ease. A friendship developed. I have come to appreciate his love of simplicity and the outdoor life (by bicycle of course), and his visible generosity to others. In my case an invitation to work from his home and office on one occasion (as he was also on sabbatical) ensured that I could carry out a research stay in Germany. With some proximity and some distance to Joachim and his interest in Irish topics, one can observe what ease, humour and appreciation of Irish-Otherness accompanies him as he moves from German to Irish terrain. To my mind something of his learning journey echoes Muneo Yoshikawa's personal reflections on moving across two cultural spaces:

> I am now able to look at both cultures with objectivity as well as subjectivity; I am able to move in both cultures, back and forth without any apparent conflict [...] I really am not concerned whether others take me as a Japanese or an American; I can accept myself as I am. I feel I am much freer than ever before, not only in the cognitive domain (perception, thoughts etc.) but also in the affective (feelings, attitudes, etc.) and behavioural domains (quoted in Kim 2009: 59).

Joachim, I wish you a long and happy retirement with (more) time for cycling,

---

* Claire O'Reilly (Dr. phil. 2001, University of Limerick in collaboration with the University of Regensburg) is Lecturer in German at University College Cork with responsibilities for the BComm International Programme (Academic Coordinator). She has published in the field of *Kulturkontakt* following a number of strands within Irish-German Studies, i. with Niamh O'Mahony in 2009: *Societies in Transition: Ireland, Germany and Irish-German Relations in Business and Society since 1989*, ii. *The Expatriate Life: A Study of German Expatriates and their Spouses in Ireland – Issues of Adjustment and Training* (2003) and more widely considering questions pertaining to intercultural training, iii. *Interkulturelles Training in Deutschland. Theoretische Grundlagen, Zukunftsperspektiven und eine annotierte Literaturauswahl* (with Maik Arnold, 2005). An edited monograph (with Veronica O'Regan) on the Irish in Germany is forthcoming entitled: *Ireland and the Irish in Germany: Reception and Perception*.

travelling, reading, self-generosity, if there is such a word, and the good health to enjoy all of these.

Introduction and Background

In his book *The Ethics of Travel* Syed Islam (1996) advances that there are two very different kinds of travel experience: the nomadic traveller, being inquisitive and participative, is intrinsically motivated to "come face to face with the other" (vii) experiencing the intensity of encounter (cf. ibid.: 209). Against this the sedentary traveller is described by Islam as "failing to encounter difference" (ibid.) and engaging in location-swapping, without seeking understanding of the Other. Aspects of this idea and not fully engaging with the host culture can be seen in the sentiments of a student following her Year Abroad (YA):[1]

> I would like to return (to Austria). I have learned from mistakes. I wish I did more learning while over there, now I would like to spend a year working there and make FULL advantage of the opportunity which I did not do during my year abroad unfortunately (Q_10, Austria [city not mentioned], 2009-2010).[2]

A visible sense of regret pervades these lines. What were these mistakes? What barriers prevented learning taking place? One common misconception held by many students is that being immersed in a second language community in tandem with language courses will create fluent and native sounding foreign language speakers (cf. Freed 1995: 5). A further fallacy or at the least a partial truth accompanying language learning is that physical presence in the second culture will help to develop cultural and intercultural

---

[1] The term I use here, the Year Abroad (YA) is also known as Residence Abroad and Study Abroad denoting the same phenomenon: students remain registered in their home countries and return home to finish their degree after one year's sojourn abroad. This can be distinguished from international students who leave their country of origin to study for the entire duration of a programme abroad.

[2] Note on abbreviation: Q stands for questionnaire; I for interview. The majority of interviewees and received questionnaires are based on feedback from students at University College Cork. Five of the eleven interviewees were from University College Dublin, abbreviated here to UCD.

competence (cf. Coleman & Parker 2001), an idea which echoes Sharon Wilkinson's concept of a culture myth (cf. Pellegrino 1998).

As the introduction so far would suggest, the author found in an Irish university setting that it is not a foregone conclusion within a formal educational setting that students realise and embrace the learning potential associated with the YA.[3] Many of our students, teenagers not too long ago of the Celtic Tiger era, fail to maximize learning opportunities while abroad.[4] Against this background the idea behind this paper was born, namely to examine the YA experiences of students in Germany, and to examine the qualitative experience of the *Kulturkontakt* regarding Irish-German exchange. The research for this paper is based on feedback from students at various intervals over an 11-year period. Research commenced in 2002[5] and comprises snapshots of the student experience since this time: Face-to-face interviews were held with 11 students *during* their YA (2002) and with 5 *returned* YA students (2009-2010). The 2002 interviews were the basis for questionnaires developed later and completed by 50 students *on returning* from the YA commencing in 2006 and up to 2013. Students were from both Business (BComm International) and Arts and Humanities programmes. As the focus of this paper is on Irish students in Germany, the particular Irish

---

[3] For the students discussed in this paper the YA is a compulsory part of their undergraduate programme completed in Year 3 (of a 4-Year programme). They all have partaken in the EU-funded ERASMUS programme (European Region Action Scheme for the Mobility of University Students).

[4] Students can fulfil their programme and credit obligations, but still come home having made little visible linguistic advancement or displaying a higher level of differentiated cultural thinking. This observation that many students do not return home with the competences one might hope for has been found in YA studies within different contexts (e.g. Freed *et al.* 2004, Tsoukalas 2008 Murphy-Lejeune 2008).

[5] The author first commenced research in Year Abroad studies in 2002: The project consisted of an analysis of the learning experience of Irish students both at university and within the socio-cultural environment in Germany (with Dr. Gisela Holfter and Prof. Dr. emer. Alexander Thomas and funded by the Royal Irish Academy in collaboration with the DAAD). Interviews – lasting 55-90 minutes – with eleven Irish students were carried out by the author at the University of Regensburg and at the University of Nuremberg-Erlangen, and unpublished interview excerpts from this sample are included in this paper.

context within the YA academic landscape will first be described to provide a backdrop to the study in question.

Irish Studies in the YA Context: Germany as Destination

Despite a recognised superabundance of information on the subject of international students and the study abroad experience, only in recent years have publications grown in number focusing on non-mainstream contexts. One such area, and a relatively new field of YA research interest, pertains to German-Irish exchanges, despite the fact that the German academic exchange service (DAAD) has been sponsoring Irish students to Germany as far back as the 1950s.[6] Studies on Irish students in Germany have added to research in terms of Second Language Acquisition (SLA) and concerning non-language outcomes of the YA. Concerning SLA research Riana Walsh (2004) found, in the context of (15) Irish students in Germany, that oral confidence was a major outcome of the YA, but that students require more linguistic guidance to maximise opportunities during the YA. Anne Barron (2003) conducted a longitudinal study of (33) Irish students at German universities concerning their socio-pragmatic competence, examining speech acts of requests, offers, and refusals of offers. While she did note greater use of native-like formulations and greater knowledge in how to use such formulations appropriately, she found that only "rarely was the L2 norm actually reached" (Barron 2003: 238). Another PhD-project by Kristin Brogan with (55) Irish students in Germany focusing on factors that positively influence Second Language Acquisition during the YA, found that not all students increased their SLA, but intercultural learning is one of the outcomes. Moving outside of the predominant language focus in YA studies, Jean Conacher (2008) examined issues of identity and acculturation of (6) Irish ERASMUS students in Germany. This research is positioned within a similar context: although language issues do feature, the overall learning experience in academic and non-academic terms is to the fore, and although

---

[6] Student reports from and since this time are unfortunately not accessible for analysis, as they are only intended for internal DAAD use.

numbers are small in research terms, they are mostly in line with YA studies of Irish students studying German to date.

Irish students have been going to Germany in increasing numbers over time (see Table 1), with the DAAD sponsoring over 800 Irish students since the 1950s (cf. DAAD 2007: 16).

Table 1: Overview of Numbers of Irish Students in Germany, 1972-2013					
Year	*Number*	*Year*	*Number*	*Year*	*Number*
1972 - 1973	78	1986 - 1987	360	2000 - 2001	536
1973 - 1974	83	1987 - 1988*	418	2001 - 2002	518
1974 - 1975	95	1988 - 1989	215	2002 - 2003	506
1975 - 1976	110	1989 - 1990	475	2003 - 2004	479
1976 - 1977	144	1990 - 1991	604	2004 - 2005	408
1977 - 1978	147	1991 - 1992	740	2005 - 2006	435
1978 - 1979	164	1992 - 1993	826	2006 - 2007	413
1979 - 1980	179	1993 - 1994	477	2007 - 2008	353
1980 - 1981	201	1994 - 1994	521	2008 - 2009	386
1981 - 1982	224	1995 - 1996	596	2009 - 2010	369
1982 - 1983	220	1996 - 1997	568	2010 - 2011	409
1983 - 1984	260	1997 - 1998	622	2011 - 2012	475
1984 - 1985	305	1998 - 1999	559	2012 - 2013	466
1985 - 1986	338	1999 - 2000	573		
Table compiled by author based on statistics provided by the German Federal Statistical Office; computations DZHW / www.wissenschaft-weltoffen.de.					
* Of these figures, 112 Irish students first took part in 1987-1988 when the ERASMUS programme commenced. A total of 31,597 students from Ireland have travelled on ERASMUS grants since 1987.					

Table 1 illustrates the numbers of Irish students studying in Germany since 1972, the year such differentiated records commenced. The period with the largest number of students followed the fall of the Berlin Wall in 1989 when numbers increased steadily until 1993. As can be expected, interest in foreign markets and in Germany goes hand-in-hand with the ebb and flow of domestic markets: The period of the Celtic Tiger, especially during the years 2004-2008, was seemingly less interesting for Irish students, but the recession in Ireland has sparked new interest in Germany, as can be seen with recent increases in Irish student numbers in Germany. Today, 1.4 per cent of international higher education students in Germany come from Ireland with 0.7 per cent of foreign students in Ireland from Germany (cf. OECD 2013: 321). These figures comprise all student numbers, but it is undoubtedly the case that students on exchange, ERASMUS or otherwise, are an important part of ongoing interstate (Irish-German) relations, and they often go on to occupy important business-related, political and diplomatic positions in later careers.[7] Thus, and not only for this reason, the quality of their YA experience can be influential in forming important hetero-images of the host nation and in turn influence later career decisions.

Research Findings

Analysing the fifty questionnaires,[8] a number of recurring themes could be identified which, following Mayring's (1997) approach to content analysis, were grouped, placed into categories, and then evaluated. Challenges in academic adjustment featured most notably in the sample of students in question here.

<u>1. Academic Adjustment and Language Adjustment</u>
Excerpts from face-to-face interview (I) data and questionnaire (Q) data serve to illustrate the YA experience from the students' perspective. In response to the question *'How are your academic studies progressing?'* students remarked:

---

[7] Some examples of how study abroad periods shaped Irish individuals in later careers can be read in Claire O'Reilly & Veronica O'Regan, eds. (2014, forthcoming), *Ireland and the Irish in Germany: Reception and Perception*, Baden-Baden: Nomos.

[8] All students interviewed were Irish nationals. The experiences in this study were based on self-ratings only, and the study did not include third-party evaluations, university language tests, or control groups as part of its methodological design. Therefore, these considerations must be seen as limitations to evaluating actual outcomes of the YA of this student sample. However, the value of interviewing students qualitatively while abroad opens a window to understand the students in their individual contexts in addition to them reconstructing their experiences on returning home. I would like to thank respondents for sharing their YA experiences with me.

> In terms of lectures you are left totally up to yourself to choose them and to fill out forms. Foreigners are a bit lost with this; it is a bit complicated. We had no help with this, or registering for exams. I found it really hard getting up at 7.30am because if you weren't in the queue for 8.00am you wouldn't get to register. (I_1_UCD, Regensburg, 2001-2002)

> The university system on the continent is very different from here. I believe the learning experience would have been better if a better understanding of the system was given beforehand, i.e. registration problems. And because registration problems existed, I was very much restricted in terms of what classes I could attend, and so, my learning experiences were affected. (Q_11, Munich, 2006-2007)

> The learning experience at university was a good experience but quite challenging. It was very hard to follow the business German lectures. (Q_10, Nuremberg-Erlangen, 2012-2013)

As the sample quotes reveal, challenges in the academic environment started outside of the classroom, and before the commencement of the semester. Furthermore, the German academic system necessitated some adjustment:

> The longer class times and the large class size took a bit of getting used to. I found the way the university year is split into two semesters much more practical and manageable than our university system. (Q_7, Erlangen, 2006-2007)

> The lectures were very difficult to follow due to the fact that they were a lot longer than lectures in Ireland – some were close to two hours without a break. (Q_9, Marburg, 2012-2013)

This was particularly the case concerning the in-class experience:

> In student interaction in courses – even if there were 500 people in the room, 5 people might be talking at home, whereas over here everyone has their hands up and they are fighting to get their word in. (I_3, UCD, 2001-2002). I_4 agrees. (I_3&4_UCD, Regensburg, 2001-2002)

> German students always seem to be on time and they do the work, and there is a lot more interaction in class here. (I_5, Nuremberg-Erlangen, 2001-2002)

> People are a lot more willing to put their hand up in lectures and say something, whereas at home they sit back and wait for someone else to say something. It might have something to do with school, and I think Germans are more confident from home as well. (Q_2, Marburg, 2006-2007)

A running thread throughout the interview scripts is the language challenge students faced at University:

> I enjoyed the *Leseverständnis* in German, but the first history lecture I went into, I was totally lost. It has got better but I still have to concentrate really hard and I still get lost. (I_2, UCD, Regensburg, 2001-2002)

> We are not able to stand our own ground as well here due to the language problem. We are stumbling over our words and not getting it right (…). At least at home you can fight back more than over here. (I_4, Nuremberg-Erlangen, 2001-2002)

> They have a barrier when it comes to ERASMUS students. But it is the same in UCD. I don't walk up to ERASMUS students and say, "Hi my name is O., what is your name?", "Do you want to speak English with me?" So I don't blame them at all. But I think there is this barrier there and until you are introduced by one of their friends into this group, you are not accepted. You have to establish a friendship to get into a group and be accepted. (I_5_UCD, Nuremberg-Erlangen, 2001-2002)

The loss of learning to students based on their friendship and language patterns is obvious. Moreover, the academic experience and overall academic success may have been more positive for students with the benefit of host national friendships (and lowered rates of dropping out as Westwood and Barker found in 1990).[9] Other benefits of such friendships have included sociolinguistic competence which has been found to be significantly positively affected by contact with native speakers (cf. Regan, Howard & Lemée 2009: 139). Thus, in light of these findings, there does appear to be a loss of learning on a number of levels for Irish students in Germany.

---

[9] Westwood & Barker (1990) studied a programme between visiting and host national students that focused on cultural interpretation, communication, general information, confidants and friends.

Overall, when analysing the data concerning the university experience, comments revolved around the key aspect of understanding both content through the L2, and adapting to a different academic system. The in-class experience was also found to necessitate adjustment with more participation by German students. On a positive note, there is evidence of positive academic and intellectual exchange occurring, with students commenting on different teaching methods and styles. The academic side of their year abroad presented more challenges for the Irish student than experiences in the wider socio-cultural environment. There were, however, difficulties and obstacles to learning in both academic and socio-cultural environments.

2. Obstacles to the Learning Experience during the YA Sojourn

Analysing all questionnaires and the interview data collectively from 2002-2013, three factors were identified that prevented students fully immersing themselves in the L2.

i. Peer Groups and Choice of Language

As identified above, staying in groups with co-nationals is considered unproductive in terms of learning outcomes. Irish students remaining in English-speaking circles could with hindsight evidently see that these patterns acted as a deterrent to greater language and cultural learning, and for some regret was evident:

> I loved living in Germany. The only regret I have is spending so much time with the other Irish students even though I made very good German friends. I also had to work and the easiest place for me to get a well-paying job was in an English pub, which hindered my acculturation experience. (Q_7, Nuremberg-Erlangen, 2006-2007)

> I probably should not have made a lot of English-speaking friends. It diluted a lot of what I learnt. (Q_2, Munich, 2009-2010)

> I spent too much time with fellow ERASMUS students, who were mainly of an English-speaking background. My circle of friends meant that I didn't have much opportunity outside of class to interact on a social basis with Germans. (Q_13, Munich, 2010-2011)

> I lived with a Korean girl who spoke very little German. I didn't learn anything German living with her. I spent a lot of time then with ERASMUS students and learned what we called "ERASMUS Deutsch". (Q_13, Leipzig, 2006-2007)

As discussed under the academic experience above, the new language was a repeated challenge for Irish students particularly in the early months abroad. This may be one of the reasons why students found that German students chose to speak English with them, despite their attempts to keep conversations in the L2.

ii. Speaking English with (Home and) Host Students
Irish students appeared to be lacking confidence in the first months to switch to German when German students spoke English with them, as the sample of quotes below reveal:

> I found the Germans were more interested in practicing their English, but with a little persistence they will speak German. (Q_4, Nuremberg-Erlangen, 2009-2010)

Even though this student did persist and speak German, she identified this one aspect as a factor hindering her acculturation:

> The fact that the Germans always want to speak English prevented my acculturation experience from being more positive. (Q_4, Erlangen-Nuremberg, 2009-2010)

Others found:

> It was often difficult to speak German to certain people who only wished to speak English. This was often frustrating and disheartening [...]. People whom I encountered who only wished to speak English did affect my acculturation to an extent. (Q_2, Hannover, 2010-2011)

> There were occasions where Germans heard my accent and then started speaking English. (Q_7, Konstanz, 2012-2013)

This fact encouraged others to spend more time in ERASMUS circles:

> One of the main parts of ERASMUS is speaking the language of the country and Germans will only speak English to non-Germans. This is very annoying; therefore, most of my other friends were ERASMUS students. (Q_11, Munich, 2006-2007)

Although the sentiments do lack a sense of differentiation, these findings are in line with similar studies of Irish students abroad. One study (Brogan 2011) found concerning language experience during the YA that 32 per cent of native German students refused to speak German with Irish ERASMUS students, and that at the most, only 25 per cent of students were speaking German 30-49 per cent of the time. Staying with Irish students in Germany, Conacher (2008) found that students – all of whom had higher than average grades and were clearly motivated to invest time and energy integrating into German life – spent between 40 and 60 per cent of their time speaking German (cf. Conacher 2008: 11). She observes that students were disappointed with this and that *"Ihre Hauptenttäuschung ergab sich aus der Tatsache, dass sie trotz aller Versuche kaum in deutsche Bekanntenkreise einbrechen konnten und eine Art 'gläserne Barriere' erkannten"* (ibid.: 14). Affirming findings here, Conacher contends that as students felt they were an outsider-group from the main German student population, this increased the draw to the ERASMUS group who shared similar experiences and the need to integrate. Overall, therefore, it can be maintained that as students experienced feelings of frustration when they found that host students predominantly wished to practice their English, this increased the pull to staying in predominantly English-speaking circles.

iii. Multimedia Usage and Breaks in Stay
Where multimedia usage could have been a factor positively influencing L2 gains, and was the case for some ("I read a lot of German books, newspapers and watched German TV, this helped my adapting to living in Germany"), for many, multimedia proved to be a significant obstacle to learning (students mentioned Facebook, and being on Skype in the evenings to family members). This observation is echoed by Ehrenreich who finds that "media opportunities are increasingly changing the quality of the YA experience itself, as it was never so easy to be connected to home even in the most remote corner of the world" (Ehrenreich 2008: 30, my trans-

lation). Also the frequency of visits home to family and friends – a vast majority of students made trips home at Christmas, over the semester break, at Easter and even for family occasions – meant that students who were speaking German, were speaking it for less time than envisaged by the academic programme and by the sending institution.[10]

Despite the above obstacles to learning, a number of positive outcomes were evident from the YA. These cannot be discussed at length here but positive outcomes were seen in perceptions of the host country nationals and of Germany; language progress was noted by many; stereotypes were occasionally challenged and there was increased self-awareness arising from the YA. Reflecting perhaps the age group of the cohort, many named benefits such as "independent living"; "living alone for the first time", "a greater sense of independence and confidence in travelling alone" (all of these quotes were from the 2012-2013 sample). There were a number of common threads when students, evaluating the merits of their YA, named several *long-term effects* that they feel will benefit their lives both professionally and personally. Becoming independent, and awareness of other foreign students at home was the most often mentioned benefit of the 2006-2007 student cohort. Against this, reflecting altered economic circumstances in later years (2009-2013), over 75 per cent of responses focused on how the YA will positively influence job opportunities and how returning to Germany to work has become a realistic option, such as "My German has improved a lot which will help greatly as I intend to move back after I have finished my degree" (Q_6, Cologne, 2012-2013). Therefore, although from an educational and institutional perspective optimal linguistic advancement was not a main finding, the positive affective associations after the year in Germany and Austria were noteworthy. This is seen especially in the many comments of students wishing to return to Germany after their degree.

---

[10] The majority of students travelled home 3-4 times during the year. There is a slight reduction in the 2012-2013 group however, reflecting perhaps the financial downturn: 60% in this sample travelled home twice, 30% travelled home three times and 10% travelled home just once.

In summary, and as seen from the interview data above, many students expressed regret at some level at not utilizing fully the learning potential during the YA. These sentiments were voiced more often by Business students than by Arts and Humanities students. Business students as a cohort seemed to grasp less clearly the explicit reasons for going abroad – to be immersed in the culture, to develop more native sounding language structures and differentiated thinking about themselves and others.

Conclusion

One challenge today for the third level educator is to help students realise the huge potential for learning that the YA offers, and to motivate them to reflect on their learning, as Goethe once mused about after only three months in Italy:

> Nothing above all, is comparable to the new life that a *reflective person* experiences when he observes a new country. Though I am still always myself, I believe I have been changed to the very marrow of my bones (Goethe 1970: 147, italics added).

In this study there is convincing evidence to integrate Riana Walsh's suggestion of incorporating linguistic guidance while abroad. This would mean that students receive ongoing guidance and feedback as to their Year Abroad goals and their patterns of day-to-day interaction, with some stimulus to adapt behaviours where necessary.[11] There are, however, a number of variables that will influence the YA and the learning outcomes. James Coleman (2010) reminds us that the YA depends on many factors, only some of which can be influenced by institutions and programme coordinators. Individual motivation, attitudes, preparation, curriculum, integration, support, tasks while abroad, debriefing on return, assess-

---

[11] This idea has been translated as a 'cultural mentor' elsewhere (see Berg 2009) and is understood to be a person who will accompany students on their YA path, helping them to be the architects of their own learning. A more detailed discussion of the teaching and learning considerations for this cohort can be found in a paper by the author entitled: "Teaching for Understanding the Year Abroad: Thoughts on Fostering the Reflective Learner", in *Mountain Rise. The International Journal for the Scholarship of Teaching and Learning*, 2014, 8/2, 1-23.

ment and L2 maintenance are all influencing factors (cf. Coleman 2010).

Perhaps in the case of the 19-year old Irish student in Germany or Austria, it is not realistic to expect linguistically proficient, culturally and interculturally competent individuals after 10 months abroad. There is evidence, however, that students are motivated to return to Germany after graduation, to continue learning and speaking German, and are still culturally interested after their Year Abroad. This is fertile ground for them to continue on a learning journey that will develop with time, to return to the opening quote by a student "I would like to return (to Austria). *I have learned from mistakes*". If one reflects on the objectives of ERASMUS to include enabling students to benefit educationally, linguistically and culturally from the experience of learning in other European countries,[12] there is evidence that there is some progress towards meeting these goals. There is, however, grounds to suggest that the Year Abroad is not being fully utilized for linguistic gains and that students can learn from the barriers to learning seen in this study. One main conclusion, therefore, is the need to reflect with students prior to departure on strategies for maximising individual learning experiences once abroad, and to foster in students a sense of self-ownership of individual learning paths during the YA. In this way, Goethe's notion of the conscious and reflective student abroad may in some way be realised.

Sources

Barron, Anne (2003), *Acquisition in Interlanguage Pragmatics. Learning How to Do Things with Words in a Study Abroad Context* (Pragmatics and Beyond New Series 108), Amsterdam – Philadelphia: Benjamins.

Berg, Michael Vande (2009), "Intervening in Student Learning Abroad: A Research-Based Inquiry", *Intercultural Education*, 20, Supplement 1, 15-27.

---

[12] Cf. http://ec.europa.eu/education/lifelong-learning-programme/erasmus_en.htm (22 October 2013).

Brogan, Kristin (2011), "Students as Citizens of the World – the Study Abroad Experience", unpublished conference paper, in *UCC Graduate Conference*, UCC Cork, Department of German, UCC, 4-5 May.

Coleman, James A. & Linda Parker (2001), "Preparing for Residence Abroad: Staff Development Implications", in John Klapper, ed., *Teaching Languages in Higher Education. Issues in Training and Continuing Professional Development*, London, CILT, 134-162.

Coleman, James A. (2010), "What is the Year Abroad for? Insights and Principles for Inform Assessment", paper presentation (*Assessing the Year Abroad*), University of Bath, 26 June.

Conacher, Jean (2008), "'Home Thoughts on Abroad': Zur Identität und Integration irischer Erasmus-StudentInnen in Deutschland", in *German as a Foreign Language*, 2, 1-20.

DAAD (2007), *Verbleibstudie Irland, Abschlussbericht* (unpublished report).

DAAD (2013), *Wissenschaft weltoffen. Daten und Fakten zur Internationalität von Studium und Forschung in Deutschland*, Bielefeld: Bertelsmann, http://www.wissenschaftweltoffen.de/publikation/wiwe_2013_verlinkt.pdf (22 October 2013).

Ehrenreich, Susanne (2008), "Sprachlernsituation Ausland. Sprachbad-Mythen und Lingua-Franca-Realitäten", in Susanne Ehrenreich, Gill Woodman & Marion Perrefort, eds., *Auslandsaufenthalte in Schule und Studium. Bestandsaufnahmen aus Forschung und Praxis*. Münster – New York: Waxmann, 105-122.

Freed, Barbara (1995), "Language Learning and Study Abroad", in Barbara Freed, ed., *Second Language Acquisition in a Study Abroad Context*, Amsterdam – Philadelphia: Benjamins, 3-34.

Freed, Barbara, Norman Segalowitz & Dan Dewey (2004), "Context of Learning and Second Language Fluency in French: Comparing Regular Classroom, Study Abroad, and Intensive Domestic Immersion Programs", *Studies in Second Language Acquisition*, 26, 275-301.

Goethe, Johann Wolfgang (1970), *Italian Journey, 1786-1788*, transl. W.H. Auden and Elizabeth Mayer, London – New York: Penguin Classics.

Islam, Syed (1996), *The Ethics of Travel: from Marco Polo to Kafka*, Manchester: Manchester University Press.

Kim, Young Yun (2009), "The Identity Factor in Intercultural Competence", in Karla Deardorff, ed., *The SAGE Handbook of Intercultural Competence*, Los Angeles – London: SAGE, 53-84.

Mayring, Philipp (1997), *Qualitative Inhaltsanalyse. Grundlagen und Techniken*, Weinheim: Deutscher Studien Verlag.

Murphy-Lejeune, Elizabeth (2008), "The Student Experience of Mobility, A Contrasting Score", in Mike Byram & Fred Dervin, eds., *Students, Staff and Academic Mobility in Higher Education*, Newcastle: Cambridge Scholars Publishing, 12-30.

OECD (2013), *Education at a Glance. OECD Indicators*, http://www.oecd-ilibrary.org/education/education-at-a-glance-2013_eag-2013-en (19 March 2014).

Pellegrino, Valerie (1998), "Student Perspectives on Language Learning in a Study Abroad Context", *Frontiers. The Interdisciplinary Journal of Study Abroad*, Fall, 91-120.

Regan, Vera, Martin Howard & Isabelle Lemée (2009), *The Acquisition of Sociolinguistic Competence in a Study Abroad Context*, Bristol: Multilingual Matters.

Tsoukalas, Ioannis (2008), "The Double Life of Erasmus Students", in Michael Byram & Fred Dervin, eds., *Students, Staff and Academic Mobility in Higher Education*, Newcastle: Cambridge Scholars Publishing, 131-152.

Walsh, Riana (2004), "The Year Abroad – A Linguistic Challenge", *Teanga: The Irish Yearbook of Applied Linguistics*, 14, 48-57.

Westwood, Marvin J. & Michelle Barker (1990), "Academic Achievement and Social Adjustment among International Students: A Comparison Groups Study of the Peer-Pairing Programs", *International Journal of Intercultural Relations*, 14, 251-263.

Elmar Schenkel (Leipzig)*
Velozipedische Kulturwissenschaft.
Über Roland Girtlers Radtour nach Italien

Für den in diesem Band Geehrten ist das wichtigste Fahrzeug sicherlich das Fahrrad. Es muss der Spekulation überlassen bleiben, wie viele seiner Ideen zur Kultur auf zwei Rädern entstanden sind, irgendwo zwischen Gohlis und der Beethovenstraße oder in den Auenwäldern von Leipzig. So dürfte es ihn interessieren, dass ein österreichischer Soziologe und Kulturwissenschaftler einen großen Teil seiner Feldbeobachtung und Theorien über Randkulturen und Kulturkontakte auf dem Fahrrad entwickelt hat. Roland Girtlers radgestützte Studien zu Gaunern, Prostituierten, Rebellen, Wilderern, Pilgern und Vaganten mögen als Ansporn dienen für ähnliche Arbeiten, durchaus auch in theoretischer Hinsicht: Radeln zur Erkenntnis. Vielleicht können diese Hinweise dienlich sein für den in dieser Festschrift Geehrten, wie man seine Tage im Ruhestand verbringen kann. Eine Pilgerfahrt (auch ohne Heilige und Wallfahrtsorte) auf dem Rad, mit offenen Augen und Gelassenheit, mit gelegentlichen Sinnsprüchen und heiteren Begegnungen, guter Lektüre und gutem Tee, wäre nicht die schlechteste Idee, die neue Lebensphase zu eröffnen.

What is truth? said jesting Pilate, and would not stay for an answer.
(Francis Bacon)

Was ist Kultur? fragte Pilatus einst – *nicht*, und wenn wir heute antworten sollten, so könnten wir zurück fragen: von welchem Fahrzeug aus? Das Fahrzeug ist ein Medium, das Geschwindigkeit und Nähe zum beobachteten Objekt vorgibt. Ich sehe Dinge anders, wenn ich sie zu Fuß angehe, mit dem Auto anfahre oder dem Hubschrauber anfliege. Das Fahrzeug ist die Botschaft, um McLuhan abzuwandeln. Selbst Bacon hat Bewegung angedeutet, als er

---

* Elmar Schenkel, geb. in Lippetal bei Soest, Büronachbar des Geehrten, Radler, Schreiber, Maler. Von 2011-12 transsilvanischer Dorfschreiber in Katzendorf/Cata. Zum Verhältnis von Fahrrad und Literatur veröffentlichte er *Cyclomanie*. Neuere Bücher: *Reisen in die ferne Nähe. Unterwegs in Mitteldeutschland* und *Die Stille und der Wolf – Essays.*

hinzufügte, Pilatus habe nicht auf die Antwort gewartet. Pilatus saß schon in einem anderen Fahrzeug, er war ungeduldig, und es passte ihm nicht zuzuhören. Es sollte ja nur ein Scherz sein.

Wer also nach Kultur fragt, muss angeben, wie er oder sie sich ihr nähert. Die Bewegungsart gibt – wie jedes Medium – den Maßstab vor, der wiederum Phänomene erschafft oder verschwinden lässt. Wenn also ein Kulturwissenschaftler seine Studien hauptsächlich vom Fahrrad aus betreibt, so mag dies Auswirkungen auf seine Gegenstände und deren Beobachtung haben. Gadamers philosophischem Klassiker wäre ein *Fahrrad und Methode* gegenüber zu stellen, Hermeneutik als Velozipedik umzudeuten: das Umfahren des Gegenstandes als eine Form der allmählichen Bedeutungserhellung. Darin würde, in bester britischer Manier, weniger theoretisiert als beobachtet, wobei der eigene, bewegliche Standpunkt immer (selbstironischer) Teil des Prozesses bliebe.

Roland Girtler, der 1941 in Spital am Pyhrn (Oberösterreich) geboren wurde, ist sehr heimatbewusst, hat er sich doch unter anderem mit seinen Eltern, die als Landärzte tätig waren, soziologisch beschäftigt. Ebenso mit Klosterschülern, denn ein solcher war auch er, nämlich im berühmten Kloster Kremsmünster. Seine ersten Studien betrieb er Anfang der 1970er Jahre in Indien, unter anderem in Gujarat und Mumbai, später widmete er sich europäischen Randkulturen – neben den oben genannten wären noch die Landler zu erwähnen, bei denen es sich um von Maria Theresia vertriebene Protestanten handelt, die sich in Siebenbürgen, im heutigen Rumänien, niederließen (*Verbannt und vergessen – der Untergang der Landler in Siebenbürgen*, 1992). Bekannt wurde er auch mit seinen „10 Geboten der Feldforschung" (2009). Darin empfiehlt er einen Umgang mit den zu erforschenden Menschen und Gruppen auf Augenhöhe und nicht zuletzt auch dieses, das zehnte Gebot:

> Du mußt eine gute Konstitution haben, um dich am Acker, in stickigen Kneipen, in der Kirche, in noblen Gasthäusern, im Wald, im Stall, auf staubigen Straßen und auch sonst wo wohl zu fühlen. Dazu gehört die Fähigkeit, jederzeit zu essen, zu trinken und zu schlafen. (ibid.)

In seinem Büchlein *Vom Fahrrad aus* (2011) skizziert Girtler einige seiner Methoden und Beobachtungen und hebt das Radeln als perfekte Position des Kulturwissenschaftlers hervor. Der Radfahrer sieht sich in einem anderen Zeitrahmen als der Autofahrer und unterliegt weniger dem Diktat des ‚Zeit ist Geld'. Als Radler bleibt er subversiv, etwa wenn er kurz einen Kongress in Alpbach besucht, wo die gelehrten Hochschulwochen stattfinden: „Diesmal möchte ich mir das Getue nur kurz ansehen, als Außenseiter, als jemand, der nicht dazugehört, der auf seinem Fahrrad die Weisheit der Teilnehmer lediglich am Rande bemerkt." (2011: 34) Die Zeit reicht, um sich ein Bild zu machen und eine kleine kulturwissenschaftliche Vignette des Gelehrten einzuschieben, von dem man sich durch den Raddress unterscheidet: „Die wohl wichtigsten Symbole dieser Gemeinschaft weiser Leute sind: eine gelehrte Sprache, geflissentlicher Ernst und die Vorstellung, ein Träger der Wahrheit zu sein. […] Wissenschaft hat ernst zu sein, zumindest solange, als man nicht beim gemeinsamen Büfett steht." (ibid.: 37) In einem weiteren Essay sieht er gar Ähnlichkeiten zwischen den Sprachen der Wissenschaftler und der Ganoven, die beide Spezialjargons entwickelt haben (ibid.: 81). Ihm schwebt dagegen eine heitere Wissenschaft vor, eine, die sich den Menschen zuwendet und ihnen hilft, ihre Herzen zu öffnen. Also was ist Wahrheit, wenn sie schon nicht auf Konferenzen zu finden ist? „Mein Bier, welches ich hier am Abend trinke, ist für mich die Wahrheit schlechthin." (ibid.: 42) Dieser Ausspruch ist natürlich nicht universell gültig. Wahrheit ist subjektiv, wollen wir daraus schließen, und sie ist flüssig (es darf auch Tee sein). Explizit entschuldigt sich der Vegetarier Girtler am Ende seines Reisebuches *Die Lust des Vagabundierens* gar: „Jenen Leuten, die sich daran stoßen sollten, daß ich hier und da Bier und Rotwein auf würdige Leute trinke, sei gesagt, daß ich dies nur aus rituellen Gründen tue. Grundsätzlich trinke ich kaum Alkohol, und wenn, dann nur sehr mäßig." (2001: 336). Das Ritual wird in diesem Buch allerdings täglich und manchmal mehrmals täglich ausgeführt. Daran ist gar nichts auszusetzen – ich finde es eher schade, dass er sich entschuldigen zu müssen glaubt. Denn das Getränk erfrischt ihn nicht nur, es bietet auch Gelegenheit, ein Fazit über seine täglichen kulturgeschichtlichen Erkenntnisse zu ziehen. Zudem lockert es die Zunge, man kommt ins Gespräch.

Bei der Reise, die er in *Die Lust des Vagabundierens* (2001) schildert, handelt es sich um eine Pilgertour per Rad von Österreich nach Assisi und zurück. Solche Pilgertouren sind inzwischen wieder sehr modern geworden, spätestens seit Shirley MacLaine und Hape Kerkeling den Jakobsweg bewanderten. Davon grenzt sich Girtler jedoch ab – immer ist er ein Kritiker des Mainstream gewesen, so auch hier. Der Jakobsweg, oder besser der Kult des Heiligen Jakob, verkörpert ihm Islamfeindlichkeit und Ketzerbekämpfung. Näheres dazu schrieb er in seinem Buch *Irrweg Jakobsweg. Die Narbe in den Seelen von Muslimen, Juden und Ketzern* (2005). Girtler hat andere Heilige, die ihm besser gefallen, etwa den hl. Antonius von Padua und insbesondere den hl. Franziskus von Assisi. Sie stehen für eine liebende Kirche, die sich mit den Armen solidarisiert und die daher besser zu Girtlers sozialem Denken passen. Dazu eine alte Liebe zu Italien, zur italienischen Mentalität, und schon geht die Reise los: über die Alpen nach Venedig, über Padua und Bologna nach Assisi und zurück über Siena, Florenz und Ravenna durch die Dolomiten nach Osttirol.

Es ist aber keine Radtour wie es jede andere sein könnte, gespickt mit Erlebnissen, Wetterkapriolen und Begegnungen. Dies alles findet sich hier natürlich auch, doch ist es durchdrungen vom Blick des Kulturwissenschaftlers. Girtler findet auf dieser Reise seine alten Themen wieder: die Vagabunden und Wilderer ebenso wie die Ketzer und Aufmüpfigen, die gegen den ausbeuterischen Adel rebellierenden Bauern und Protestanten, die Siebenbürger Landler und Reisenden, die Pilger, Vaganten und Studenten. Dazu kommt das wache Ohr für die Sprache, sei es das Italienische, Lateinische, Österreichische, Etruskische oder Ladinische, ein Hineinhorchen in die Geschichte der Wörter, die so manchen Aufschluss über Völkerwanderungen und kulturelle Einflüsse geben. Girtler hat zudem nicht nur Heilige als Helden, sondern auch große Einzelne wie den gotischen König Theoderich (Dietrich von Bern), den sagenhaften Zwergenkönig Laurin oder Dante im Visier. Jeder Ort ist mit deren Geschichten besetzt. Manches weiß der Reisende von vornherein, manches schnappt er auf, anderes muss er sich in Broschüren erlesen.

Immerhin ergibt diese Reise für den Leser eine Art Kulturgeschichte, die von der Vorzeit der Etrusker bis hin zu den Kämpfen zwischen Österreichern und Italienern im Ersten Weltkrieg reicht. Einige Höhepunkte seien herausgehoben. In Venedig erinnert er sich an Marco Polo, der ihm wie ein reisender Kulturwissenschaftler erscheint. Auch er habe die fernsten Fernen aufgesucht und Berichte mitgebracht über die damaligen Randkulturen – so wie sie von Europa aus gesehen wurden. In Padua grüßt er den hl. Antonius, der ihm in seiner Menschen zugewandten Art gefällt und auch darin ein Muster für kulturelles Verstehen darstellt. Da Girtler jemand ist, der dauernd etwas sucht oder verlegt hat, ist Antonius genau der richtige Heilige, ihm zu helfen (2001: 116). (Ich darf hinzufügen, dass meine Mutter als gute Katholikin auch alles wieder fand, weil sie Antonius anrief. Der protestantische Geehrte möge ob dieses Volksglaubens nachsichtig sein.)

Jedoch ist Girtler nicht der Askese oder Sinnesverachtung zugewandt. Das zeigt sich darin, dass der zweite ‚Heilige', den er nach seinem Besuch in Venedig verehrt, Casanova ist. Auch in diesem sieht er einen Verwandten, er lobt ihn ob seiner Schläue und seiner Beweglichkeit. Immer wieder breitet Girtler die Arme aus und lässt sie alle zu sich kommen: „Ich glaube überhaupt, dass echte Heilige Vagabunden sind, ebenso wie wahre Gelehrte und Dichter." (2001: 104)

In Bologna – noch weiß er nichts von den Spaghetti Bolognese, die auch Bologna-Prozess heißen und von dem wir sehr wohl wissen, wem oder was es den Prozess gemacht hat, der universitären Freiheit und Mobilität nämlich – erinnert er an die älteste Universität Europas mit ihren bis heute teils andauernden Gebräuchen. Ich durfte dies selbst vor einigen Jahren erleben, als ich zufällig unter den Arkaden der Universität ging und eine Gruppe von Studenten einen neugeweihten Doktor empfing. Sie taten es mit lautem Gesang und riefen „Dottore! Dottore!" Dann musste dieser eine launige Rede auf offener Straße halten. Der Kulturwissenschaftler sieht hier Initiationsrituale aus alten Zeiten. Girtler, der überall

Verwandte sucht, findet sie auch unter den Studenten, denn diese waren im Mittelalter meist unterwegs, wie ihre Lehrer auch.

In Assisi schließlich erzählt er uns viel über den hl. Franziskus, der sich von einem kriegerischen Playboy zu einem wahren Heiligen wandelte, der all seine Habe den Armen gab und mit den Tieren sprach. Es lohnt sich, seine Lebensgeschichte heute zu lesen, da der jetzige Papst Franziskus in dieser Tradition steht. Girtlers Sympathie und Bewunderung hat er allemal.

In Siena erfahren wir etwas über ein weiteres Initiationsritual, das Pferderennen auf dem schönsten Platz der Welt, *Il Campo*. Florenz bringt ihm, neben den Wundern der Renaissance, zuallererst Dante ins Gedächtnis. Dieser ist auch ein Ausgestoßener, der vom Rande her agieren muss, nachdem ihn die papsttreuen Guelfen aus Florenz vertrieben hatten. Damit hat er wieder alle Sympathie des radelnden Gelehrten, der am liebsten alle seine historischen Favoriten auf Fahrrädern sähe. Den hl. Franziskus und den hl. Antonius etwa ernennt der fröhliche Wissenschaftler spontan zu den Patronen des Radfahrens. Dante erscheint ihm zudem als früher Vertreter des vereinigten Europas (2001: 240). Der andere Dichter, den Girtler besingt, ist Francesco Petrarca, nicht nur als Begründer des Sonetts, sondern auch und vor allem, weil er ein Bergsteiger war und als erster über seinen Gang auf einen Berg in der Provence, den Mont Ventoux, geschrieben hat – zu einer Zeit, als Berge verpönt waren. Dante, der ja in seiner *Commedia* viel klettern muss, wird von ihm ebenfalls zum Bergsteiger ernannt.

Weitere historische Figuren, denen er begegnet und die ihm zumeist Respekt und oft Sympathie einflößen, sind Paracelsus, der Wanderarzt, der Gotenkönig Theoderich in Ravenna, dessen Grab er aufsucht, sowie der Kartograph Waldseemüller, dem Amerika seinen Namen verdankt und der dies bald danach bereute, weil er einem Fehler aufgesessen war. Ab 1513 dachte er nämlich, Amerika sei kein eigener Kontinent und nannte es wieder *terra incognita*! Die Reise endet im Reiche des Zwergenkönigs Laurin, der sich mit Dietrich von Bern herumschlagen musste – und Girtler weiß nicht, wem er jetzt die meiste Sympathie geben soll. Danach geht der Autor eine alte, befreundete Wildererfamilie besuchen.

Ich habe es unterlassen, die vielen Gespräche aufzuzählen, die Girtler während seiner Tour in Gaststätten, Pizzerien, Hotels, an Tankstellen und Straßenrändern mit Einwohnern und anderen Touristen führte. Manchmal sind sie nur *small talk*, der den Tag leichter macht, manchmal versucht er, in das Innere eines Ortes vorzustoßen durch das richtige Fragen. Das hat er schließlich in seiner Feldforschung gelernt. Für diese Art von Kommunikation hat er den Begriff „ero-episches Gespräch" erfunden. Das heißt, dass gefragt und erzählt wird und der Forscher sich selbst einbringt als Person (2001: 256). Dabei hilft ihm gelegentlich sein Talent, mit vier Bällen zu jonglieren, denn das macht Eindruck und erleichtert den Zugang zu Fremden.

Aber vor allem das Fahrrad spielt immer wieder eine Rolle in solchen Anbahnungen. Etwa, wenn er einen Platten hat und auf die Hilfe anderer angewiesen ist oder wenn er sich vor einem Gewitter unterstellen muss. Den meisten nötigt der Sechzigjährige Respekt ab, da er den schweren Weg über die Alpen nach Assisi geschafft hat – und das ist allemal eine gute Voraussetzung für Gespräche. Zwischendurch philosophiert er gerne über den Unterschied zwischen Autofahrern und Radlern – das ist etwa so wie zwischen Fleischessern und Vegetariern (Girtler ist ein solcher, wie er allenthalben bei der Bestellung von vegetarischen Pizzen mitteilen zu müssen glaubt). Und er ist natürlich auch ein großer Leser. Seine Lieblingsbücher sind *Don Quijote*, die *Göttliche Komödie*, *Simplicius Simplicissimus* und *Spaziergang nach Syrakus* von J.G. Seume. Alle diese Bücher haben mit Ruhelosigkeit zu tun, mit Wandern, Exil, Reisen in der Fremde, mit Fahrten ins Unbekannte hinein. Daher erklärt er einmal einer Dame, dass er sich wie ein Vagabund fühle, der nie genau wisse, wohin sein Weg führe (2001: 238). Insofern ist seine italienische Radtour auch ein Bild der Reise, auf der wir uns alle befinden.

Quellen

Girtler, Roland (1992), *Verbannt und vergessen – der Untergang der Landler in Siebenbürgen,* Linz: Veritas.

--- (1995), *Randkulturen: Theorie der Unanständigkeit,* Wien: Böhlau.

--- (1998), *Wilderer – Soziale Rebellen in den Bergen,* Wien: Böhlau.

--- (2000), *Die alte Klosterschule. Eine Welt der Strenge und der kleinen Rebellen,* Wien: Böhlau.

--- (2001), *Die Lust des Vagabundierens. Eine Pilgerreise mit dem Fahrrad nach Assisi,* Wien: Böhlau.

--- (2005), *Irrweg Jakobsweg. Die Narbe in den Seelen von Muslimen, Juden und Ketzern,* Graz: Steirische Verlagsgesellschaft.

--- (2007), *Das letzte Lied vor Hermannstadt,* Wien: Böhlau.

--- (2009), „Die 10 Gebote der Feldforschung", http://www.qualitative-forschung.de/fqs-supplement/members/Girtler/girtler-10Geb-d.html (12. März 2014).

--- (2011), *Vom Fahrrad aus,* Wien: LIT Verlag.

Gabriele Linke (Rostock)*
Aufbruch zu neuen Welten:
Fahrräder und andere Verkehrsmittel in schottischen autobiographischen Texten

Unsere Fahrräder, Fahrradfahrwetter und Fahrradtouren spielten in den persönlicheren Kommunikationen mit Joachim Schwend über viele Jahre hinweg eine Rolle. Unser Hang zum Fahrradfahren gab uns, neben dem kollegial-fachlichen Austausch, immer ein verbindendes Thema, für das Grenzen und Entfernungen bedeutungslos waren. Was läge da näher, als auch hier verwandte Erfahrungen zu betrachten, zumal in dem ihm so vertrauten Schottland?

In Anbetracht der schier endlosen Küstenlinie Schottlands und seiner überwiegend bergigen und teilweise dünn besiedelten Landschaften scheint es ganz offensichtlich, dass Fortbewegungsmittel in Schottland und in den Lebensgeschichten seiner Bewohner auch heute immer wieder eine große Rolle spielen. Da sind nicht nur die schottischen Auswanderer, die auf Schiff und Bahn angewiesen waren, sondern auch *Glaswegians* und andere Stadtbewohner, die für ihren Weg zur Arbeit und andere besondere oder alltägliche Verrichtungen die Straßenbahnen und Busse unverzichtbar fanden. Aber auch weniger prominente Fortbewegungsmittel bestimmten das Leben mancher Menschen. Wer kein Geld, aber Zeit hatte, fuhr mit dem Fahrrad nach Oxford, um dort sein Stipendium anzutreten, und in der Kindheit konnte ein Roller den Kontakt zur Welt herstellen.

Hier soll es eher um die kleinen, alltäglichen Fortbewegungsmittel gehen als um die großen und schnellen Maschinen für weite und

---

* Gabriele Linke promovierte 1987 an der FSU Jena auf dem Gebiet der Angewandten Sprachwissenschaft und arbeitet seit 1992 auf dem Gebiet der Cultural Studies. Sie habilitierte sich mit einer Arbeit zu populären Liebesromanen des Verlags Harlequin Mills & Boon. Seit 2001 ist sie Professorin für britische und amerikanische Kulturstudien an der Universität Rostock und arbeitet, unter anderem, auf den Gebieten Autobiographie, Film, und Geschlechterstudien.

lange Reisen, aber auch darum, wie man – globale, und deshalb auch schottische – Kultur studieren kann, indem man Verkehr studiert (eine Idee, die unter anderem Peter Sloterdijk in seinen *Globen II* (1999) ausführte). Wie dicht liegen Ausgangspunkt und Ziel beieinander, und wie wichtig sind sie? Welche Beziehungen werden durch Mobilität verwirklicht, beendet oder neu gestiftet? Ist die Gewissheit einer Rückkehr wichtig? Antworten auf diese und andere Fragen können erhellen, wie sich Personen sozial verorten, eine kulturelle, soziale oder familiäre Zugehörigkeit leben, aufgeben, oder anstreben. Sie können die Bedeutungen, soziale Wichtigkeit und Auswirkungen von Orten, Räumen, Distanzen und Grenzüberschreitungen offenlegen, sowohl Fluchten aus Räumen als auch Zuflüchte sichtbar machen. Wie aber schreiben Menschen in Schottland im 20. Jahrhundert über ihre Beförderungsmittel, und welche Grenzen werden mit deren Hilfe überschritten?

Autobiographischen Texten kommt hier ein besonderer Ort zwischen dem Dokumentarischen und dem Fiktionalen zu. Auch wenn heute die Selektivität und (Re)Konstruiertheit autobiographischer Erinnerungen außer Frage stehen, wirkt, nach Philippe Lejeune (1989), doch der autobiographische Pakt zwischen AutorIn und Leserschaft, der garantieren soll, dass dem autobiographischen Text nachprüfbare Lebensdaten zugrunde liegen und die AutorInnen sich subjektiv um Wahrhaftigkeit bemühen. So beziehen sich die Texte einerseits auf historisch konkrete Verkehrsmittel, andererseits werden nur die Aspekte erzählt, die Spuren in der Erinnerung hinterlassen haben und für die nachträgliche Sinnstiftung in der Lebensgeschichte besonders wichtig sind, weil neue Territorien und Bereiche sozialer Erfahrungen und Entfaltung erobert wurden. Die Bedeutungen, die Menschen ihren Fortbewegungsmitteln zuschreiben, sind wichtige Teile gesellschaftlicher Sinnstiftung. Abschließend sei vermerkt, dass die zitierten Texte von AutorInnen verfasst wurden, die überwiegend in der zweiten Hälfte des 20. Jahrhunderts gelebt haben und den unteren Schichten der Bevölkerung Schottlands entstammen.

Die Grenze zum Erwachsenwerden ‚erfahren'
In ihren Kindheitserinnerungen *This Is Not About Me* beschreibt die Schriftstellerin Janice Galloway die Vorform des Fahrrads, den Roller, als Mittel der Erweiterung ihres Aktionsradius, denn zunächst ermöglicht er der fünfjährigen Janice, allein zum Strand zu rollern, mit einem Sandeimerchen am Lenker. Galloway hebt hervor, dass es damals noch normal war, dass Fünfjährige allein am Strand herumliefen und Eltern Selbständigkeit und Unbeaufsichtigtsein zuließen. Die einsamen Ausflüge zum Strand bringen natürlich Abenteuer und Begegnungen neuer Art, wie die Bekanntschaft mit dem Jungen Colin, der aus Angst vor seinem Vater nicht nach Hause gehen will. Bezüglich der Bedeutung ihres Rollers vermutet Galloway, „[t]he scooter must have opened up my sense of adventure" (Galloway 2009: 106). Die fünfjährige Janice nimmt sich mit ihrem Roller auch eines Tages vor, einer geregelten Arbeit nachzugehen, sucht sich eine Aufgabe auf einem kleinen Platz hinter einem Kino, auf dem sie Risse im Beton mit Kies füllen will, und weist dem Roller eine zentrale Funktion in ihrem ‚Arbeitstag' zu:

> 1. scooter to work with a head held high, park scooter sideways near gravel; 2. scoop up said gravel […] in spade to half-fill bucket, balance half bucket load on the scooter handle carefully for journey to the broken slabs; […] 4. scooter back to gravel pit and start again from step one. (Galloway 2009: 107)

Nach wenigen Tagen gibt sie auf, weil ihre Arbeit immer wieder im Alltag zunichte gemacht wird, aber dem Roller kommt bei ihrem Projekt eine wichtige Rolle zu: Auf dem Weg zu und bei der Arbeit und wenn Lasten zu bewegen sind, müssen Transportmittel hinzugezogen werden, die dem Gewicht der Arbeit entsprechen, sie aufwerten und die Arbeiterin stolz machen, so dass sie hoch erhobenen Hauptes dahinrollen kann, wie unter 1. beschrieben – mit Roller und Sandeimerchen werden hier freudvoll wichtige Muster des Erwachsenenlebens eingeübt, wird ‚spielerisch' die Grenze zwischen spontanem, zweckfreiem Kinderspiel und planvoller, routinierter Erwachsenentätigkeit überschritten.

Robert Douglas tritt als Fünfzehnjähriger allmählich in die Welt der Erwachsenen ein, und auch die Straßenbahn trägt ihren Teil zu diesem Übergang bei. Zum einen gibt sie männlichen *Glaswegians* die Gelegenheit, „The Art of Alighting from a Moving Tram" zu praktizieren und zu vervollkommnen: „This was a rite of passage. Part of being a man. To exit gracefully from a tram in motion – the faster it was going the better – made one appear 'dead gallus'" (Douglas 2005: 283). Zum anderen trägt sie ihn zu seiner Lehrstelle in der North British Locomotive Company. In der morgendlich vollen Straßenbahn fühlt er sich stolz den Arbeitern zugehörig, die, wie er, ausgestattet mit Frühstückspaketen und praktischer Kleidung, schweigend und Zeitung lesend ihrem Tagewerk entgegenrattern. Am Ende des Tages beschließt er, von nun an auch eine Abendzeitung zu kaufen und auf der Heimfahrt zu lesen: „Aye. Just like aw the other Working Men" (ibid.: 289). Der Unterschied zum Schulweg wird für ihn durch die Straßenbahnfahrt sinnlich erlebbar, und das Befolgen der Arbeiter-Rituale in der Straßenbahn gibt ihm die Möglichkeit, sein neues Zugehörigkeitsgefühl zu den Arbeitern und seinen glanzvollen Status als Verdiener auszudrücken.

Christina Hall wächst als Tochter von Kleinbauern, *Crofters*, auf South Uist in den Äußeren Hebriden auf und logiert während ihrer Grundschulzeit bei Verwandten auf der benachbarten Insel Barra, denn oftmals leben Familienmitglieder über die Inseln verstreut. Die erste Schiffspassage, die sie als Neunjährige allein unternimmt, lässt sie eine neue Art von Selbstständigkeit und familiärer Anerkennung erreichen. Sie reißt von ihren Tanten auf Barra aus, um an der Hochzeit eines Cousins auf Benbecula teilzunehmen. Mit ihren Ersparnissen bricht sie auf, nimmt den Bus nach Castlebay und die Fähre nach Lochboisdale. Die Schiffspassage auf der *Loch Earn* prägt sich der unerfahrenen Reisenden als „the worst possible means of getting from A to B in the history of travel" (Hall 1999: 33) ein. Sie wird, wie viele andere Reisende, seekrank, versucht die verschiedenen unbeschreiblichen Gerüche zu beschreiben und fühlt sich sterbenselend. Sie nimmt jedoch die Unannehmlichkeiten der Fahrt in Kauf, um zur Hochzeit zu kommen, und ihre Unabhängigkeit und Starrköpfigkeit werden belohnt. Ihre Sorgen über ihre Weiterreise erweisen sich als unbegründet, denn ihr Vater erwartet sie bereits in Lochboisdale, und für die anderen Kinder ist die Schiffsreisende eine Heldin. Das gute Ende ihres großen Kindheitsabenteuers zeigt, dass die Fährpassagen den Zusammenhalt zwischen Familienmitgliedern über das Wasser hinweg ermöglichen, aber diese Beziehungen auch auf die Probe stellen. Die Bereitschaft zur Überwindung der See zwischen den Inseln stellt eine wichtige Voraussetzung für das Erwachsenwerden dar. Folgerichtig werden in Halls Erzählung ihre eigenständigen Mühen um die Stärkung der Familienstrukturen als ein Schritt zum Erwachsenwerden anerkannt.

Weite Wege zum sozialen Aufstieg
Wenn man vom Zusammenhang von Wohn- und Arbeitsort und der Zugehörigkeit zu sozialen Klassen ausgeht, ergibt sich als Konsequenz, dass, wer sozial aufsteigen möchte, sich räumlich bewegen muss und das Überschreiten sozialer Grenzen im Allgemeinen das Überwinden von räumlichen involviert. Ralph Glasser, als Sohn armer jüdischer Emigranten 1920 in den Gorbals – dem berühmtesten Arbeiterviertel Glasgows – geboren, aufgewachsen und als Textilarbeiter beschäftigt, fühlt sich schicksalhaft und unlösbar seinem dem Glücksspiel verfallenen Vater verbunden. Er wagt in seiner Jugend nicht, dieses unsichtbare Band zu durchtrennen: „If only I could walk away from all this!" (Glasser 2006: 194) Als er, in Abendkursen gebildet, ein Stipendium an der Universität Oxford gewinnt, gelingt es ihm, Konventionen, Pflicht- und Schuldgefühle zu überwinden und ein gebrauchtes Fahrrad zu erwerben, um nach Oxford zu radeln. Die Reaktionen der älteren Generation auf seine Flucht aus den Gorbals variieren. Während der Vater seines Freundes die Reise nach Oxford als „romantic, heroic quest" sieht (ibid.: 236), kann sein eigener Vater nur einen prosaischen Akt „to better [him]self" und ein schicksalhaftes Ereignis erkennen, aber Glasser vermutet auch, dass sein Vater die Parallelen zwischen seiner eigenen Reise aus der osteuropäischen Heimat in den *melting pot* Glasgows und der Reise seines Sohnes nach Oxford erkennt – in beiden Fällen führt sie zu einer Welt „light years distant from these [his] roots" (ibid.), was nicht nur geographisch, sondern nationalkulturell-ethnisch im Falle des Vaters und bezogen auf soziale Klassenzugehörigkeit im Falle des Sohns zu verstehen ist.

Schon als er sein Fahrrad aus der Wohnung schiebt, verändert sich sein Raumgefühl: „Indeed the place was already receding from me."

(ibid.: 235) Glasser schwelgt in der Beschreibung des Verkehrsmittels, das ihn von den Slums der Gorbals zur Universität in England bringen soll. Das Fahrrad verfügt über eine Gangschaltung und einen Dynamo zur Beleuchtung; in einer wasserdichten Satteltasche sind Wäsche, Lebensmittel und sogar ein Primuskocher verstaut (ibid.) – alles Zeichen dafür, dass es sich um die Reise seines Lebens, um ein großes und langes Abenteuer handeln wird, für das er gerüstet sein will. Er plant lange Tagesstrecken und preiswerte Übernachtungen in den Unterkünften des *Cyclists' Touring Club*. Auf seinem Weg über die kahlen Höhen der Cheviot Hills erfährt er die Erschöpfung und Einsamkeit des *in-between*-Seins vor der eigentlichen Grenzüberschreitung, aber er wird auch durch ermutigende Begegnungen gestärkt und rollt nach fünf Tagen wohlbehalten nach Oxford hinein. Bei seiner Ankunft ermöglicht ihm sein Fahrrad, dass er die Oxforder City, die er als nahezu absolute Gegenwelt zu den Gorbals empfindet, immer wieder in alle Richtungen durchqueren, sich so mit ihr sofort vertraut machen und sie sich aneignen kann. Dieses Hochgefühl auf dem Fahrrad prägt ihn, auch wenn er die Stadt mit ihren Colleges im Weiteren als *the citadel* bezeichnet, zu der man sich den Eingang schwer erkämpfen muss. Nach der Aufnahme in das College verliert das Fahrrad seine große Bedeutung und geht ein in den Alltag einer Stadt, in der kaum etwas mehr als „a short bicycle ride" (ibid.: 249) von den Colleges entfernt ist. Es hatte ihn, den *Gorbals boy*, aber von Nord nach Süd, von den Slums zur Universität und aus der Welt jüdischer Immigranten und Arbeiter in den von bürgerlichem und aristokratischem Lebensstil geprägten Mikrokosmos der Universität Oxford getragen.

Aber auch innerhalb einer Stadt gibt es territorial-soziale Grenzen, die immer wieder neu gezogen werden und überschritten werden müssen. Meg Hendersons Familie gehörte zu den vielen Arbeiterfamilien, die in den 1950ern aus den Mietskasernen von Glasgow nach Drumchapel zogen, das neben Castlemilk und anderen ein neues Hochhaus-Wohngebiet vor den Toren Glasgows war und seinen Bewohnern modernen Komfort versprach. Henderson, die sehr kritisch die Veränderungen in Glasgow nach dem Zweiten Weltkrieg kommentiert, beklagt den Verlust der engen sozialen Netzwerke der alten ‚Slums' von Glasgow und sieht in der Entfernung zu den zurückgebliebenen Menschen und den langen Wegen zur Arbeit einen großen Nachteil. Jedoch erinnert sie sich an ihre erste Busfahrt als eine Reise durch eine ihr bis dahin fremde Welt von Bäumen, Rasen und breiten Straßen, später durch Felder, bis sie zum neuen Wohngebiet kommen. Da es in Drumchapel keine Schulen gibt, organisiert die Schulbehörde ein „bussing", das Henderson und andere „Catholic overspill children" (Henderson 1994: 101) täglich zu einer katholischen Mädchenschule im wohlhabenden West End von Glasgow befördert. Dort verbringt sie die glücklichsten Jahre ihrer Schulzeit, erfährt Wertschätzung und Ermutigung, und in dieser kurzen Zeit wird der Grundstein für ihre spätere Arbeit als Journalistin gelegt.

Auch Schiffspassagen liegen in manchen Fällen auf dem Weg zu höherer Bildung und sozialem Aufstieg. Das Leben auf den Äußeren Hebriden bot Kindern viele Freiheiten und Abenteuer, aber zum Schulbesuch mussten sie oftmals auf eine andere Insel oder, für eine weiterführende Bildung, auf das Festland. Christina Hall besucht in der Oberstufe eine katholische Mädchenschule in Fort William. Für sie verbinden sich viele Erinnerungen mit den Fährpassagen, die sie vor und nach allen Ferienzeiten zur oder von der elterlichen *Croft* beförderten. Die Oberschulzeit war ein Test des Familienzusammenhalts, denn um an die Schulen auf dem Festland zu gelangen, musste man sechs Mal im Jahr den Minch queren, wozu Hall bemerkt: „The journeys alone would be enough to put many people off […] they were a necessary evil, and we were so proud of having joined ranks of the chosen" (Hall 1999: 120). Die Reise ist immer „unfailingly awful" (ibid.), und Hall bekennt: „I prayed for death many times during my seasick school journeys […]" (ibid.). Sie fügt hinzu, dass selbst Seeleute, die den Golf von Biskaya gut überstanden, den Minch fürchteten, nicht nur wegen schlechten Wetters und Strömungen, sondern auch wegen der miserablen Schiffe. Hall selbst errechnet, dass sie zwischen ihrem 14. und 20. Lebensjahr mindestens 216 Stunden auf See verbringt, und sie „fed the herring" jedes Mal (ibid.: 121). Es ist bemerkenswert, dass sie die regelmäßigen unangenehmen Schiffspassagen für einen Grund hält, der manche davon abhält, eine höhere Bildung anzustreben, die in den 1950er Jahren nur auf dem Festland möglich war. Die schrecklichen Seefahrten ertragen Hall und andere aber auch aus Stolz, die Prüfungen für die höhere Schule bestanden zu haben, und sehen sie als einen Preis, der für die Chancen auf einen besseren Beruf oder ein Studium zu zahlen ist. Hall wird später Lehrerin, aber ihrer Familie auf South Uist bleibt sie ihr Leben lang innig verbunden. Die Querung des Minch und das Schiff selbst sind zwar mit negativen Assoziationen verbunden, aber die Reise trennt nicht nur, sondern verbindet zugleich, prüft und fördert den Aufstiegswillen der Jugendlichen und ihre Selbstständigkeit, aber auch ihre Fähigkeiten, soziale und emotionale Beziehungen zu erhalten; die Schiffe wie auch der Strom von Menschen zwischen den Hebriden und dem Festland stiften Verbindungen zwischen Inseln und Festland als Teilen Schottlands, und dennoch ist der Minch eine Barriere, die immer wieder neu zu überwinden ist.

Grenzen zwischen privatem und öffentlichem Raum
Schiffspassagen spielen bei der Überschreitung der Grenzen zwischen privatem und öffentlichem Raum keine Rolle, wohl aber Fahrräder, die nicht nur von Männern, sondern von Anfang an auch von Frauen genutzt wurden. Den Frauen dienten sie als Mittel zum Verlassen der häuslichen Sphäre und zur Erweiterung ihres Aktionsradius, was im 19. Jahrhundert fast zu einer *moral panic* führte, wie einschlägige Frauengeschichten berichten. Im 20. Jahrhundert behauptet das Fahrrad mit verschiedensten Funktionen seinen Platz im Leben vieler Frauen.

In der Lebensgeschichte der Hebamme Anne Bayne spielt das Fahrrad eine Rolle, weil es ihr als berufstätiger Frau Bewegung im öffentlichen Raum ermöglicht und der Respekt, der dem Hebammenberuf gezollt wird, sogar dem Hebammenfahrrad zugute kommt. Dieses besitzt in Baynes Erzählung keine Bremse, aber der Polizist hält an der Haymarket-Kreuzung in Edinburgh, an der sich fünf Straßen treffen, den Verkehr immer an, so dass sie ohne zu bremsen über die Kreuzung segeln kann. Sie findet nie heraus, ob er wusste, dass das Fahrrad keine Bremsen hat, oder ob er mit dem Gedanken „Here comes the nurse" („Anne Bayne": 102) seiner Achtung vor ihrem Beruf und der angenommenen Dringlichkeit ihrer Fahrten Ausdruck verlieh – aber sie ist sich sicher: „Nurses had a great respect" (ibid.: 99). Dieses Bewusstsein ihrer wichtigen Aufgabe in den Gemeinden und ihres hohen sozialen Ansehens spielt in vielen Lebensgeschichten schottischer Hebammen eine große Rolle, und so erzählen einige Anekdoten vom Respekt und den Privilegien, die Hebammen genießen, wenn sie sich kreuz und quer durch den öffentlichen Raum bewegen. Bayne berichtet, wie sie eine Stelle in Tullibody antritt, das sie als ein „little elite introverted mining village" bezeichnet (ibid.: 103), wobei das Wort „elite" keineswegs überrascht, denn Bergarbeitersiedlungen wurden lange Zeit als traditionelle Gemeinwesen idealisiert, die durch klare (hierarchische) soziale Strukturen und feste moralische Wertvorstellungen geprägt waren, unter welchen Gutnachbarlichkeit und Gemeinsinn eine besondere Rolle zukam. Bayne bekommt von der Kommune in den 1950er Jahren einen Vespa-Roller mit Gebrauchsanweisung und fährt dann zu einer Tankstelle, um nach dem nötigen Benzin-Öl-Gemisch zu fragen. Der Tankwart versorgt sie drei Jahre lang mit Gemisch und sagt ihr am Ende, alles sei bezahlt, es gebe keine offene Rechnung. Bayne berichtet zufrieden: „So that's the kind of thing that went on. I've nae doubt that it was miners who did that" (ibid.: 104). Ihre Erzählung zeugt vom Stolz auf den Respekt und die Fürsorglichkeit, mit denen das Bergarbeiterdorf ihre Arbeit belohnt, aber auch sichert, dass die Hebamme in ihrem Bezirk immer schnell zur Stelle sein kann.

Diese Privilegien wirken jedoch nur im Arbeitsbezirk der Frauen und wenn sie vermutlich zu ihrer wichtigen Arbeit unterwegs sind; die Frauen stellen meist die Nutzung von Fahrrad und Motorroller auch nur als Teil ihrer beruflichen Mobilität dar. Allerdings rühmt sich Ann Lamb, geboren 1902, die oft mit dem Fahrrad (auch hier wieder einem gebraucht gekauften!) zu Patientinnen fuhr: „I rode the bicycle, I was a great lass on the bicycle and I had fun" („Ann Lamb": 15). Anne Chapman hingegen beobachtet, dass im Glasgow der 1940er und 50er Jahren die meisten Hebammen zu Fuß gingen oder die Straßenbahn nahmen, während sie selbst radelte und auch die Frauen der „gypsies" in ihren Zeltlagern außerhalb der Stadt versorgte („Anne Chapman": 65-66). Die Möglichkeit der sehr individuellen Mobilität, die das Fahrrad den Frauen in der Stadt verschaffen konnte, wurde also nur von wenigen genutzt, und diese nahmen dann das Fahrrad als einen erwähnenswerten Teil ihrer Lebensgeschichte wahr, durch den sie sich von den Bus- oder Bahnnutzerinnen unterschieden. Zweifellos war das Fahrrad für die radelnden Hebammen – berufstätige und in der Öffentlichkeit sichtbare Frauen – ein Ausdruck von Kraft, Selbstvertrauen, Unabhängigkeit und selbstbewusster Beanspruchung des öffentlichen Raums.

Jenseits der Stadtgrenzen
In den Großstädten Schottlands brachten Bus und Straßenbahn viele Jahrzehnte lang die ärmeren Stadtbewohner zur Erholung vor die Tore der Stadt. Robert Douglas beschreibt seinen ersten Tagesausflug mit der Straßenbahn nach Milngavie, einem Dorf damals außerhalb Glasgows, mit einer Gruppe Freunde. Aufgeregt sieht er, dass die Stadtgrenze passiert wird und am Ende die Schienen einfach aufhören. Er reflektiert erstmalig über den Unterschied zwischen Stadt und Land, über die niedrigen Häuser und das Fehlen von Mietskasernen und über den Unterschied zwischen einem Park in Glasgow und „the countryside", „aw natural and open" (Douglas 2005: 148). Obwohl sich die Straßenbahn auf immer gleichen Wegen im Stadtgebiet bewegt, überschreitet sie doch auch an einigen Stellen Grenzen und ermöglicht den Fahrgästen ein weiteres Entfernen von der Stadt, auch wenn sie selbst an der Endstation wieder umkehrt. Insbesondere für den reiseunerfahrenen Robert Douglas eröffnen sich ganz neue Welten von Wasser, Wald, Wiesen und Gerüchen – werden doch die Gerüche von Metall, Öl, Holz und Menschen ersetzt durch die Düfte des Waldes und der Blumen. Am Ende steht eine Straßenbahn „in solitary splendour" (ibid.: 153) mit der Verlockung einer schienengesicherten Heimkehr. So trugen die Straßenbahnen, die Erholung suchende Städter in die ländlichen Randgebiete brachten, trotz ihrer begrenzten Routen viel dazu bei, dass der enge Stadtraum sich öffnete, dass seine Grenzen auch für die unteren sozialen Schichten durchlässig und die Offenheit unbebauter Räume ‚erfahrbar' wurden. Aber auch Busse bringen dem Straßenbahnliebhaber Douglas neue Erfahrungen. Nach der 11+-Prüfung erschließt sich ihm auf einer Schulfahrt nach Linlithgow und Edinburgh erstmals schottische Geschichte jenseits der Sehenswürdigkeiten von Glasgow, und seit dieser Augen öff-

nenden Fahrt verbindet er dieses Wissen mit *Alexander's 'Bluebird'-* Bussen (ibid.: 187).

Für Meg Henderson sind es immer Busse, die sie an den Wochenenden in ihrer Jugend zum Loch Lomond und zu einer Jugendgruppe befördern, wo sie mit Paddeln, Wandern und Campen eine Gegenwelt zu ihrem problembeladenen Alltag und in der Gruppe, „the Crowd", eine Ersatzfamilie findet (Henderson 1994: 174). Wie die Straßenbahn sind Busse hier das Bindeglied zwischen dem oftmals durch soziale Enge und Konflikte geprägten Leben in Glasgow und „the country", dem immer eine befreiende, ausgleichende, stärkende und heilende Wirkung zugeschrieben wird, und sie wirken wie ein Ventil, durch das die sozialen und emotionalen Spannungen in der Stadt und in den Familien zumindest zeitweilig gelöst werden.

Auch Mae Stewart, die auf eine Kindheit in der Jute-Stadt Dundee zurückschaut, berichtet von der wichtigen Rolle der Busse für die Familien, die in der Nachkriegszeit statt Urlaub ein paar „days oot" (Stewart 2009: 51) nahmen und mit Bussen für den Tag an den Strand fuhren. Im Sommer in der „holiday fortnight", wenn fast alle Fabriken in Dundee geschlossen waren, strömten die Arbeiterfamilien bei entsprechendem Wetter täglich mit dem Bus an den Strand, anders als die „toffs", die Flugzeuge nahmen und in Hotels wohnten (ibid.). Das Verlassen der Stadt und die Ankunft in der Gegenwelt des Strandes haben für die Arbeiterfamilien einen hohen Wert als Ausdruck der Zugehörigkeit zur Arbeiterklasse, aber auch des zeitweiligen Verlassens der Arbeitswelt. Jenseits der Stadtgrenzen werden Familienleben, ein gewisser Wohlstand und Naturverbundenheit zelebriert. Für alle aber öffnen Straßenbahnen und Busse das Tor zu anderen Welten – zu Strand, Wald und See, zu Dörfern, geschichtsträchtigen Bauten und anderen Städten, und sie bieten zugleich die Gewissheit der möglichen Rückkehr.

Kulturgut Eisenbahn in Krieg und Frieden
Wurden bis jetzt nur Gefährte auf Verkehrswegen innerhalb der britischen Inseln betrachtet, soll abschließend noch eine unfreiwillige Grenzüberschreitung zur Sprache kommen, bei der die

Eisenbahn nicht vorrangig als Transportmittel über Grenzen fungiert, sondern, im Kontext von Krieg und Kriegsgefangenschaft einen transkulturellen Symbolwert erhält. Eric Lomax, der sich selbst als „the railway man" bezeichnet, arrangiert wichtige Stationen seines Lebens um Bahnhöfe und Eisenbahnen herum, die in seiner Kindheit, seinem Beruf und in seinem militärischen Einsatz im Zweiten Weltkrieg auf der malaiischen Halbinsel sowie als japanischer Kriegsgefangener beim Bau der Burma-Siam-Eisenbahn eine Rolle spielen. Er beginnt seine Lebenserinnerungen mit einer Reflexion über Duncan Mackellars Gemälde des St. Enoch-Bahnhofs in Glasgow in den 1880er Jahren. Er findet im Bild die Trauer und Einsamkeit von Reisenden und Zurückgelassenen, aber auch die Ambivalenz von Bahnhöfen ausgedrückt, zu der sowohl die beendeten Reisen als auch die Melancholie des Abschieds, die Kosten der Reise und die Unvermeidbarkeit der Trennung, kondensiert im Pfeifen einer Dampflokomotive, gehören. In seiner Kindheit erstreckt sich seine Faszination jedoch auf alle Schienenfahrzeuge einschließlich Straßenbahnen, und als Grund dafür gibt er an: „There was something infinitely reassuring in the predictability of the system" (Lomax 1996: 5). Ähnlich wie Douglas sieht er Schienen als Garanten von Verlässlichkeit und Ordnung sowie als Bollwerk gegen die Willkür des sonst eher chaotischen Verkehrs und Lokomotiven als „the most beautiful machines produced in the industrial revolution" (ibid.: 16).

Lomax wird später beim Militär zum Nachrichtenoffizier ausgebildet und 1941 nach Singapur verschifft. Nach der katastrophalen Niederlage der Briten auf der malaiischen Halbinsel geht Lomax in japanische Kriegsgefangenschaft und muss zunächst beim Bau der Siam-Burma-Eisenbahnlinie mitarbeiten, der überwiegend mit knochenbrecherischer Handarbeit von Kriegsgefangenen und anderen Arbeitskräften vorangetrieben wird. Lomax kommentiert: „Railways have always broken the bodies and spirits of their builders" (ibid.: 86). Im Rückblick bewertet er das Kriegsgefangenenlager und seine Arbeit als „involuntary professional railwayman" (ibid.: 107) jedoch ‚relativ' positiv, denn sie verlangte technische Kenntnisse und wurde von japanischen Ingenieuren geleitet. Seine Technikkenntnisse helfen ihm, menschliche und kulturelle

Grenzen etwas zu überwinden, und selbst hier sieht er sich noch in der Lage, die Schönheit von Maschinen zu genießen, zum Beispiel „the joy of [the] sudden appearance" der schönsten Lok, die er je gesehen hatte, „a beautifully preserved, turn-of-the-century machine built by Krauss of Munich, its origin described on a magnificent brass plate" (ibid.: 106), und es folgt ein poetisches Loblied auf die Lokomotive.

1943 endet seine Zeit beim Eisenbahnbau; es folgt, da im Lager illegale Radios gefunden worden waren, eine Zeit der Lagerwechsel, Misshandlungen und Folter. Ein letztes Mal werden in dieser Zeit Eisenbahnen noch schmerzhaft wichtig für ihn – man hat bei ihm eine handgezeichnete Karte der Eisenbahnlinie gefunden und foltert ihn, um herauszufinden, wozu sie dienen sollte. Lomax versucht, seine Folterer zu überzeugen, dass er ein „railway enthusiast" sei, der ein Souvenir haben wollte, und überschüttet sie mit technischen Informationen über Eisenbahnen in Großbritannien, die für Japaner unglaubwürdig klingen, den Übersetzer überfordern und dazu führen, dass seine Folter verstärkt fortgesetzt wird (cf. ibid.: 141). Das überaus Britische dieses Eisenbahnenthusiasmus, der, wie Lomax erklärt, der Industriellen Revolution entsprang, wird von der japanischen Militärpolizei nicht erkannt und gewürdigt. Nicht in jedem Fall hilft also Technik bei der Überwindung von Grenzen.

Lomax' Lebenserzählung bringt eine globale und imperiale Dimension in meine kleine Sammlung von Transport- und Grenzüberschreitungsgeschichten, denn sein Leidensweg als Kriegsgefangener lässt am Rande immer wieder die soziale und kulturelle Bedeutung von Eisenbahnen aufscheinen, sei es in imperialen technischen Projekten, in der globalen Präsenz bestimmter Maschinen, die weltweit Bewunderung und Identifikation hervorrufen können, oder in der Teilhabe am (britischen und schottischen) kulturellen Gedächtnis, in dem die Pionierleistungen der Industriellen Revolution einen wichtigen Platz einnehmen und Eisenbahnwissen mit Sicherheit und Heimat konnotiert ist.

Eine Zusammenschau der autobiographischen Erinnerungen lässt erkennen, dass die Benutzung von Verkehrsmitteln immer den

Aktionsradius und den Wissens- und Erfahrungshorizont der Fahrenden erweitern und das Einüben von identitätsstiftenden sozialen Verhaltensweisen, die einen neuen Status markieren, fördern kann. Transportmittel ermöglichen die Ortswechsel, die Bildung, sozialen Aufstieg, familiäres Glück, Erleben von Bewegungsfreiheit und Natur bedeuten können. Schienenfahrzeuge versprechen besondere Berechenbarkeit und Zuverlässigkeit und bieten so, mehr als andere, Geborgenheit und eine sichere Rückkehrmöglichkeit. Die Antwort auf die Frage, inwieweit diese lebensgeschichtlichen Interpretationen der Autorinnen und Autoren aus Schottland ‚schottisch' sind, bleibt nun der Leserschaft überlassen.

Quellen

„Ann Lamb" (2000), in Lindsay Reid, *Scottish Midwives. Twentieth-Century Voices,* Dunfermline: Black Devon Books, 11-16.

„Anne Bayne" (2000), in Lindsay Reid, *Scottish Midwives. Twentieth-Century Voices,* Dunfermline: Black Devon Books, 93-114.

„Anne Chapman" (2000), in Lindsay Reid, *Scottish Midwives. Twentieth-Century Voices,* Dunfermline: Black Devon Books, 63-68.

Douglas, Robert (2005), *Night Song of the Last Tram. A Glasgow Childhood*, London: Hodder.

Galloway, Janice (2009), *This Is Not About Me*, London: Granta.

Glasser, Ralph (2006), *The Ralph Glasser Omnibus: Growing Up in the Gorbals – Gorbals Boy at Oxford – Gorbals Voices, Siren Songs,* Edinburgh: Black and White.

Henderson, Meg (1994), *Finding Peggy. A Glasgow Childhood*, London: Corgi Books.

Hall, Christina (1999), *To the Edge of the Sea. Schooldays of a Crofter's Child*, Edinburgh: Birlinn.

Lejeune, Philippe (1989), *On Autobiography,* hrsg. v. Paul Eakin, übers. v. K. Leary, Minneapolis: University of Minnesota Press.

Lomax, Eric (1996), *The Railway Man,* London: Vintage.

Sloterdijk, Peter (1999), *Globen. Sphären: Makrosphärologie,* Band II, Frankfurt/Main: Suhrkamp.

Stewart, Mae (2009), *Dae You Mind Thon Time? Tales from the Dundee Tenements*, Edinburgh: Black & White.

Gert Hofmann (Cork)[*]
„Dass alle heiligen Orte der Erde zusammen sind um einen Ort ..." Hölderlins Frankreichreise und die Geburt einer neuen Poetik

Ich lernte Joachim Schwend bei unseren Begegnungen in Irland als einen inspirierten Reisenden kennen, nicht allein als einen hochgebildeten Kenner des Landes, sondern als einen faszinierten Freund, dem die Landschaft zur Inspirationsquelle wird, und der sich den Menschen bei aller reflektierten Zurückhaltung gleichwohl mit menschlich rückhaltloser Zuneigung und Sensibilität zu öffnen vermag.

Die poetische Signatur inspirierter Reiseerfahrungen markiert epochale Schwellenmomente der Literaturgeschichte. Hölderlins Überwindung des ästhetischen Idealismus in der schreibenden Reflexion auf die Erlebnisse seiner Bordeauxreise kann hierfür als Beispiel dienen:

> Die heimathliche Natur ergreift mich auch umso mächtiger, je mehr ich sie studire. Das Gewitter, nicht blos in seiner höchsten Erscheinung, sondern in eben dieser Ansicht, als Macht und als Gestalt, in den übrigen Formen des Himmels, das Licht in seinem Wirken, nationell und als Prinzip und Schicksaalsweise bildend, daß uns etwas heilig ist, sein Drang im Kommen und Gehen. Das Karakteristische der Wälder und das Zusammentreffen in einer Gegend von verschiedenen Karakteren der Natur, daß alle heiligen Orte der Erde zusammen sind um einen Ort und das philosophische Licht um mein Fenster ist jezt meine Freude; daß ich behalten möge, wie ich gekommen bin, bis hierher. (Hölderlin, Brief an Böhlendorff, Sommer 1802, StA 6,1: 433)

Dieser Auszug aus einem Brief Hölderlins an seinen Freund Casimir Ulrich Böhlendorff vom Sommer 1802 wird in seiner Bedeutsamkeit erkennbar, wenn man weiß, dass es sich um einen der letzten

---

[*] Gert Hofmann lehrt deutsche und vergleichende Literaturwissenschaft am University College Cork und an der Universität Rostock. Zur Zeit ist er als Gastprofessor an der Hankuk University of Foreign Studies in Seoul tätig.

Briefe Hölderlins vor seinem psychischen Zusammenbruch handelt, gleichsam um einen der letzten Akte eines bewussten Aufbegehrens dagegen. Hölderlin schrieb ihn wenige Wochen nach der Rückkehr von der letzten großen Reise seines Lebens, nach Bordeaux, auf der er zweimal das gesamte Südfrankreich zu Fuß durchquert hatte, auf dem Hinweg im Winter von Strasbourg zunächst nach Lyon, sodann über die „gefürchteten überschneiten Höhen der Auvergne, in eiskalter Nacht, in Sturm und Wildniß, und die geladene Pistole neben mir im rauhen Bette" (An die Mutter, 28. Januar 1802, ibid.: 429). Fünf Monate später, auf dem Rückweg, erlebt er „die traurige einsame Erde" Südfrankreichs, seine „Hirten [...] und einzelne Schönheiten, Männer und Frauen, die in der Angst des patriotischen Zweifels und des Hungers erwachsen sind" (Brief an Böhlendorff, Sommer 1802, ibid.: 432). In einem flirrend heißen Sommer ergreift ihn einerseits „das gewaltige Element, das Feuer des Himmels", aber auch „die Stille der Menschen, ihr Leben in der Natur [... ihr] Körper, die Art, wie sie in ihrem Klima wuchsen, und die Regel, womit sie den übermüthigen Genius vor des Elements Gewalt behüteten." (ibid.) Die elementaren Kräfte der Landschaft und des Klimas Südfrankreichs verdichten sich in Hölderlins Perzeption zum „Athletischen" des Körpers eines „südlichen" Menschentyps, das ihn, umgeben von den „Ruinen des antiquen Geistes", mit dem „eigentlichen Wesen der Griechen bekannter" (ibid.) macht.

Die Wanderungen durch Frankreich, teilweise lebensgefährlich, in jedem Fall excessive Anstrengungen bis an die Grenze der totalen physischen und psychischen Erschöpfung, bedeuten in Hölderlins Biographie einen Einschnitt, der sich an seinem Schreiben und Denken deutlich ablesen lässt. Die überstandenen Lebensgefahren der Hinreise versetzen ihn zunächst in den Zustand einer Euphorie des ‚Neugeborenseins', der das Gefühl des hoffnungslosen Scheiterns seiner bisherigen Etablierungsbemühungen in der literarischen und intellektuellen Öffentlichkeit Deutschlands (die dominiert wird vom Diskurs des Idealismus) zu überstrahlen vermag und, wiederum in körperlichen Metaphern, eine gewisse moralische Unabhängigkeit verspricht: „Ich bin nun durch und durch gehärtet und geweiht [...] Ich denke, ich will so bleiben, in der Hauptsache. Nichts fürchten und sich viel gefallen lassen." (An die Mutter, ibid.: 430)

Die manisch-psychedelische Ergriffenheit von den „Karakteren der Natur" südfranzösischer Landschaft, der die „athletischen Körper" der „einzelnen Menschen" wie Signaturen einer „zärtlichen Reflexionskraft" eingeschrieben erscheinen, lässt die Erfahrungen der Rückreise dann zur mäeutischen Bedingung eines völlig neuartigen somatisch-ästhetischen Denkens werden, das sich im radikalen Gegensatz zum metaphysisch-ethischen Diskurs seiner Zeitgenossen positioniert. Beide Erfahrungen, einerseits die immer bestehende Möglichkeit einer „Neugeburt" bzw. einer *‚gebärenden'* Selbstreflexion, die unabhängig ist sowohl von den Bedingungen der sozial etablierten Lebenswelt, als auch von den transzendentalen Signifikaten des intelligiblen Subjekts, andererseits das Vermögen einer *körperlich* verdichteten Reflexionskraft, welche den elementar wirksamen Naturkräften in ganz unterschiedlichen Landschaftsräumen (die „fremde Natur" in Südfrankreich, die „heimathliche Natur" in Schwaben) auf je eigene Weise zu entsprechen vermag, verbinden sich hier zum Ansatz einer neuartigen „Poetik des Leibes", welcher seiner Zeit weit voraus ist und uns auch die Neu-Lektüre von Hölderlins Gesamtwerk unter dem Gesichtspunkt einer anti-idealistischen korporalen Ästhetik ermöglichen könnte. Solche Poetik diskreditiert den metaphysisch-ethisch ausgerichteten Diskurs des Idealismus und seinen hierarchischen Geist-Körper-Dualismus und stellt ihn gewissermaßen (aber anders als Marx) ‚vom Kopf auf die Füße'.

Beide Erfahrungen sind Grunderfahrungen des Reisens, und beide Erfahrungen sind zentriert in der Subjektivität eines fundamentalen Körper-Sinnes, der zum Agens für den Prozess des Schreibens wird.

Für den Heimgekehrten spiegelt das „philosophische Licht um mein Fenster" – Widerschein des Wetterleuchtens am Himmel – durch seinen „Drang im Kommen und Gehen" etwas von dieser ästhetischen Dynamik seiner Reiseerfahrung, die nicht nur eine Dynamik der Bewusstwerdung ist (das wäre ein romantischer Gedanke), sondern vielmehr eine Dynamik der Raumerfahrung in der gegenseitigen Ausgesetztheit von Körper und Landschaft, von Erde und Licht, Verschlossenem und Offenem. Snježana Zorić und ich haben diese Dynamik als „Topodynamic" zu beschreiben versucht, als

Emergenzdynamik des Raums im Verhältnis zur Bewegung des Reisenden. Dort heißt es zu eben diesem Zitat Hölderlins:

> Hölderlin praises the errant light appearing around his "window" as delightful, and he calls it "philosophical." Such imagery approves of the "window", the threshold device between inside and outside, between withdrawal to oneself and exposedness to the world, as a genuine place of living encounter and delightful enlightenment; but it also invokes the mindfulness – and open-mindedness – of the philosopher as the indispensable condition to dwell on this threshold as a confusing place of mutually pervasive intro- and extroversion – the two incompatible but nevertheless equally defining impulses of the human experience. Living experience engenders the human Self in its very exposedness to the Other, as an ongoing process of metamorphosis, not as static re-construction of approved identities. (Hofmann & Zorić 2012: 11)

Unterwegs, in der Befindlichkeit des Reisens, erweist sich jener Schwellenraum zwischen „Kommen" und „Gehen" als der eigentliche Entfaltungsraum des Menschseins. In der labilen Balance des Schwellenraums als eigentlichem Verweilort des Reisenden müssen sich Lebensgeschichten immer wieder neu entscheiden. Markierte Schwellenorte in der Landschaft verstehen sich umgekehrt meist als Erinnerungsorte unerklärlicher Schicksale oder als heterotopische Übergangsorte im Sinne Foucaults, Nekropolen z.B. oder heilige Haine – Orte, die niemals vollständig einzuschreiben sind in das gesicherte Koordinatensystem etablierter Bedeutungen und Erkenntnisse. In jedem Fall erweist sich auch bei unserer Lesart Hölderlins, was Casey längst behauptete: Orte sind Ereignisse – und Landschaften? Das Konzert eines unaufhörlichen ereignishaften Geschehens.[1]

Wenn es sich nun also beim Reisen um die eigentliche Lebenskunst handelt – Kunst der Bewegung des Menschen im Raum, und Kunst der Bewegung des Raums im Menschen, im Prozess seiner niemals zu vollendenden Selbst-Werdung – dann trifft dasselbe in gleichsam

---

[1] „Rather than being one definite sort of thing – for example, physical, spiritual, cultural, social – a given place takes on the qualities of its occupants, reflecting these qualities in its own constitution and description and expressing them in its occurrence as an event: places not only *are*, they *happen*." (Casey 1996: 26-27)

hochkonzentrierter Form auf den Akt des Schreibens zu. Die Bewegung von Mensch und Raum im Verhältnis zueinander resultiert in erschütternden und beglückenden Momenten der Begegnung, Impulsen zur Identitätsdurchkreuzung und Bedeutungskrisen, die aber wiederum in Akten des Schreibens Raum zu greifen und zu schöpfen vermögen. Erst durch die Einschreibung der körperlichen Exponiertheit des Reisenden in Akte der Literatur und Kunst wird die Landschaft zum Habitat menschlichen Lebenssinns.

Wahrheit und Authentizität haben selbst „keinen Ort", sie werden, nach Giorgio Agamben, nur manifest in einer Dynamik des „giving space or giving a place to non-truth – that is, as a taking place [and] exposure of its innermost impropriety." (Agamben 1993: 12,3) Das hat aber zur Folge, dass der Gedanke der Wahrheit als Authentizität qua Identität eines transzendentalen Bewusstseins, wie er die Philosophie der europäischen Neuzeit, Aufklärung und des transzendentalen Idealismus prägte, nicht in der Lage ist, den Raum in seiner Ausgedehntheit und Vielgestaltigkeit adäquat als selbständiges (und bedeutungsgenerierendes) Phänomen zu erfassen. Unter dem Eindruck seiner Frankreichwanderung vollzieht Hölderlin genau an diesem Punkt eine dramatische Umkehr. Die Wahrheitsreflexion philosophischer Erkenntnis wird einer „zärtlichen Reflexion" ästhetischer Wahrnehmung untergeordnet, die nicht mehr in der Authentizität (in sich ruhenden, abstrakten Begrifflichkeit) eines transzendentalen Subjekts verbürgt ist, sondern in der Weltzugewandtheit eines lebendigen Körpergefühls, für das auch nicht mehr die Proportionalität des klassischen griechischen Kunstwerks zum Beispiel genommen werden kann – wohl aber das reale „Athletische" jener lebendigen Menschen Südfrankreichs, denen Hölderlin auf seiner Wanderung zufällig begegnet war:

> Diß bestimmte ihre Popularität, ihre Art, fremde Naturen anzunehmen und sich ihnen mitzutheilen, darum haben sie ihr Eigentümlichindividuelles, das lebendig erscheint, sofern der höchste Verstand im griechischen Sinne Reflexionskraft ist, und diß wird uns begreiflich, wenn wir den heroischen Körper der Griechen begreifen; sie [also ihre Popularität qua Reflexionskraft] ist Zärtlichkeit, wie unsere Popularität. (StA 6,1: 432, v22f.)

„Popularität" verweist hier auf den „nationellen" „Karakter" der Griechen als „südlichen Menschen", der sich sowohl in der athletischen Bildung ihrer Körperlichkeit, wie auch in der landschaftlichen Bildung des Raumes (des Lichts, des Klimas, der Erde etc.) artikuliert. Aber Hölderlin gibt dem Gedanken des „Nationellen" hier noch eine neue, interessante Wendung. „Nationell" wird nicht allein im Sinne von „vaterländisch" gebraucht, sondern auch im Sinne von „originell", etymologisch konnotiert mit der lateinischen Wurzel des Wortes im Verb *nasci* = „geboren werden". Hölderlins Hoffnung auf einen neuen „Anfang" der deutschen Dichtung im Zeichen ihrer eigenen „nationellen" Charakteristik, die im vorletzten Abschnitt des Briefes deutlich ausgesprochen wird, verbindet sich also zugleich mit einer ganz konkreten, körperhaften Vorstellung von *Geburt* und *Gebären*, die wiederum dem sinnlich pointierten Gedanken einer gleichsam *körperzentrierten* – nicht bewusstseinszentrierten – Erkenntnisweise („zärtlichen" „Reflexionskraft") Rechnung trägt, welcher den Hauptteil des Briefes ausmacht und sich erst der Begegnung mit den fremden „Karakteren" der Landschaft und Lebenswelt Südfrankreichs verdankt.

Zuletzt wird genau das, was zuvor in einer ausführlichen Argumentation gerade als das „Eigenthümlichindividuelle" des griechischen „Verstandes" identifiziert wurde, eine körperzentrierte, eher somatisch als mental sich artikulierende Reflexionskraft, auch mit der „Popularität" der Deutschen assoziiert: die „Zärtlichkeit" ihres Reflexionsvermögens. Das überrascht zunächst, aber schon im folgenden Abschnitt wird deutlich, dass nur deshalb, weil die „zärtlich" erotische Reflexionskraft den griechisch-südlichen Verstand in seiner nationellen Charakteristik nicht nur bestimmt, sondern zugleich auch transzendiert, in ihr etwas von jenem „Höchsten der Kunst" erkennbar wird, das für keine „nationelle" Charakteristik mehr in Anspruch genommen werden kann.

Zärtlichkeit ist eine Form der Kommunikation und Reflexion, die vom Sinnlich-Erotischen dominiert wird, die sich nicht zwischen Subjekt und Objekt im intelligiblen Modus der erkennenden Aneignung vollzieht, sondern zwischen verschiedenen Subjekten, dem Eigenen und dem Anderen in der Weise einer körperlich berührenden Annäherung.² Insofern deutet sich an, dass sich hier für Hölderlin die Intentionalität der Kunst im idealistischen Sinne überhaupt umkehrt: sie zielt nicht mehr auf die Idealisierung des beweglichen Phänomens zur festen Form einer Idee, die erkennbar wäre, sondern umgekehrt auf die „Phänomenalisierung" aller transzendentalen Formen, Begriffe, Ideen und Vorstellungen zu ihrer eigenen, völlig souveränen aber beweglichen und im menschlichen Körper zentrierten „Zeichen"-Sprache, einer Sprache der Kunst, die „alles Ernstlichgemeinte" (nicht nur die Begriffe der Vernunft) in der Zeichenhaftigkeit des sinnlichen Phänomens „stehend und für sich selbst erhält". Kunst nährt sich allein aus einer „zärtlichen" Reflexion auf die „Karaktere" der jeweils umgebenden Landschaft, ohne einer transzendentalen (oder sonstwie metaphysischen) Bedeutungsreferenz zu bedürfen.

Eine Zeile, die sich in den Handschriften zur Hymne „Mnemosyne" findet, lässt sich als Erläuterung zu dieser Briefstelle lesen: „Ein Zeichen sind wir, deutungslos, und haben fast die Sprache in der Fremde verloren". Die Hymne betrauert den Tod der Mnemosyne, der Göttin des mythischen Gedächtnisses, aber nicht den Totalverlust der Sprache, die als poetisches „Zeichen" offenbar auch den Verlust aller ehemals verbürgten Deutungen übersteht. Deutlich wird hier, dass sich für Hölderlin, anders als für Schiller, Kunst und Dichtung keinesfalls als Medium verstehen lassen. Kunst kann nicht einfach nur Instrument der Überführung menschlicher Bildung aus dem Zustand physischer Notwendigkeit in den der sittlichen Freiheit sein. Hölderlins Überlegungen fügen sich überhaupt nicht mehr unter das metaphysische Regime einer praktischen Idee, welche der sinnlichen Kunst ihren philosophischen oder historischen Endzweck vorschreibt – auch nicht im Sinne einer geistigen Synthese von Sinnlichkeit und Sittlichkeit. Hölderlin synthetisiert nicht, sondern verschärft die Kantischen Gegensätze noch, indem er ihre Ordnung umkehrt. Sein Denken richtet sich auf die reflexive Dynamik des Hervorgangs der lebendigen Kunst als vergänglicher aus

---

² Vgl. Emmanuel Levinas 1999 und 2003 zum philosophischen Diskurs der Erotik seit Platon, und zur Phänomenologie des Eros als einer Kommunikationsform mit dem Anderen in seiner Andersheit diesseits des Erkennens.

dem leibhaften Leben des Künstlers als Individuum – im Modus der „Zärtlichkeit" – nicht auf deren Autorisierung durch eine bleibende Idee. Im Namen einer ästhetisch emanzipierten Kunst und Dichtung verkehren sich die philosophischen Hierarchien des idealistischen Menschenbilds in ihr Gegenteil: der Vorrang des Intellektuellen über das Sinnliche und die logische Apriorität des transzendentalen Begriffs über den empirisch individuellen Fall verlieren ihre Geltung. Ein winziger philosophischer Gedankenfetzen, den Hölderlin ungefähr zur Zeit des Entstehens des zweiten Böhlendorffbriefes in das sogenannte Homburger Folioheft notiert, gleichsam wie als Überschrift über ein darauffolgendes hymnisches Fragment, gibt dafür das Prinzip an: Die „Apriorität des Individuellen über das Ganze". (in Uffhausen 1989: 146; cf. Burdorf 1993) Unmittelbar darunter findet sich ein Hymnenfragment, das mit Versen beginnt, die Friedrich Beißner folgendermaßen rekonstruiert:

> Vom Abgrund nämlich haben
> Wir angefangen und gegangen
> Dem Leuen gleich, in Zweifel und Ärgerniß,
> Denn sinnlicher sind Menschen
> In dem Brand
> Der Wüste
> Lichttrunken und der Thiergeist ruhet
> Mit ihnen. Bald aber wird, wie ein Hund, umgehn
> In der Hitze meine Stimme auf den Gassen der Gärten
> In denen wohnen Menschen
> In Frankreich
> Der Schöpfer
> Frankfurt aber, nach der Gestalt, die
> Abdruck ist der Natur zu reden
> Des Menschen nemlich, ist der Nabel
> Dieser Erde, diese Zeit
> Auch ist Zeit, und deutschen Schmelzes (StA 2,1: 250)

Ich will hier nur darauf hinweisen, dass in diesem Fragment dieselbe Thematik und Begrifflichkeit zur Sprache kommt wie in den Böhlendorffbriefen (und anderen poetologischen Schriften der Zeit, z.B. den Sophokleskommentaren): die Abgründigkeit des Lebens, Not und Notwendigkeit des „Anfangens" für eine neue Art des Dichtens, die Bedeutung des „Nationellen" in diesem Zusammenhang für die „Stimme" des Dichters (sowohl im Sinne des „Vaterländischen" als auch des „Originellen"), der „Thiergeist" als Inbegriff aller sinnlich-leibhaften Seelenvermögen, damit also auch die Körperverhaftetheit dieser Stimme (und ihres nationellen Charakters), ebenso die Sinnlichkeit der südlichen Landschaft und ihres Sonnen-Lichts, das körperliche Empfinden der Hitze (in Opposition zur konventionellen Lichtmetaphorik der Aufklärung), in der sich die Stimme bewegt, und auch die Unterschiedlichkeit der nationellen Charaktere der Natur (in Südfrankreich und in Deutschland), welche auf die Stimme als körperlich affizierbare einwirken. Schließlich findet sich hier der Verweis auf jene „Gestalt" (Susette Gontard), die „Abdruck der Natur des Menschen" ist, in Frankfurt, dem „Nabel dieser Erde", die gleichsam zur Quelle jener „Zärtlichkeit" wird, die ins Zentrum der ästhetischen Reflexion in den Böhlendorffbriefen rückt: als das, was das „Höchste der Kunst" charakterisiert, das Griechen und Deutsche gemeinsam haben (die gleichsam erotische „Mitte", in der sich alle Charaktere der Welt berühren).

Hier scheint sich also zu bestätigen, dass Hölderlin in dieser letzten Phase seiner poetologischen Arbeit in der Tat bereit war, einen radikalen Schritt zu tun, und die Möglichkeitsbedingungen ästhetischer Reflexionskraft und künstlerischer Produktion nicht in der transzendentalen Verfassung eines intelligiblen Bewusstseins, sondern in den sensiblen oder gar physiologischen Bedingungen individueller *Korporalität* als Quelle („nationeller") künstlerischer Originalität aufzusuchen, die Bedingungen der *conditio humana*, der Sterblichkeit und ihrer gefühlten Anerkennung, der Fragilität des Körpers und seiner Exponiertheit an die Kräfte der Natur und Geschichte, die eine Landschaft prägen. Die faktische *Not* wird zur Kreativkraft eines gelebten Daseins in seiner Abgründigkeit *und* Bedeutsamkeit; sie offenbart sich dem Reisenden nur durch seine körperliche Exponiertheit an jene Kräfte der Natur und Geschichte, die eine Landschaft als Wohn-Raum für Menschen an jedem Ort anders charakterisieren – eine Erfahrung, die Clifford Geertz zum Ausgangspunkt seiner modernen anthropologischen Theorie machte: „no one lives in the world in general." (Geertz 1996: 262)

Die Korporalität des poetischen Impulses bei Hölderlin, seine „Zärtlichkeit", führt denn auch nicht zur Synthese wahrer Begriffe, sondern zur Kontingenz einer gleichsam berührenden Wahrnehmung, zum topographischen Miteinander des „nationell" Verschiedenen am Ort der Dichtung. So ergibt die eingangs zitierte Bemerkung Hölderlins ihren literarischen Sinn: Allein das landschaftlich koagulierende „*Zusammentreffen* in einer Gegend von verschiedenen Karakteren der Natur, daß alle heiligen Orte der Erde zusammen sind um einen Ort" ist die „Freude" des heimgekehrten Dichters (StA 6,1: 433, Z. 42ff.) – es ist die Freude des Schreibens. Oder aber, noch pointierter, in dem eben bereits zitierten Gedichtfragment „Vom Abgrund nemlich": „Allda bin ich / Alles miteinander." (StA 2,1: 250)

Quellen

Agamben, Giorgio (1993), *The Coming Community*, übers. v. Michael Hardt, London – Minneapolis: University of Minnesota Press (Originaltitel: *La comunità che viene*, Turin 1990).

Burdorf, Dieter (1993), *Hölderlins späte Gedichtfragmente: „Unendlicher Deutung voll"*, Stuttgart – Weimar: Metzler.

Casey, Edward S. (1996), „How to Get from Space to Place in a Fairly Short Stretch of Time: Phenomenological Prolegomena", in Steven Feld & Keith H. Basso, Hrsg., *Senses of Place*, Santa Fe: School of American Research Press, 13-52.

Geertz, Clifford (1996), „Afterword", in Steven Feld & Keith H. Basso, Hrsg., *Senses of Place*, Santa Fe: School of American Research Press, 259-262.

Hölderlin, Friedrich (1943-1985), *Sämtliche Werke* (Große Stuttgarter Ausgabe, hier zitiert als StA), hrsg. v. Friedrich Beißner, Stuttgart: Kohlhammer.

Hofmann, Gert & Snježana Zorić, Hrsg. (2012), *Topodynamics of Arrival. Essays on Self and Pilgrimage*, Amsterdam – New York: Rodopi.

Levinas, Emmanuel (1999), *Die Spur des Anderen. Untersuchungen zur Phänomenologie und Sozialphilosophie* (4. Auflage), übersetzt, herausgegeben und eingeleitet von Wolfgang Nikolaus Krewani, Freiburg i. Br. – München: Karl Alber.

Levinas, Emmanuel (2003), *Die Zeit und der Andere*, übersetzt und mit einem Nachwort versehen von Ludwig Wenzler, Hamburg: Felix Meiner.

Uffhausen, Dietrich, Hrsg. (1989), *Friedrich Hölderlin. „Bevestigter Gesang". Die neu zu entdeckende hymnische Spätdichtung bis 1806*, Stuttgart: Metzler.

Kathleen Starck (Landau)*
Die Regionen, der Professor und ich

Die Autorin studierte von 1994 bis 1997 bei Jochen Schwend britische Kulturstudien und arbeitete bis 2002 als wissenschaftliche Mitarbeiterin an seinem Lehrstuhl. Heute ist sie selbst Professorin für britische Kulturwissenschaft. Die regionalen Schwerpunkte der Leipziger Kulturstudien beeinflussten durchaus auch ihre Forschungs- und Reisetätigkeit, wie der folgende persönliche Beitrag verdeutlicht.

„They took the soup." Dieser Satz wird nach Aussage meines Begleiters, des Betreibers einer Jugendherberge auf der westirischen Insel Achill Island, immer noch über manche alteingesessene Familien gesagt. Ein Satz, der noch heute bewirkt, dass sich manche Familien nicht grün sind. Weil ihre Vorfahren damals, während der großen Hungersnot in den 1840ern, die Suppe der englischen Armenküchen angenommen haben. Im Gegenzug zwangen die Engländer die Iren, mitten in der Landschaft völlig sinnlose Steinmauern zu errichten. Die Suppe sollte schließlich verdient sein. Es ist 2002, ich bin unterwegs in Irland, schaue auf die immer noch herumstehenden *dry stone walls* und bin überzeugt, ich selbst hätte niemals genügend Stolz besessen, um lieber zu verhungern als mich von der englischen Kolonialmacht demütigen zu lassen. Gleichzeitig lässt der Suppensatz in mir sofort Bilder aus meinem Studium aufsteigen.

---

* Kathleen Starck ist Professorin für Cultural Studies im Fach Anglistik der Universität Koblenz-Landau, Campus Landau. Ihre Forschungsinteressen liegen in den Bereichen Gender Studies, postkoloniale/transkulturelle Studien, Kulturen des Kalten Krieges (insbesondere Film), Populärkultur, Postsozialismus und zeitgenössisches britisches Drama. Sie ist Autorin des Buches *'I Believe in the Power of Theatre.' British Women's Drama of the 1980s and 1990s* (WVT, 2005) und Herausgeberin der Bände *When the World Turned Upside-Down: Cultural Representations of Post-1989 Eastern Europe* (C-S-P, 2009), *Between Fear and Freedom. Cultural Representations of the Cold War* (C-S-P, 2010), *Von Hexen, Politik und schönen Männern – Geschlecht in Wissenschaft, Kultur und Alltag* (LIT, 2013) sowie Mitherausgeberin des 2014 erscheinenden Bandes *Political Masculinities* (mit Birgit Sauer). Darüber hinaus hat sie zahlreiche Aufsätze in den Bereichen Gender Studies/Masculinity Studies publiziert.

Wir sitzen in einem dieser fensterlosen „Bunkerräume" des alten Seminargebäudes der Universität Leipzig. Damals, Mitte der Neunziger, als der Büroturm „Weisheitszahn" noch die Kollegen und Kolleginnen der Universität beherbergte, der Fahrstuhl nur in bestimmten Etagen hielt, damit man nicht zu lange auf ihn warten musste, und kein Logo, weder des MDRs noch einer anderen Firma, auf dem Dach prangte. Die Luft im „Seminarbunker" ist, wie immer, schlecht. Wir sehnen uns nach Tageslicht und Sauerstoff. Was uns hier hält, ist trotzdem nicht nur der berühmte Seminarschein, den man am Ende bekommt und als Prüfungszulassung vorlegen muss. Es ist der Professor (auch wenn er diesen Titel erst später verliehen bekam), der gerade mal wieder vom Thema abschweift, so dass man Mühe hat, sich zu erinnern, was genau das Thema eigentlich ist. Ach, ja, da war doch was mit so einer Hungersnot. Und die Engländer haben nicht wirklich geholfen, sondern Mais geschickt, mit dem die Iren nichts anfangen konnten. Sie kannten ihn nicht und versuchten, ihn roh zu essen. Und dann war da auch noch dieser Satiriker, der empfahl, man möge doch Babypos essen, die wären so schön zart. Mein Professor für britische Kulturstudien wusste scheinbar immer unendlich viele Extras zum eigentlichen Thema zu erzählen. Historische Anekdoten, Querverbindungen zur Literaturgeschichte, Dinge aus der eigenen Forschung. Das hat mich tief beeindruckt, auch wenn ich manchmal den Faden verloren habe.

Dass der Professor jede Menge Humor besitzt, habe ich so richtig erst in meiner mündlichen Abschlussprüfung entdeckt. Das Thema habe ich lange vergessen – vermutlich drehte es sich auch um eine der Regionen der Britischen Inseln. Aber ich weiß noch, dass ich auf eine Frage, mit der ich gerechnet hatte, antwortete: „Das habe ich mir gedacht, dass Sie das fragen werden." Der Professor konterte: „Und was haben Sie sich gedacht, was Sie dann antworten werden?" Darauf ich: „Ich habe mir gedacht, dass ich antworten würde ..." Und dann sagte ich ihm, was ich mir vorher als Antwort zurechtgelegt hatte. Wir haben herzlich gelacht, und ich hatte Spaß an meiner Prüfung. Das sollte man sich auf der Zunge zergehen lassen: Ich hatte Spaß an meiner mündlichen Abschlussprüfung.

Eine weniger lustige, aber ebenso regionenbezogene Erinnerung lässt weitere Facetten des professoralen Charakters erahnen: Ich stehe in einem Museum in Berlin und sehe auf eine Schautafel, die die Hexenverfolgung in Europa erklärt. Mir fällt ein, dass ich einmal eine Seminararbeit zum Thema Hexenverfolgung in Schottland geschrieben habe. In der Universitätsbibliothek gab es nicht so viel Material. Und Google Books war noch nicht erfunden. Kurzerhand gab mir der Professor eine Diskette (ja, die gab es damals noch) mit seiner noch unveröffentlichten Habilitationsschrift, in der sich ein Kapitel mit der schottischen Hexenverfolgung beschäftigt. Die Hausarbeit ist bei einem meiner vielen Umzüge verloren gegangen. Aber das Thema Hexenverfolgung interessiert mich nach wie vor. Gerade vor ein paar Wochen habe ich auf einer Webseite zur Ahnenforschung Auszüge aus Gerichtsakten gelesen, die illustrieren, wie die Logik der Hexenverfolgung, der Geständnisse, der Folter und des Widerrufens in Mecklenburg funktionierten. Was mich zu einer weiteren regionalen Differenz bringt, die für den Professor und für mich von Bedeutung ist: die zwischen Ost und West.

Darüber haben wir uns, glaube ich, nie wirklich unterhalten. Wie das so ist, mit dem Osten und dem Westen. Schließlich ist der Professor als Wessi in den neunziger Jahren an eine ostdeutsche Universität gekommen. Als viele noch eine „Buschzulage" für nötig hielten, angeblich, damit man überhaupt qualifizierte „Aufbauhelfer" in den Osten locken konnte. Wie hat er die Ossis erlebt? Und wie sind sie ihm begegnet? Waren die Studierenden anders als die im Westen? In seiner Forschung jedenfalls interessiert er sich sehr für Identitäten und Transformationsprozesse. Ein Thema, das auch mich selbst in meiner eigenen Arbeit immer wieder beschäftigt. Wahrscheinlich musste ich erst aus Leipzig und dem Osten weggehen, um das zu reflektieren. Ironischerweise arbeite ich, das Ostkind, nun an einer Universität in Rheinland-Pfalz, unweit der akademischen „Heimat" des Professors in Mainz/Germersheim. Nicht zuletzt deswegen habe ich gerade das Buch *Dritte Generation Ost* gelesen, eine Art Manifest von heute ca. Dreißigjährigen mit ostdeutschen Wurzeln, die die Beschäftigung mit der ostdeutschen Herkunft befördern möchten. Ich bin zwar nicht mit allen dort geäußerten Meinungen einverstanden, aber so ein Buch wäre vielleicht eine interessante Grundlage für ein Ost-West-Gespräch mit dem Professor.

Nach meinem Studium habe ich beim Professor am Lehrstuhl gearbeitet. Eines meiner ersten Seminare widmete sich den Äußeren Hebriden, ganz im Sinne des am Fachbereich bestens etablierten Schottland-Schwerpunktes. Aus heutiger Perspektive befürchte ich, das Seminar war nicht besonders gut. Aber die schottischen Western Isles interessieren mich immer noch. Der Professor betreute auch die Doktorarbeit meines damaligen Freundes. Und der wollte die Abwanderung junger Menschen von den Äußeren Hebriden erforschen. Also war auch ich mehrmals dort. Geforscht habe ich nicht, aber den Westen Schottlands immer mehr lieben gelernt. Die Stille an den breiten Stränden, die aussehen, als befänden sie sich in der Karibik. Die Kühe, die plötzlich am Strand auftauchen. Die Seehunde, die nachts heulen und einem sofort klar werden lassen, warum die Insulaner so viele Spukgeschichten zu erzählen wissen. Die totale Dunkelheit, in der man sprichwörtlich die Hand vor Augen nicht sehen kann. Die Einheimischen, die sich am Nachmittag mal eben ein *wee dram* gönnen, das den russischen *sto gramm* nicht unähnlich ist, danach mit dem Auto die einzige Straße der Insel nach Hause fahren, um dann das Auto selbstverständlich offen und mit steckendem Zündschlüssel vor ihrem Haus abzustellen. Und getrampt sind wir. Kreuz und quer durch Schottland. Wenn ich allein unterwegs war, waren meine Fahrer meist mehr um meine Sicherheit besorgt als ich selbst. Einmal stellte uns ein älterer Herr pikante Fragen nach FKK-Stränden. Da würden doch alle Deutschen ständig hingehen. Ein anderes Mal musste ich einen ausgestopften Hahn auf meinem Schoß halten, der zuvor auf dem Beifahrersitz gesessen hatte. Und dann war da noch diese Fahrt nach Portree auf der Insel Skye. Der Fahrer war bekifft, und den Rücksitz teilte ich mit einem sabbernden Hund. Danach erschien mir Portree gleich noch viel schöner. Wir waren damals auch auf den Orkney-Inseln. Mein Professor fiel mir wieder ein, als wir dort diverse Kirchen- und Burgruinen erkundeten und an vielen lasen, wie lange diese Orte noch unter norwegischer Herrschaft standen. Das musste auch in irgendeiner seiner Lehrveranstaltungen aufgetaucht sein. Die Steinzeitsiedlung Skara Brae war unglaublich. Unsere Vorfahren hatten tatsächlich schon *sideboards*. Damals konnte man noch zwischen den Mauern, quasi direkt in den Wohnungen der Steinzeitmenschen, herumlaufen, die heute nur noch von hinter einer Absperrung zu besichtigen sind.

Aber zurück zum Professor. Er händigte nicht nur seine unveröffentlichte Habilitationsschrift an „kleine" Studierende aus, sondern stellte seinen Mitarbeitern sogar seine Vorlesungsskripte zur Verfügung. Mit den Worten „damit ihr mehr Zeit für eure Dissertation habt". Vielleicht ist es nicht klug, das zuzugeben, aber dieses Skript zur Geschichte des britischen Parlaments verwende ich zuweilen heute noch in meinen Seminaren. Auch sonst war der Professor sehr daran interessiert, seinen Mitarbeitern genügend Zeit für die Anfertigung ihrer Dissertationsschriften zu lassen. Ich kann mich nicht erinnern, neben der Lehre, Abnahme von Prüfungen und Begutachtung von Seminar- und Abschlussarbeiten mit zusätzlichen Aufgaben betraut worden zu sein. Gut, ich habe an einigen Treffen der Kulturstudienlehrenden der Neuen Bundesländer teilgenommen. Aber das habe ich nicht als zusätzliche Aufgabe, sondern eher als fachliche und persönliche Weiterbildung erlebt. Erfuhr ich doch zum Beispiel auf einem dieser Treffen, dass man Theoretiker wie Gramsci oder Foucault auch im Original bzw. in der Übersetzung lesen könne und nicht immer auf Zusammenfassungen ihrer Thesen von anderen Autoren zurückgreifen müsse. So lachhaft dies heute rückblickend klingt, für mich als ganz junge wissenschaftliche Mitarbeiterin war das durchaus eine wertvolle Anregung.

Einmal sagte uns der Professor, dass er eigentlich Wahl-Ire wäre. Als ich, neugierig geworden, das erste Mal hinflog und Rundreisen durch Nord- und Südirland in einem Minivan für Backpackers machte, verstand ich ihn. Auch wenn es seltsam klingt: es gibt dort definitiv das grünste Grün. Es ist sogar grüner als in West Yorkshire, wo ich mein Auslandsstudium absolvierte und erstmals Bekanntschaft mit „grünstem Grün" machte. Außerdem stimmen die Klischees eben manchmal doch: In Galway gab es überall Musik, Dingle war trotz Touristenscharen einmalig schön, in Tralee wimmelte es nur so von aufgebrezelten jungen Mädchen, die „Rose of Tralee" werden wollten, bei der Überquerung des Shannon sah ich meinen ersten Delfin. Nur den Blarney Stone habe ich lieber nicht geküsst. Ich weiß, dass ich niemandem einen Gefallen getan hätte, wenn ich zu meinem losen Mundwerk noch zusätzlich „the gift of the gab" erhalten hätte. Lange im Gedächtnis ist mir auch meine Stippvisite bei den Anhörungen zum *Bloody Sunday* im nordirischen (London)Derry geblieben. Wir saßen auf der Besuchergalerie und sahen lauter Anwälte und Zeugen, die alle vor Monitoren saßen. Auf den Monitoren und groß auf die Wand projiziert war eine Karte. Darauf gab es verschiedene Markierungen und Kreuze. Ein Zeuge war gerade dabei, der Kommission zu erklären, wann er sich bei der für viele Nordiren tödlich endenden Demonstration dreißig Jahre zuvor wo befand, wo sich britische Soldaten postiert hatten und von wo Schüsse abgegeben wurden. Ich glaube nicht, dass mir ohne die Lehrveranstaltungen in British Cultural Studies und meine Arbeit am Institut für Anglistik bewusst geworden wäre, wie geschichtsträchtig die Veranstaltung war, bei der ich da für einen Moment zusehen durfte. Heute, gut vierzig Jahre nach dem *Bloody Sunday*, gibt es viele wissenschaftliche Veröffentlichungen zur *Bloody Sunday Inquiry*. Sie illustrieren, wie voreingenommen die ersten Anhörungen kurz nach dem Vorfall waren. So voreingenommen, dass man zu dem Ergebnis kam, die britische Armee treffe keine Schuld. Mit den neuen Anhörungen gelangte man zu einem völlig anderen Ergebnis, und schließlich entschuldigte sich die britische Regierung offiziell für das Verhalten ihrer Armee.

Wie der Professor bin auch ich mehrfach nach Irland zurückgekehrt. Dabei habe ich u.a. die wunderbare Insel Sherkin vor der Küste Südirlands für mich entdeckt und sogar meinen Mann, der alles andere als anglophil ist, ein wenig mit meiner Begeisterung für diese und ähnliche Landschaften angesteckt. In Dublin „erlebte" ich 9/11. Als Gender-Forscherin zögere ich, dies aufzuschreiben: ich hörte die Radionachricht der einstürzenden *Twin Towers* erstmals in einem Schuhgeschäft. Dann verfolgte ich die unglaublichen Fernsehbilder mit vielen internationalen Gästen einer Dubliner Jugendherberge. Die berühmt-berüchtigte Rede von George Bush, in der er ankündigte, dass man die Verantwortlichen „aus ihren Löchern ausräuchern würde", hörte ich im Radio des Linienbusses von Dublin nach Belfast. Meinem Bruder schenkte ich zum Abitur ein Wochenende in Dublin, und er verliebte sich sofort in die Stadt, wenn nicht in das ganze Land, als jemand im Pub einfach so ein Gespräch mit ihm begann und ihn in Irland willkommen hieß. Die Liebe verschlug mich nach Cork, ich wohnte während einer Sommerschule eine Woche in Limerick und bestaunte als Touristin segregierte protestantische und katholische Wohnviertel in Belfast – und wieder erinnerte ich mich an vergessen geglaubte Kommentare und Anekdoten aus Seminaren wie „Anglo-Irish Coexistence", die ich Jahre zuvor besucht hatte. In einem Pub im Belfaster Zentrum lernte ich, was ein *snook* ist (eine abgetrennte Sitznische mit direktem Zugang zur Bar), trank mein erstes *Black'n'Black* (Guinness mit *blackcurrant*-Sirup, eher ein Nachtisch als ein Bier). Ob ich mich nun selbst als „Wahl-Irin" bezeichnen würde, weiß ich nicht, aber dass der Anstoß zu dieser anhaltenden Faszination vom Professor kam, ist mehr als wahrscheinlich.

Ähnliches gilt auch für die schottische „Region" (die natürlich genau wie Irland eine Nation ist, wie der Professor betonte), und zwar auch diesseits der Hebriden – obwohl gerade die Insel Skye eines der Urlaubsziele „in the middle of nowhere" ist, die ich erst kürzlich wieder mit meinem Mann aufsuchte. Als Doktorandin flog ich jahrelang zum *Fringe Theatre Festival* nach Edinburgh und benutzte dort die Universitäts- und Nationalbibliotheken. Ich weiß nicht, ob es mit des Professors Ausführungen zum *Scottish Enlightenment* zu tun hatte, aber in Edinburgh erlebte ich auch erstmalig die Vorteile eines Smartphones, das in den Händen eines englischen Freundes den Weg zu unserem Hotel anzeigte. Der Professor selbst hätte sicher in dieser Stadt keinen elektronischen Wegweiser benötigt, schließlich hat er dort geforscht und gelebt. Ein wenig „Forschung" betrieb auch ich vergangenes Jahr in der schottischen Hauptstadt, als ich eine Gruppe Studierender dorthin begleitete. Der Professor hätte sicher seine helle Freude an der Debatte im schottischen Parlament gehabt, bei der wir als Gäste im Saal sitzen durften. Es ging darum, ob im Referendum zu Schottlands Unabhängigkeit eine oder zwei Fragen gestellt werden sollten. Ein Punkt, den wir im Anschluss auch mit einem Angehörigen der Universität Edinburgh diskutierten. Spannend wäre es auch gewesen, den Professor bei Alan Riachs Vortrag an der Universität Glasgow dabei zu haben, dem einzigen Lehrstuhlinhaber Großbritanniens für schottische Literatur. Ich hätte doch gern gewusst, ob der Professor die Ausführungen des Kollegen zur schottischen Nationalliteratur teilt, zu der er selbst so viel geschrieben und in seinen Seminaren erzählt hat. Natürlich „erforschte" ich Schottland auch jenseits der Hauptstadt und der akademischen Gefilde: so verpasste ich in Aberdeen wegen bummelnder Freunde ein *open air* Silvester-*ceilidh* (traditioneller schottischer Tanzabend), verzweifelte am Dialekt eines Taxifahrers in Dundee, kaufte in Glasgow mein erstes *Big Issue*, die bekannteste britische Obdachlosenzeitung, und aß überraschend gut indisch in der nördlichsten Stadt Schottlands, Inverness. Manchmal bietet dieses Land auch Zuflucht. Als vor knapp drei Jahren meine Mutter viel zu früh und sehr plötzlich verstarb, flog ich spontan für eine Woche auf die Orkney-Inseln. Um allein zu sein mit mir und den Wellen und einer Landschaft, die anderen unwirtlich erscheinen mag. Es hat ein bisschen geholfen.

Natürlich habe ich keine Ahnung, wo genau der Professor in Irland oder Schottland unterwegs war und ist. Aber er hat in mir die Neugier geweckt und genährt, die mich heute noch immer wieder in diese Gegenden führt. Nach Wales verschlug es mich bisher leider nur einmal – mag das an den Forschungsschwerpunkten meines Professors liegen, und daran, dass Wales in meinem Studium quasi nicht auftauchte? Auch das sollte ich ihn vielleicht mal fragen. Zuletzt gefragt habe ich ihn, inzwischen als Kollegin, ob er ein Gutachten in einem Berufungsverfahren übernehmen könnte. Leider musste er, aus mir völlig verständlichen Gründen, ablehnen. In diesem Zusammenhang gab er mir augenzwinkernd den Rat, nie Studiendekanin zu werden. Schon gar nicht in unseren Zeiten universitärer Dauerreformen. Ich werde mein Bestes tun, seinen Rat zu befolgen. Für diesen und andere Ratschläge, seine vielen Anregungen und für seine Unterstützung, als Studentin und Mitarbeiterin, an dieser Stelle ein großes Dankeschön.

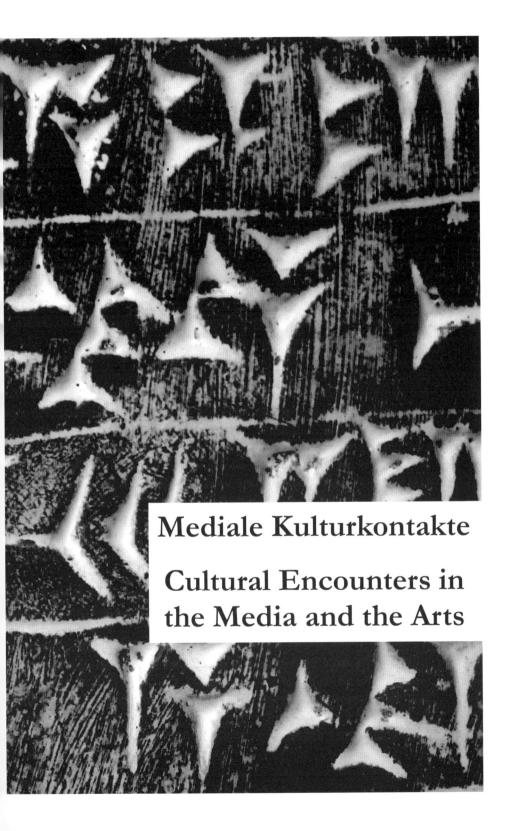

Mediale Kulturkontakte

Cultural Encounters in the Media and the Arts

Ian Campbell (Edinburgh)[*]
Understanding and Misunderstanding Scottish Fiction

Joachim Schwend has been a steady friend through decades of work on Scottish literature (on which he was writing when we met) and in my many visits to Germany. His unfailing good humour, through everything, is something to remember with gratitude. My sudden immersion in Germany and in the work of Germersheim was a rich source of potential misunderstanding for someone taking his first stumbling steps in German. He was a sure and patient guide.

This is intended as a general prelude to reading and re-reading Scottish fiction with an eye to detail and above all to uncertainties in the text – something I spent many happy hours doing with Joachim Schwend decades ago. And offering classes in Scottish literature in Germany, in Germersheim and in Göttingen, underlined to me the value of holding up to a familiar text the challenge of understanding in a second language, and explaining to the holder of that second language what the reader in the original thinks the meaning is. Misunderstanding is a rich topic for the student of Scottish fiction. It offers to some the kinds of pitfall that a visitor to a foreign country and its language might encounter. More interestingly, it can be seen as a sophisticated narrative device easily overlooked in the rush to categorise a nation's literature, or make value judgements based on unfamiliarity. Many of the examples I choose relate to a country in rapid change and flux – no strange topic to a German audience – and I suggest the use of misunderstanding is a deliberate and fruitful way of communicating between author and reader.

---

[*] Ian Campbell was born in Lausanne, educated in Swiss and Scottish schools, Aberdeen (MA) and Edinburgh (PhD) Universities. Since 1967 he has been on the staff of Edinburgh's English Literature department, and retired in 2009 from the chair of Scottish and Victorian Literature. He has taught in Canada, USA and widely in Europe. One of the senior editors of the CARLYLE LETTERS project, he publishes in Victorian literature, and in Scottish literature of many periods.

Introducing *A Window in Thrums*, J.M. Barrie has a particularly interesting opening:

> On the bump of green round which the brae twists, at the top of the brae, and within cry of T'nowhead Farm, still stands a one-story house, whose whitewashed walls, streaked with the discoloration that rain leaves, look yellow when the snow comes. In the old days the stiff ascent left Thrums behind, and where is now the making of a suburb was only a poor row of dwellings and a manse, with Hendry's cot to watch the brae. The house stood bare, without a shrub, in a garden whose paling did not go all the way round, the potato pit being only kept out of the road, that here sets off southward, by a broken dyke of stones and earth. On each side of the slate-coloured door was a window of knotted glass. Ropes were flung over the thatch to keep the roof on in wind.
>
> Into this humble abode I would take any one who cares to accompany me. But you must not come in a contemptuous mood, thinking that the poor are but a stage removed from beasts of burden, as some cruel writers of these days say; nor will I have you turn over with your foot the shabby horse-hair chairs that Leeby kept so speckless, and Hendry weaved for years to buy and Jess so loved to look upon. (Barrie 2005: 1)

On the face of it, this is naturalistic description with a decided social slant: the narrator's superiority to the house described is reinforced by the "still" in the first sentence, a sense of time-warp and backwater. The direct appeal is to the reader to suspend socially-based attitude, with emotive language (beasts of burden), financial criteria (humble abode), reference to other writers (some cruel writers of these days). Yet to see Barrie's introduction in this light is to misunderstand an altogether cleverer strategy. Certainly he is attempting to embrace the reader in shared experience. Yet the very next paragraph shows that the reader's initial experience will not be quite as inclusive as expected.

> I speak of the chairs, but if we go together into the "room" they will not be visible to you. For a long time the house has been to let. Here, on the left of the doorway, as we enter, is the room, without a shred of furniture in it except the boards of two closed-in beds. The flooring is not steady, and here and there holes have been eaten into the planks. You can scarcely stand upright beneath the decay-

ing ceiling. Worn boards and ragged walls, and the rusty ribs fallen from the fireplace, are all that meet your eyes, but I see a round, unsteady, waxcloth-covered table, with four books lying at equal distances on it. There are six prim chairs, two of them not to be sat upon, backed against the walls, and between the window and the fireplace a chest of drawers, with a snowy coverlet. On the drawers stands a board with coloured marbles for the game of solitaire, and I have only to open the drawer with the loose handle to bring out the dambrod. In the carved wood frame over the window hangs Jamie's portrait; in the only other frame a picture of Daniel in the den of lions, sewn by Leeby in wool. Over the chimney-piece with its shells, in which the roar of the sea can be heard, are strung three rows of bird's eggs. Once again we might be expecting company to tea. (ibid.: 1-2)

The last sentence is masterly. "We" may be expecting company to tea, but the reader is not of the party. It becomes clear that *A Window in Thrums* is an exercise in double narrative, one visible to Barrie in imagination and memory, and one accessible to the reader only at Barrie's pleasure, when in each chapter he re-creates incidents from the imagined world of his characters – in a setting he vividly remembers from childhood Kirriemuir – and in this opening has already accounted that all is vanished. The immediacy of the experience co-exists with the realisation that realistic though this Scotland is, it is beyond the reader's experience. This, in short, is not Scotland. It is localised, of the past, and in ruins whatever the excellence of the realistic writing.

Another Scottish writer who achieved the same double vision by surprisingly similar means, two generations earlier, was John Galt whose *Annals of the Parish* have been misunderstood in the same way as Barrie's Kirriemuir fiction has been categorised and often undervalued. The opening chapter of Galt's supposed diary of a country minister is as deftly misleading as Barrie's introduction to Kirriemuir.

In the same year, and on the same day of the same month, that his Sacred Majesty King George, the third of the name, came to his crown and kingdom, I was placed and settled as the minister of Dalmailing. When about a week thereafter this was known in the parish, it was thought a wonderful thing, and everybody spoke of me and the new king as united in our trusts and temporalities,

> marvelling how the same should come to pass, and thinking the hand of Providence was in it, and that surely we were preordained to fade and flourish in fellowship together; which has really been the case: for in the same season that his Most Excellent Majesty, as he was very properly styled in the proclamations for the general fasts and thanksgivings, was set by as a precious vessel which had received a crack or a flaw, and could only be serviceable in the way of an ornament, I was obliged, by reason of age and the growing infirmities of my recollection, to consent to the earnest entreaties of the Session, and to accept of Mr Amos to be my helper. [...] So, on the last Sabbath of the year 1810, I preached my last sermon, and it was a moving discourse. There were few dry eyes in the kirk that day; for I had been with the aged from the beginning – the young considered me as their natural pastor – and my bidding them all farewell was, as when of old among the heathen, an idol was taken away by the hands of the enemy. (Galt 2002: 3)

As with Barrie's narrator, Galt is through the persona of the country minister inviting the reader to apply preconceptions. Balwhidder is obviously a man of limited experience and worldly sophistication, as his comments on the royal accession prove. His tendency to equate his own ministry with the King's reign is deliberately made ridiculous by the author. Yet the overall effect is curiously similar to Barrie's; here is a vanished Scotland being recreated through the narrative of someone who had been there. And here, too, is the arching experience of someone who has seen change and lived through it, indeed seen change denied to the first-hand experience of the reader.

> When it was known that I was to preach my last sermon, every one of those who had been my hearers, and who had seceded to the Canaille meeting, made it a point that day to be in the parish kirk, and to stand in the crowd, that made a lane of reverence for me to pass from the kirk-door to the back-yett of the manse. And shortly after, a deputation of all their brethren, with their minister at their head, came to me one morning, and presented to me a server of silver, in token, as they were pleased to say, of their esteem for my blameless life, and the charity that I had practised towards the poor of all sects in the neighbourhood; which is set forth in a well-penned inscription, written by a weaver lad that works for his daily bread. Such a thing would have been a prodigy at the beginning of my ministry; but the progress of book-learning and education has been wonderful since. (ibid.: 155-156)

Galt's narrator is as elusive as Barrie's worldly and experienced voice. For while Balwhidder in the story is determinedly provincial in outlook and experience (a trip to Glasgow and a trip to Edinburgh in fifty years the limits of his wider world), there is a subtext in *Annals of the Parish* as plangent in its description of irrevocable change as Barrie's account of the end of the weaving communities of his youth in Kirriemuir. Balwhidder's parish may seem remote and untouched by progress, but a careful reading of the fifty years' diary entries shows that industry has come (the weavers in the cotton-mills), the Church has suffered splits (the Canaille meeting house), and the intelligent working class who in the 1760s would have taken their instruction from the pulpit now have their own ideas not only on religion but on politics – witness the extraordinary entry for 1790 when the minister notes the arrival of a new bookseller who takes in "a daily London newspaper for the spinners and weavers, who paid him a penny a-week a-piece for the same; they being all greatly taken up with what, at the time, was going on in France." (ibid.: 104) Not, you note, that the minister shows any real interest in what was going on in France.

And here lies the root of much misunderstanding of those who have read *Annals of the Parish* as an agreeably provincial and undemanding study of Scottish country life. Galt has animated the narrative by an extraordinary gap between the narrator's naturalistic writing (consistently agreeable) and his apprehension of the change around him – lamentable. Balwhidder is stuck in not only the past, but in his own past. The changing years make it quite plain to the reader that his parish is emptying fast of the kind of churchgoing loyalty which filled the early chapters. Not only do the new incoming weavers have the Canaille meeting house and its more interesting preaching to go to – so do Balwhidder's own parishioners who find his preaching (as even he admits) too boring to tolerate.

And this lies at the root of the misunderstanding of the first and last chapters of *Annals of the Parish*. When Balwhidder preaches his last sermon, the church is filled with those who realise it's the end of an era. But most of them have not been there for years. Defecting to other places of worship, or simply defecting, they have come back one time for an extraordinary occasion, not really because of Balwhidder's preaching (however much he may misunderstand the occasion) but because in some way they understand it is the end of an era.

The result achieved is exactly the one Grassic Gibbon depicts when he describes the auditors at the unveiling of the war memorial at the conclusion of *Sunset Song,* with the names of the villagers in Kinraddie who did not return from the battlefields of France. They know there is something important implicit in the occasion, "the young ploughmen they stood with glum, white faces, they'd no understanding or caring, it was something that vexed and tore at them, it belonged to times they had no knowing of." (Gibbon 2006: 255-256) But the readers do, and the scene has a central role in the action of the great trilogy of *A Scots Quair,* which carries the events right to the here and now of publication of *Grey Granite* in 1934, challenging the reader out of retrospective comfort to the shock of the present.

Critics of retrospective Scottish fiction, such as *Annals* and *Window in Thrums,* have been repelled by the assumption that they depict an unthreatening Scotland of the past, choosing to overlook the change and challenge from which modern Scotland emerged. This, specifically, is the charge leveled at much of the "Kailyard", and often with justice. Yet in the two examples here there is the beginning of a counter-argument: it is possible to depict that attractive past for which there was so obviously a demand while using narrative strategies which allowed for more than one simultaneous reading. Why else would George Douglas Brown have begun *The House with the Green Shutters* with a brilliant pastiche of a Kailyard opening, Barbie sleeping under the summer dawn, if not to raise one set of reader expectations before crushing them in the hyper-realist plot which followed? Brown's novel uses the familiar characters and settings of Kailyard – the gifted son at University, the local hero, the hardworking schoolmaster – only to subvert them by exposing their inadequacy as vehicles to express the complexity of a Scotland changing daily – in Brown's case, the horse and cart business on which the prosperity of the House with its shutters is built, overcome by the advent of the railway age which destroys John Gourlay's business in a matter of years (cf. Brown 2001). Grassic Gibbon's Kinraddie is similarly destroyed in the course of *Sunset Song*; indeed when Chris returns to her father's farm in the second novel, very shortly after she left it, it is all but unrecognizable as arable farming has given way to sheep-grazing. When Balwhidder's luckless successor in the pulpit of Dalmailing begins his ministry, he will have a steep learning curve to overcome the inertia of the previous half-century.

Scottish fiction, read in this way, exhibits a rich variety of ways in which a commercially acceptable, or fashionable, picture of an unchanging Scotland can be subverted when a critical reading overturns initial impression, or superficial understanding of plot. Jeanie Deans may be comfortably settled at the end of Sir Walter Scott's *The Heart of Midlothian* thanks to Argyle's patronage, a new farm and new resources, but it is partly because the old setting of the earlier parts of the novel has become untenable through political and social change – and through Jeanie's own life changing as well. Likewise her father's death marks the end of something she simply cannot understand, though Scott uses Davie Deans' emotional traumas to hint at the appalling sufferings of an earlier Covenanting era, without explicitly evoking them as he was to in *Old Mortality*. The Davie Deans who can hardly bring himself to make a joke at his daughter's engagement –

> On this occasion David Deans was delivered of his first-born joke; and apparently the parturition was accompanied with many throes, for sorely did he twist about his physiognomy, and much did he stumble in his speech, before he could express his idea, 'That the lad being now wedded to his spiritual bride, it was hard to threaten him with ane temporal spouse in the same day.' He then laughed a hoarse and brief laugh, and was suddenly grave and silent, as if abashed at his own vivacious effort. (Scott 1982: 439-440)

– is not merely there for the near-comic effect, but to indicate a lifetime's emotional thwarting and all the near-tragic effect it had on his daughters. Not till Davie's death can Jeanie's family settle to the pattern Scott obviously saw as a standard for a peacetime Scotland. Not till Redgauntlet's exile with the Pretender at the end of *Redgaunt-*

let can the Union settle to restoring peace and prosperity without the shadow of a further Jacobite uprising: the cause, as he realises with anguish in the novel's climactic moment, "is lost for ever" (Scott 2011: 396).

To continue with Scott, on another level, he uses misunderstanding at every stage of *The Heart of Midlothian* skilfully to advance the plot. Davie Deans' misunderstanding of the widow Butler thwarts a possible attachment in the loneliness of his widower's position. The Laird of Dumbiedykes is simply incompetent in forwarding his suit with Jeanie since he has no understanding of women and courtship. More seriously, Davie's lack of empathy with both daughters comes close to bringing the novel to tragedy. It leads Effie to acts of rebellion and to her incarceration in the Tolbooth: it produces one of the best scenes in the book when Jeanie and her father discuss Effie's plight – and their positions as witnesses who could save Effie – without really making sense to one another.

In London, Scott subtly uses misunderstanding to highlight the confrontation between Jeanie (whose very accent and dress invite misunderstanding in England) and royalty. The interview between Argyle and Queen Caroline is a masterful handling of words not fully understood or misheard, speeches misinterpreted – a near-disaster turned at the end into triumph not through rational argument but through "eloquence" and sympathy. To push the point further, it is possible to argue the scene has been misunderstood by readers ever since. The Queen, at parting, presses a housewife-case on Jeanie with a very large banknote inside. Do Queens carry such cases around just in case they are needed when they meet strange supplicants from foreign parts of their country? It can at least be argued, and argued convincingly, that Caroline was ready to concede the point and had the present for Jeanie all ready – a politician herself, she sees that this will soften Scottish antagonism to the royal family, and perhaps even more importantly make a powerful ally at court in London – Argyle – strongly indebted to her. (cf. Scott 1982: 359-370) Perhaps we have been misunderstanding *The Heart of Midlothian* for many years.

This is not a discussion of misunderstanding so much as an indication that fiction can probe a deeper analysis while offering entertainment and a picture of Scotland which is commercially successful. After all, Grassic Gibbon could have become rich (and with a growing family would have welcomed the income) by replicating over and over the basic plot and setting of *Sunset Song*, rather than using that novel to indicate the sunset of a whole way of life (his own teenage years of the First World War) and moving on in the other novels of his trilogy to show the social struggles and economic difficulties of Scotland in the 1920s and 1930s. The popularity of *Sunset Song*, compared to *Cloud Howe* and *Grey Granite*, is some indication of reader preference for the attractive picture in that first novel. Yet the challenge lies not in *Sunset Song*'s selection as Scotland's most popular novel, but in the author's courageous decision to destroy the very picture of Scotland he evoked in that nostalgic book. To stop with the first novel is to misunderstand Grassic Gibbon's intention and his view of his country; to read the Kailyard without the corrective dose of twentieth-century realism is to misunderstand the potential of literature to depict the complex totality of a society.

One does not have to wait till the twentieth century to see how understanding and misunderstanding have surrounded the country's literature. Peter Garside and Cairns Craig have done much to draw attention to the complexities of Hogg's *Confessions of a Justified Sinner*, despite the novel's enormous success in the last decade (cf. Craig 1996; Hogg 2002). For while attention is rightly drawn to the characters of Gil-Martin and Wringhim, the author's most brilliant invention perhaps is the narratorial voice at the beginning and the end, and inconspicuously throughout. So many voices clash in that novel, so much unreliability, that perhaps the only reliable voice would belong not to the narrator as one might expect, but of all people to Gil-Martin – if we felt we could believe him. Even Wringhim, dull of ear and of intellect, has moments when he does not quite believe his mentor – "I could not help thinking, that I perceived a little derision of countenance on his face as he said this, nevertheless I sunk dumb before such a man" (Hogg 2002: 94). Wringhim is hardly quick on the uptake: "You may call me Gil-

Martin. It is not my *Christian* name; but it is a name that may serve your turn" (ibid.: 89). The uncertainties which stalk the pages of all the interlocking and imperfect narratives in Hogg's book are reminiscent of the authorial voice of *Wandering Willie's Tale*, of *Markheim*, of McKellar in *The Master of Ballantrae* – even, sometimes, of Rev. Balwhidder in *Annals of the Parish* when he occasionally reveals himself to be a little cleverer than we thought. Anyone who takes Henry Jekyll's "full confession" at the end of Stevenson's novel at face value is misunderstanding indeed.

Many Scottish authors were acutely aware that their readers might not comprehend the full effect of their discourse. Socially, an author like Hogg might be looked down on specifically because he used a marvellously flexible array of Scottish voices and registers. Authors like Stevenson and Buchan proved themselves perfectly adept in both standard English and Scottish registers. Hogg actively pilloried those who laughed at Scottish voices by giving the 'best' characters in the *Confessions* a strong Scottish voice, while many of the dubious or wicked spoke the finest English – and Gil-Martin the best, along with a comprehensive (but inaccurate and deeply misleading) command of quoted Scripture.

It was Grassic Gibbon in a wide-ranging critique of his contemporaries in Scottish writing who made a trenchant observation which still has value.

> However the average Scots writer believes himself Anglicized, his reaction upon the minds of the intelligent English reader [...] is curiously similar to that produced by the English poems of Dr Rabindranath Tagore. The prose – or verse – is impeccably correct, the vocabulary is rich and adequate, the English is severe, serene [...] But unfortunately it is not English. The English reader is haunted by a sense of something foreign stumbling and hesitating behind this smooth façade of adequate technique: it is as though the writer did not *write* himself, but *translated* himself. (from "Literary Lights", in *Scottish Scene* (Hugh MacDiarmid and LGG, London, Jarrolds, 1934), quoted after Gibbon 2007: 146)

This paper has tried to turn this insight back on itself. The Scottish writer, it has been suggested, can be aware of this doubleness, can use it to transmit a flexible and sometimes ambiguous number of meanings to the reader, in alternating between language levels, in assuming a retrospective viewpoint which disguises a keen appreciation of change and the present, in exploiting the ingrained assumptions (born of the Kailyard) that Scottish is somehow older, lower in class, less capable of rich fullness than standard English. And it has been the opportunity to read Scotland's fiction from a distance, especially in working with groups overseas, that has brought the rich potential of misunderstanding into focus. As Grassic Gibbon continued in his essay, "for the truly Scots writer it [his native discourse] remains a real and haunting thing, even while he tries his best to forget its existence and to write as a good Englishman" (ibid.: 146-147). Well, perhaps not. Gibbon was ironically pushing his point too far. Language is a living thing, and in Scottish fiction its life lies as much in its potential for ambiguity and perhaps even misunderstanding, as it does in its rich potential to describe the changing country.

Sources

Barrie, James Matthew (2005), *A Window in Thrums* (First Edition 1889), intro. Ian Campbell, Edinburgh: Saltire Society.

Brown, George Douglas (2001), *The House with the Green Shutters* (First Edition 1901), intro. Cairns Craig, Edinburgh: Canongate Classics.

Campbell, Ian (1990), "The Grassic Gibbon Style", in Joachim Schwend & Horst W. Drescher, eds., *Studies in Scottish Fiction: Twentieth Century* (Scottish Studies 10), Frankfurt/Main: Peter Lang, 271-287.

Campbell, Ian (1993) "Glossing (glossing)", in *Scottish Studies/Études Écossaises* [hors série]: *Proceedings of the Scottish Workshop of the ESSE Conference, Bordeaux 1993*, Grenoble: Université Stendhal, 59-77.

Craig, Cairns (1996), *Out of History: Narrative Paradigms in Scottish and English Culture*, Edinburgh: Polygon.

Galt, John (2002), *Annals of the Parish – The Ayrshire Legatees – The Provost* (First Editions 1821/2), intro. Ian Campbell, Edinburgh: Saltire Society.

Gibbon, Lewis Grassic [James Leslie Mitchell] (2006), *A Scots Quair* [*Sunset Song – Cloud Howe – Grey Granite*] (First Editions 1932-34), ed. and intro. Ian Campbell, Edinburgh: Polygon.

Gibbon, Lewis Grassic [James Leslie Mitchell] (2007), *The Speak of the Mearns* (First Edition posth. 1982), ed. Ian Campbell, Edinburgh: Polygon.

Hogg, James (2002), *The Private Memoirs and Confessions of a Justified Sinner* (First Edition 1824), ed. Peter Garside, Edinburgh: Edinburgh University Press.

Scott, Walter (1982), *The Heart of Midlothian* (First Edition 1818), ed. Claire Lamont, Oxford: World's Classics.

Scott, Walter (2011), *Redgauntlet* (First Edition 1824), ed. Kathryn Sutherland, Oxford: World's Classics.

Jürgen Ronthaler (Leipzig)*
Royal Representation and Self-Representation: Analysing Images of British Royalty in Photographs and Other Media

Jochen Schwend has always been a critical admirer and evaluating teacher of the role of the British monarchy (and some members thereof) in the history of the British Isles as well as in contemporary culture. Not only does he seem to have a certain private liking of Prince Charles (dating even back to times when the latter was mostly ridiculed), but he definitely showed his attitude and insight in various fields and during several events: Two of them shall suffice to prove it. First, there are his lectures on the British monarchy taught to generations of students since the early 1990s. Inextricably linked to them is the analysis of pictures, i.e. paintings, photographs, cartoons etc., and their intended and unintended representational markers. As I see it, Jochen Schwend thereby connects two fundamental – and nowadays often contrary – aspects of British cultural studies: namely the critical inclusion of one's own perspective (here a certain liking of the British monarchy) into the informed deciphering or decoding of this subject's role and meaning in the larger historical and cultural processes. Secondly, when in the 1990s and particularly in 1997 on account of the death of Diana, Princess of Wales, all the world foresaw the imminent fall of the British monarchy, Jochen Schwend decided to differ and steadfastly (as well as learnedly) held true to the view that the present British monarch and her monarchy will probably have to change, but will nevertheless survive these troubles – and others to come. Judging from 2014, one could hardly have been more right.

With more than 80 percent of Britain's population – according to the polls at Queen Elizabeth's Diamond Jubilee in 2012 – in favour of the Queen and almost as many in favour of constitutional

---

* Jürgen Ronthaler is Senior Lecturer in British Literature at the University of Leipzig. His research and teaching interests include Shakespeare and his adaptations, postmodernist novels, detective fiction, especially in pastiche, and their media adaptations. Evidently, he also has an interest in British Royalty and their representations. He has published on some of these topics, as well as given classes, lectures and papers at several German and European Universities.

monarchy as the British way of running the state; with billions of people watching the double events of the Jubilee in 2012 and 2013 (accession and coronation); with even more people watching the Olympic Games in London and the royal involvement in it; and with again innumerable people all over the world waiting for and watching the birth and progress of the Royal Heir, Prince George, in 2013, the British monarchy has never been safer since the times of Queen Victoria. For the first time in about 120 years (and as an exceedingly rare event at any time) a Queen can look forward to three generations of heirs apparent alive, and she wishes, of course, to present them proudly. The image of the phoenix rising out of the ashes of the "annus horribilis" 1992 and its aftermath presents itself easily.

Drawing on representations of British monarchs and heirs before and after the present Queen, I will analyse the last 150 years of their – and other people's – efforts in purporting stability and change, distance and affection, gains and losses by way of creating their images. The first part of this paper contextualises and discusses the representation of the Royals in various media and primarily focuses on the present day situation. The second part deals with their photographic self-portrayal (in the form of commissioned photographs) spanning roughly the time from the invention of photography till now. Out of the endless amount of images portraying the royal family, I have focused here exclusively on official photos depicting royal christenings. Building upon a theoretical fundament of cultural analysis and image representation, I investigate the photos with respect to what we *ought to* see, what we *really* see, and what, perhaps, is hidden. This can be seen, too, as an investigation into cultural contact of various forms, namely royal/aristocratic vs. mass culture, historical vs. contemporary culture or, particularly, British vs. international culture(s).

Royal (Self-)Representation Then and Now
Monarchs before the invention of photography in the first half of the nineteenth century had to impress their subjects with either personal presence or carefully produced artefacts and sometimes with both. For effective ruling, being seen is essential: the necessity

obviously goes back to times immemorial and had a certain peak in the Renaissance, where the Tudor kings and queens had to actively display themselves to solidify their claim on royal power. This was especially needed by Queen Elizabeth (continuously challenged on her throne) and is shown in her ceremonial processions, which were so profitably contextualized by Steven Mullaney in *The Place of the Stage*, where he describes the interaction of royal show, rhetorics of space and the Elizabethan theatre in the "Liberties" of London (cf. Mullaney 1988: 10-12). At the same time and in the same context of developing British Cultural Materialism and American New Historicism, other authors similarly investigated *Power on Display* (Tennenhouse 1986) or *Renaissance Self-Fashioning* (Greenblatt 1980) – although mostly in the context of Shakespearean plays. They all stress the dialectically interrelated structure underlying the display of royal power: it is, as for instance with Queen Titania's representation of Queen Elizabeth, no longer a one-way street: the theatrically represented sovereign displays both power *and* the almost enlightened understanding of its beneficial wielding: otherwise one might find oneself in bed with an ass-turned-weaver and would wreak havoc on one's country. Both combined might ultimately lead to losing a royal head after the weaver's reawakening as an all-roles-playing political authority (cf. Müller 1980: 286-335).

Fortunately, the present Queen Elizabeth does not have to fear such drastic consequences of possible misrepresentations. But one does not have to go back four hundred years to see dangerous outcomes of royal misjudgement. Less than ten years before Elizabeth's birth, her imperial Russian relatives were shot; her own grandfather refusing his first cousin British asylum, which had already been granted by the government. He obviously did it to save his own throne. Something for which he even restyled his family name: as the first Windsors, he and his likewise somewhat German wife, Queen Mary, led British monarchy into a new age and era, in which the revered institution became more and more dependent on the good-will of its subjects – the acceptance negotiated and gained by public displays no longer of power but of impeccable behaviour. To make things worse (for them), the behavioural code of the Royals was no longer defined by them or court protocol alone, but by public opinion, which was in itself increasingly shaped by influential mass media. To be viewed in the right light is as vital to the Windsors as it was to the Tudors. As a consequence, the present royal family lives with the necessity of royal spectacle: "The Prince of Wales either doesn't notice or simply has become accustomed to being stared at. [...] Being a spectacle is part of what he is for." (Paxman 2006: 1)

In our increasingly visual world pictorial representation plays a key role, especially to those in power. However, artistic references to Royalty have declined to the brink of disappearance and neither theatre, literature nor the arts can be expected to augment and celebrate the role of the monarchy in today's Britain as they used to – at least till the heritage industry developed and postmodernism furthered "biopics" and country house films. The truly influential pictures – as far as public opinion goes – are distributed through the press, cinema, television and other so-called modern media. With the Internet and smart phones, Google and Wikipedia, a larger number of people than ever has unlimited access to a flood of images. At the marriage of George VI to Elizabeth Bowes-Lyon in 1923, the newly founded BBC was excluded from Westminster Abbey because the Church of England vetoed it on the grounds of not wanting a public crowd to listen to the ceremony with their hats on. At the coronations of George VI in 1937 and of Queen Elizabeth II in 1953, however, visual coverage had become vital. The change occurred swiftly, doubtlessly necessitated in the first case by the preceding constitutional crisis and in the second case by the still lingering post-war gloom, for which a fairy tale in Technicolor was thought to be a wholesome and entertaining remedy, strengthening Britain's role in the world as well as the role of its monarchy in Britain *and* the world. Before we proceed to the consideration of the royal photos, two other fields of the arts have to be mentioned briefly. Both have in a growing and influential way included Queen Elizabeth II and her family in the previous decades. This new development is mainly due to the above-mentioned postmodern interest in fictitious biographies that blur the borderline between real and invented persons and situations.

The first are some brilliant cinema productions.[1] Stephen Frears' film *The Queen* of 2006 focused on the days after Diana's death in September 1997. In the film, the visual and acoustic illusion of Elizabeth II was so dazzling that the majority of the audience probably forgot the difference between the real person and her fictional substitute. The corgis, of course, were also very convincing. In the wake of this success, other "biopics" were made that displayed fictional versions of royal and high political personages, like Tom Hooper's 2010 *The King's Speech* or Phyllida Lloyd's *The Iron Lady* (2011). A new stage, evidently, had been reached with filmed impersonations of elevated persons, when the Queen herself participated (for the first time) in a short video for the Olympic Games' opening ceremony and merged her re(g)al person with the fictitious character of the ultimate employer of the ever so popular (and British) James Bond, played by Daniel Craig. Obviously, the sequence included two royal corgis as suspicious guards of the Queen and Buckingham Palace. The second field covers the representation of the Queen and her family in fictitious texts. Since pictorial representation is the main subject here, no differentiated analysis seems possible. It is, nevertheless, important to notice that especially Queen Elizabeth II has become a well-represented character in contemporary fiction. Sue Townsend's *The Queen and I* (1992) and *Queen Camilla* (2006), Emma Tennant's *The Autobiography of the Queen* (2007), Alan Bennet's *The Uncommon Reader* (2007) and, finally, THE QUEEN [OF TWITTER: @Queen_UK]: *Gin O'Clock* (2011) are examples of texts in which the imagined present Queen plays a mostly positive role, both as Head of State and as a multifaceted individual, on whom British citizens can proudly rely. This – as constitutes my argument in the following – is also the basic aim of the official photographs: to appeal to the viewer for sympathy and understanding, i.e. to hold on to monarchy.

Official Photographs of Royal Christenings 1864-2013

Queen Victoria's family and, in particular, Prince Albert, were interested in the new photographic techniques and started as early

---

[1] The almost innumerable amount of television films, series or documentaries dealing with Royals of any time and of the present age in particular has to be left out here for reasons of space.

as the 1850s to commission photographic prints from several photographers (cf. Royal Collection), including J.J.E. Mayall,

> whose 1860 portraits of the Queen and Prince Albert became the first photographs of the royal family to be published and made available for sale to the general public [...] There are also 44 photograph albums titled *Portraits of Royal Children* produced between 1848 and 1899 [...]. (ibid.)

Consequently, the British Royal Family has used this visual communication of their personages and status (alongside more traditional forms like paintings, drawings etc.) from its very beginning and this helps us to behold continuity and change in this politically purposeful self-representation. It has to be added that the growing popularity and technical development in the photographic art since the mid-nineteenth century contested the exclusive self-fashioning of the earlier years and counteracted the intentions by presenting the public with alternative pictures. However, the palace has never ceased to present official photos of important royal events, especially those of coronations, marriages or christenings.

In briefly analysing the photos I will concentrate on elements like choice of objects, composition, arrangement, background, pose, light, perspective, gaze etc. – or what in image theory is called iconicity ("Ikonizität") (Sachs-Hombach 2006: 224-225). This 'staging' of the royal characters on what Roland Barthes called the 'connotative level' of photography (cf. ibid.: 225) reveals the abovementioned aspects of continuity and change in the conveying of the message to the viewer. Martin Schulz (2005: 9) in his book *Ordnungen der Bilder* describes the function of pictures in the following way:

> Bilder sind verantwortlich für Erfolg und Niederlage von Politikern, indem sie über ihr einprägsames *image* entscheiden, nicht minder für den erfolgreichen Verkauf eines Produktes. Längst hat sich eine ‚Bildwirtschaft' entwickelt, die den aggressiven Gesetzen der *new economy* unterliegt und in der sich der Wert der Bilder am Verkaufs- und Aufmerksamkeitswert bemißt.

It could be argued that the British monarchy has used the medium to its own 'advertising' advantage from the moment it was available until now. What, now, do these 'advertisements' reveal?

The family portrait of the future King Edward VII with his wife and son (1864)[2] seems to be one of the first photos of its kind and its composition has with variations been repeated with almost every royal baby to this day. The strong Prince of Wales, his fragile wife Alexandra and their "sweet" newborn son and Heir Apparent, Prince Albert Victor, form a kind of pyramidal trinity with a somewhat towering if protective male. Dressed in what might be called (at the time) almost casual clothes, they display an air of sober middle-class propriety. The mother looks young and virtuous, in her modest expression as in the way in which she holds the child comparable to a Madonna, the whole composition reminscent of the Holy Family. These elements alone stress three important aspects of mid-nineteenth-century ideology which the royal family was made to embrace more and more – or at least to represent. First, the political rise of the middle classes after the Reform Act of 1832; second, the so-called "invention of childhood" due to the domination of the new and nucleus middle-class family in the composition and morals of the Victorian class system, and third, the deep Christian religiosity, which at this point in British history was actually waning. Furthermore, with the rather dominant Prince/ father, the gender construction of the Victorian Age is more than apparent: the father dressed in outdoor tweed is evidently both patriarch and breadwinner, the mother in her almost angelic looks is the perfect synthesis of the "angel in the house" and "mother" ideals of Victorianism. The blurred background shows foliage and – vaguely – the diamond-patterned wall of a country house, possibly Sandringham, which Victoria had aquired in 1862 for the Prince of Wales. It directs the viewer back towards the "characters" and gives them a kind of eternally tranquil setting. This is – together with the

---

[2] For copyright reasons, the photos can unfortunately not be displayed in this publication. However, footnotes refer to websites showing the images under scrutiny – most of them can be seen at Jones 2013. For this photograph, see http://en.wikipedia.org/wiki/File:Edward_and_Alix_with_Albert.jpg (11 January 2014).

tweed and the rather direct gazes of all three – a reference to a landowning family, whereas the St. George's Cross on the dress or plaid of the Prince is the only iconographic hint at the decisive role of the boy as the second in line to the throne, to which, however, he will not accede. All in all, the photo displays a much more modest, if still self-reliant Royalty than would have been constructed a century before. The picture represents the ideas of the century's dominant class rather than the sitter's own aristocratic position. This reveals a reduced political power made up for by a "they-are-of-us" symbolism, which stresses the individual more than its function, but carefully includes symbols of Englishness and religious continuity: These are values which in themselves function as a reminder of the dynastic continuity that goes directly from God to the British Crown. It is difficult to say whether at this stage all of that was intended by the posing persons or the photographer – actually, one can only be sure of the perseverance they must have had holding that position and gaze for the very long time required by photographic techniques at the time. Possibly, they only wanted to create a private family portrait: but as with books so with images: trust the tale and not the teller.

The iconography changes completely in the highly interesting picture of Queen Victoria with the future Kings Edward VII, George V and Edward VIII, at the event of the latter's christening (1894).[3] Formal dresscode and a rich background (in both senses of the word) prevail. The location is probably Buckingham Palace. The colour tones are more varied than in the first picture, the expensive furniture, hangings and decorative items clearly visible; patterns and designs all chosen to provide an aesthetically perfect setting for this important moment. The sharper contrast and minute details might to some extent be due to the development of photographic techniques. The general impression, however, was presumably intended as a strategy of this "state photography" depicting four generations of the Saxe-Coburg-Gotha dynasty and, which is more, four of their monarchs: the very regal postures suggest "Britannia rules the waves" and, actually, the world. At the time the picture was

---

[3] Cf. Hardman 2013, second picture.

taken, this was certainly true: Britain was at the peak of its Empire. But the forces that would soon challenge it from within and outside the country were already gathering: Darwinism and Marxism had been attacking the ruling classes and their ideology for decades; women were no longer submissive and demanded participation in all fields of life, including the franchise. The Irish Question was pressing and with the growing economic and political power of the US and Germany, important markets – and with it Britain's "workshop-of-the-world position" – were threatened. The *fin de siècle* approached and more than one crisis was on the way. The self-reliant royal family group, however, displays no anxieties. Two proud men, father and grandfather of the infant, look reliably steady, even if the Prince of Wales looks somewhat vaguely into a further distance and seems to ignore his family. As we know, he had other business than family to attend to and his rather Edwardian lifestyle shows clearly in contrast to his slender son. The two heirs are placed in a composition one can find again in most of the following photos: They form a silhouette which creates a "V" that points down to the really important issue: the Queen-Empress Victoria holding her great-grandchild and watching with what looks – probably by chance – ambiguous care. With hindsight one could infer the almost paradoxical split in her life: being styled the grandmother of Europe, she did not really like children, let alone having them. However, duty came first and the son to Prince George, Duke of York, represented the future. At her age – as with Elizabeth I – the end of her century equalled the end of her: it might come at any time. So, the boy gets all of the light's attention: the elaborate lace christening gown forms the focus together with the headwear of Victoria, as if the picture wants to say: our safe future springs directly from the great Queen to this new heir. The photo also concentrates exclusively on the line of succession rather than on the extended family, thus enhancing the above-mentioned message. The more troubled crown solidifies its role by shaping itself as rich, powerful, reliant and reaching far into the future. The photo enjoyed a revival in 2013, when the present Queen and her male heirs posed in a similar manner at the christening of Prince George of Cambridge (cf. below).

The photo of Princess Elizabeth's christening in 1926 presents Britain's and the first Windsor's new Heir Presumptive to the throne.[4] Her name seems to refer both to her mother and to her great Tudor ancestor. In grand style, the photo depicts the princess in the opulent family christening gown, forming the picture's centre in terms of composition and light, the dazzling brightness of the gown even outdoing the splendour of the ladies' costumes. The splendour of the occasion captured in the picture leads the viewer to forget the even more weakened and partially threatened position of the monarchy in Britain. And an absence is telling: The Prince of Wales, uncle to Elizabeth, is missing. What the photo probably does not wish to refer to are the rumours around his playboy life that will eventually lead to his abdication in 1936. And, of course, it cannot hint at a chanceful second ascension to the throne by a younger brother, who succeeds remarkably well (much supported by his wife) in safeguarding the monarchy in extreme troubles. What the picture really shows are the monarchs that will lead Britain with the exception of the very short reign of Edward VIII to this very day.

Troubled times never cease. At the time of the christening of Prince Charles in 1948 several aspects were worrying. Next to the post-war troubles in the economy, the health of King George VI was swiftly declining, which is more than visible in the photos of the christening. Princess Elizabeth's marriage to a partly German Prince so soon after the war provided a further complication. In this respect, the birth of a new Heir Apparent was a joyous and reassuring occasion. The photo described (one of two very similar versions) takes up the display of all present and future monarchs alive and their consorts. The limited personage allows us to see more clearly the sumptuous room, its furniture and its floral decoration that form – particularly in the post-war austerity – a truly royal setting. The men are in Morning Dress, the two Elizabeths are in afternoon dresses but do not look as festive as the ladies in the previous picture. The Monarch perches rather informally on the arm of the gilded settee, the Queen looking every inch a lady at the height of

---

[4] Cf. http://www.abc.net.au/news/2013-10-25/christening-portrait-of-princess-elizabeth/5045346 (10 January 2014).

fashion. Both fix their gaze on the newly born heir. It certainly is a special family, but they seem to be fairly normal humans. Prince Philip and Princess Elizabeth as parents look proudly and directly into the camera, conveying that duty has been done. The picture is still in black and white, although colour prints would have been possible since the late 1930s. Evidently one did not want to look too common, even if a spotlight was allowed to stress the stage character of the occasion... In the other version of this photo all gazes are on Charles: In him lies the future of the monarchy and for this message every positive image is conjured up (like the background) and every problem (like the outside world, including the spotlight in this case) is hidden.

At the christening of Prince William in August 1982, times were very troublesome again. The country's economy was on the rocks, Margaret Thatcher's plans and actions to overcome the problems almost split the nation, dramatically increased unemployment, dismantled the unions and led to civil-war-like situations in the Midlands and the North. A few weeks before the christening, victory in the Falklands War had rekindled national pride. The event was ideal to underpin this newly found national identity and at the same time to counteract the economic and political problems. As with the fairy-tale romance of Charles and Diana's wedding in 1981, the show distracted the people and directed them to hail their rather splendid monarchy as a safeguard for national unity. In the several coloured photographs of the occasion four generations of Windsors display golden glory, mirth, constancy and continuity. One particular picture looks like an imitation of the previously described one, but adding the immensely popular "Queen Mum" as the mother of the monarch to the personage. Her function, however, was vital: beyond simply being the great-grandmother of William, she represented Britain's hard-fought victory in the Second World War, during which she and her husband had stayed in London or Windsor to support the war efforts and hold up the morale of the nation. The photo is taken in the same room as in the image captured in 1948, the settee is larger, but of the same make. In contrast to almost all other photos, Diana looks caringly at her child: only

Victoria had looked at the child, too, but somewhat quizzically. The Queen Mother watches both of them, Prince Charles looks at his father, and the Queen – obviously as monarch – looks into the camera. The result underlines individuality and normality; again they look special, but seem thoroughly human.

The four official pictures of the christening of Prince George in 2013 combine tradition and contemporary aspects – one would not really call it innovation. The background and setting are downscaled and the sofa has less gold. The room in Clarence House is less grand than those in Buckingham Palace and the interior looks more personal, showing several paintings, including one of G.B. Shaw, and a photo of Prince Harry. The light has also changed; it now streams in from two large windows in the back, making the atmosphere more lively and bright. In the much disputed articles the media devoted to the photos, the people depicted and the interior decoration, style and curtains were not always well-received (cf. e.g. English 2013; Tooth 2013; Rayner 2013). Nevertheless, in the photo with the whole family, the allusions to royal grandeur are prevailing, despite the men being normally dressed and the ladies certainly not overdressed. The photo seems to suggest that the occasion is both formal and normal. More than in previous cases, it breaks with the tradition of separating the sexes, i.e. men standing in the back and women sitting in the front. Genders are mixed, and so are generations. All look smilingly into the camera, which makes the picture communicative, open and inviting. The class difference, however, remains there, even if this might be explained by the tradition of family of father left, family of mother right side of the photo. But the Middleton family is certainly being elevated more than the Royals are made to look "middle class". What is really new is the depiction of the Cambridges, sitting next to each other, i.e. Prince William being the first to "lower" himself to an equal position with his wife. There is a central axis created by the cream-coloured dresses of Katherine and her sister. They lead on to and blend in with the replica of the Victorian christening gown in order to fulfil the function of the photo, namely to centre and highlight the new heir and third in line to the throne – of course, in the proper traditional frame. Roger Tooth (2013) of *The Guardian Online* comments:

> Two families at ease with themselves, a royal future sorted with plenty of heirs. But there are another two pairs of eyes that look out of the photograph: from the painting of the two sisters, Princesses Elizabeth and Margaret, on their ponies. In the background, they are looking back from an earlier, less certain, era.

The Queen herself looks happy, indeed, and stands out from the others by wearing a coat and hat of a catching blue that is repeated in the carpet, where her notorious black handbag sits within easy reach. This has – particularly on the Internet – led to new speculations on its content and importance. In the comments on the above-mentioned *Guardian* article, reasons of its being there reach from the obvious (fashion, personal or London habit) via the comical (product placement) to the downright sarcastic (holding her batteries, not trusting Cameron with the nuclear button). (ibid.) Perhaps, as THE QUEEN [OF TWITTER: @Queen_UK] (2011: 157) states in *Gin O'Clock*, she simply wants her "Royal iPhone" with the special "iRule app" (ibid.: 147) close by? The handbag might be considered marginal, but 167 comments on the *Guardian* article alone (the newspaper not being known for royalist tendencies) prove the power of these pictures and even the most random thing they show. The pictures and artefacts, for instance, have been researched, described and evaluated in detail: Even James Middleton's Battenberg beard has been compared to that of King George V in the painting on the left (Tooth 2013). What escaped Roger Tooth's scrutiny was that in the next photo of the four successors the painting of the Queen's grandfather acquires a definitive function.

This photo can only be called a clever postmodernist pastiche. The setting is the same as in the photo above, but the slightly changed angle allows a clearer view of the artefacts in the room, which give the photo a more personal touch. It is enhanced by the reduced number of people posing to those who either are or will become monarchs (i.e. if all goes its regular way). This, of course, makes the picture a direct quote of that of 1894, in which Queen Victoria proudly presents the future of her monarchy in the three living heirs. Similarities such as the position and posture of the Royals are obvious; the differences, however, are noteworthy: The painting between the two Princes now adds a further monarch to the picture and connects the distant future to the distant past, hinting at a link between the two Georges. The real innovation, however, lies in two other aspects: The first is that all four sitters smile openly into the camera (Prince George really seems already to know his role), as if inviting the viewer to partake in some form of dialogue. Even more significant is the fact that the Duke of Cambridge (instead of Queen Victoria in the older picture) holds his son, thus bringing gender equality and male responsibility into the family, values that are obviously aimed at the younger generations. In other words, stressing an essential royal continuity between past, present and future despite all changes and modifications is clearly the overall aim of the photo's strong intertextual reference.

That this occurs in another troubled period for the British nation – with devolution, high unemployment, racial tensions and problematic European relations – allows us to better understand the need for a glorious (self-)representation of the royal family as being part of a far greater need, namely that of the UK and its people to further assume their special position and sell this image to themselves and to the world. If you face a precarious present, what could serve your purposes better than to politically and privately utilize an institution that has a great and valiant past, a stable and reliable present and a projectable better future. This safeguards more than anything else the role of the British Monarchy, but forces it at the same time onto an omnipresent representational stage that is in essence not so different from the "tableaux vivants" of Good Queen Bess's Royal Progress. To be seen is to survive, to be identified with is to survive better: and if this is rightly performed it even incorporates – as recently Prince Harry's bottom and Princess Eugenie's hat told us – the less royal shows and representations.

Having looked at various representations of British Royalty, one can conclude that monarchy is not exclusively, but to a great extent, dependent on the image which the subjects receive. In an age governed by mass media with an unavoidable flood of visual impressions, this influence becomes vital. One is what one is to be seen as. This is not an entirely new thought: Shakespeare's Prospero points to something very similar "We are such stuff as dreams are made on" (Shakespeare 1958: IV.1.156-157), and his Jaques knew that "All the world's a stage / And all the men and women merely players; / They have their exits and their entrances[…]." (Shakespeare 1975: II.7.139-141) The British Royals, although no longer in control of political power, seem no 'poor players' anymore. Evidently, for the moment they have learned to wield the powers of self-representation, and as the first part of my paper shows, other people's representation (mostly) follows suit. Nobody knows what the future will bring. If, however, the Royals proceed as now, they will certainly never again rule the world, but they might cleverly act out their role via the media. And this – in our world – is almost the same.

Sources

English, Rebecca (2013), "A Portrait of a Modern Monarchy: Informal Picture Shows Happy and Relaxed Royal Family Rubbing Shoulders with the Middletons", *Mail Online*, 24 October, http://www.dailymail.co.uk/news/article-2475673/Royal-christening-official-photographs-Royal-Family-Middletons-Prince-George.html (10 January 2014).

Greenblatt, Stephen (1980), *Renaissance Self-Fashioning. From More to Shakespeare*, Chicago – London: Chicago University Press.

Hardman, Robert (2013), "Making History, a Queen and Three Kings in Waiting: The First Photograph to Show Four Sovereigns Together since the Victorian Period", *Mail Online*, 24 October, http://www.dailymail.co.uk/news/article-2476033/Making-history-queen-kings-waiting-The-photograph-sovereigns-Victorian-period.html (11 January 2014).

Jones, Barbara (2013), "Celebration – A Royal Birth and Christening", The Enchanted Manor, 8 August, http://theenchantedmanor.com/celebration-a-royal-birth-and-christening/ (6 January 2014).

Mullaney, Steven (1988), *The Place of the Stage. License, Play and Power in Renaissance England*, Chicago – London: Chicago University Press.

Müller, André (1980), *Shakespeare ohne Geheimnis*, Leipzig: Philipp Reclam jun.

Paxman, Jeremy (2006), *On Royalty*, London: Viking.

Rayner, Gordon (2013), "Prince George Christening: Portrait That Shows the Future of the Monarchy", *The Telegraph*, 24 October, http://www.telegraph.co.uk/news/uknews/prince-george/10403684/Prince-George-christening-portrait-that-shows-the-future-of-the-monarchy.html (10 January 2014).

Royal Collection, http://www.royalcollection.org.uk/collection/photographs (6 January 2014).

Sachs-Hombach, Klaus (2006), *Das Bild als kommunikatives Medium. Elemente einer allgemeinen Bildwissenschaft*, Köln: Halem-Verlag.

Schulz, Martin (2005), *Ordnungen der Bilder. Eine Einführung in die Bildwissenschaft*, München: Wilhelm Fink Verlag.

Shakespeare, William (1975), *As You Like It*, ed. Agnes Latham, London – New York: Methuen.

Shakespeare, William (1958), *The Tempest*, ed. Frank Kermode, London – New York: Methuen.

Tennenhouse, Leonard (1986), *Power on Display. The Politics of Shakespeare's Genres*, New York – Cambridge: Methuen.

THE QUEEN [OF TWITTER:@Queen_UK] (2011), *Gin O'Clock*, London: Hodder & Stoughton.

Tooth, Roger (2013), "Prince George's Christening Portrait Shows Royals in Beige but Cheerful Light", *The Guardian*, 25 October, http://www.theguardian.com/uk-news/2013/oct/25/prince-george-christening-portrait-royals (10 January 2014).

Fergal Lenehan (Jena)*
"I am aware you don't speak German – yet". Depicting Germans on Irish Television

Myles na gCopaleen (more usually known as Flann O'Brien), in his 1940s satire An Béal Bocht *(The Poor Mouth), famously pokes fun at a somewhat ridiculous German professor researching in Ireland, who records the sound of a squealing pig thinking it a rare dialect of Gaelic. Joachim Schwend could not be further from O'Brien's absurdly self-important, and hilariously realized, Teutonic professorial stereotype. Joachim is indeed very much at home discussing the parallels between the thought of Richard Kearney and Edmund Burke. He is also equally at ease flopped upon the floor of a child's playroom, crayon nestling between thumb and index finger, enjoying the interwoven speech patterns of Hiberno-English and German with which my three-year-old daughter communicates (disappointingly, Joachim failed to record the encounter for further research purposes!). Joachim has also often been personally confronted with Irish stereotypes of that entity called 'the Germans', not least during his spell teaching at the then National Institute of Higher Education, Dublin, in the 1980s. Irish-German interconnections constitute, furthermore, an intellectual interest of his; hopefully this essay may further prick this curiosity.*

Introduction: Stereotypes and Their Uses

Stereotypes are problematic prejudicial collective-based generalizations that reduce the highly complex and multifaceted nature of a mass of individuals to an easily understood, and not necessarily remotely accurate, formula. They also remain indispensible for human beings' negotiation of the world. The early-twentieth-century American intellectual Walter Lippmann (1998: 81), the first person to use the term stereotype in its modern usage, actually

---

* Dr. Fergal Lenehan teaches at the department of Intercultural Studies and Business Communications of the Friedrich-Schiller-University of Jena, Germany. He received a BA and an MA from University College Dublin and a PhD in Cultural Studies from the University of Leipzig, which was jointly supervised by Joachim Schwend. He has published articles in journals such as *Studies*, *The Dublin Review of Books*, *Irish Studies Review* and *History Ireland*, as well as numerous chapters in edited volumes.

perceives stereotypes in a positive, or at least neutral sense, as a necessary tool for the ordering and simplification of "the great blooming, buzzing confusion of the outer world". Stereotypes are necessary as it remains impossible to view "all things freshly and in detail, rather than as types and generalities" (ibid.: 88). The decisive point relates, however, to the *way* in which stereotypes are used and received (cf. ibid.: 90-91). Human beings who are aware of the complexity of the world tend to know that what they use and receive "are only stereotypes"; they "hold them lightly" and "modify them gladly" (ibid.). Stereotypes remain an indelible aspect of all forms of representation which film theorist Richard Dyer (1993: 12), drawing directly upon Lippmann, sees as not wrong in itself. Yet important questions still remain: Who controls and defines stereotypes? What interests do they serve? Stereotypes are ever present in the German-Irish relationship within popular culture. Stereotypes of Germans within Irish television constitute the topic of this essay. Special attention is given to the underlying interests that these stereotyped depictions have served.

German Characters in Irish Television Drama
Irish television has, famously, been dependent on the importation of programming from the USA and Great Britain (cf. Brown 2004: 249). Indeed, the Irish national television broadcaster Radio Telefís Éireann (RTE), from its inception in 1961, preferred to import socially conservative, consumerist US shows rather than socially conscious British drama (cf. O'Toole 2011). Irish television stations, including the more recent 1990s additions of TV3 and the Irish-language station TG4 to the already existent RTE 1 and RTE 2, have not, thus, established an extensive tradition of home-produced dramatic series or television films. German characters have, nonetheless, featured in the comparatively small number of Irish television dramas that have been made.

In 1983 RTE produced a four-part mini series, in conjunction with Britain's Channel 4, entitled *Caught in a Free State*, having earlier unsuccessfully sought German television partners (cf. Sheehan 2004: 121). Ireland's neutral position during World War Two was the focal point of the drama and the series featured the bizarre circumstances surrounding the small number of German spies who entered the Irish state in the early 1940s. The series uneasily combined highly serious historical issues with slapstick humour, seen for example in an incident in which a German agent scampers throughout the Irish countryside in drag. *Caught in a Free State* was a "generally wacky menagerie" in which all characters, both Irish and German, were basically "figures of fun" (ibid.), devoid of any attempt at complexity.

The British writer John Ardagh (1995: 336-337), in his essayistic travel book *Ireland and the Irish*, writes of the phenomenon of educated Germans moving to rural Ireland, especially the west, in a romantic and often ignorantly naive search for a green, and empty, nirvana with a slower pace of life. Ardagh describes Irish-based Germans engaged in organic farming who have successfully made and marketed their own goat's cheese. This phenomenon of the well-educated German *Aussteiger* seeking an alternative existence in Ireland dominates the dramatic representation of Germans in Irish television drama.

One of Ireland's few, and most popular, home-produced television series of the 1980s and 1990s, *Glenroe*, featured, for a period in the mid-1980s, a German character: "the Berlin environmentalist architect and *Aussteiger* Helmut Blau" (Fischer 2012: 142). The writers of county Wicklow-set *Glenroe* attempted to subvert images of the insularity of rural Ireland through their insertion of a German character into the series, thereby suggesting that small town Ireland could also retain culturally diverse elements. The series later, more famously, introduced a number of Traveller characters and engaged, to an extent at least, with the topic of anti-Traveller prejudice.[1] The

---

[1] The playwright and feminist intellectual of Traveller background, Rosaleen McDonagh, has recently criticized *Glenroe*'s depiction of Travellers; the series contained "settled people playing our parts, caricaturing our identity in a manner that was not representative" (McDonagh 2013). This is not wholly true, as an actor of Traveller origin, Michael Collins, actually played one of the three regular Traveller characters. Indeed the task of an actor is to *create* a character within a dramatic context; the actor's genuine cultural background is, with some aesthetic and linguistic exceptions, insignificant. Suggesting otherwise is, surely, taking the dramatic need for some form of authenticity to an

minor and short-term German character Helmut Blau may be seen as a precursor to the more permanent Traveller storyline, which, even if viewed critically, highlighted the very real cultural hybridity, complexity and, indeed, prejudices inherent to small town life in Ireland.

An idealistic young German falls in love with Ireland and moves to the west in a four-part TG4 Irish-language drama *Kaislean* [sic] *Klaus* (Klaus' Castle), from 2003. The character of Klaus is a quasi-archetypal naive German 'Ireland fan' whose romantic gullibility is later exploited by the locals. Klaus' ability to speak fluent Irish is not reflected upon in what is here, surely, a more than ample stretch of dramatic verisimilitude.[2] The idea that every Irish village now has its own 'local German' was also reflected in the RTE sitcom *Killinaskully*, which began in 2003 and ran until 2008. *Killinaskully* was filmed and set in county Tipperary and written by the highly popular comedian Pat Shortt, who also plays a number of roles. Unlike the little-seen and largely unknown *Kaislean Klaus*, *Killinaskully* enjoyed an astonishingly large viewership while also being simultaneously universally panned by the Dublin-based television critics; a situation which *Irish Independent* journalist John Boland (2006) has – surely oversimplistically – interpreted as representing a new Irish cultural divide, between urban and rural Irish residents.

Killinaskully depicts a stereotypical rural existence in a manner that was not, indeed, very likely to please television critics. An integral part of this stereotypical rural Irish life-world is now the presence of the 'village German': the former filmmaker Dieter Langer, presently engaged as a cheesemonger. Dieter represents a German stereotype that owes something to older stereotypes and to the trans-continental cheesiness of the Eurovision Song Contest: He is amiable yet

---

unnecessary extreme. Whether *Glenroe*'s depiction of Travellers was within the realm of caricature is another matter however; it was undoubtedly a highly stereotyped and less than multifaceted version of Traveller life, not least in terms of the Traveller characters' accent and appearance.

[2] Todorov (1977: 82) sees verisimilitude as the "relation not with reality (as is truth) but with what most people believe to be reality – in other words, with public opinion". Thanks to Dr. Joachim Fischer from the University of Limerick for informing me of the existence of *Kaislean Klaus*.

highly serious and largely unresponsive to humour, while his musical taste remains decidedly questionable (Dieter is a dedicated fan of Irish double Eurovision winner Johnny Logan). Suggesting, via this stereotype, that the Germans are especially prone to seriousness and particularly 'uncool' would, of course, also seem to presuppose that the Irish are to decide what exactly is to be deemed 'cool' and acceptable, as well as having an innate sense of humour, inherently more advanced than others. There is, ironically enough in light of how the series was critically received, a culturally arrogant outlook permeating *Killinaskully*'s depiction of Dieter, emblematic of aspects of Irish culture and society during these so-called 'boom' years.

Subtle and perceptive writing could surely, indeed, have appropriated successful comedy from this rural Irish-German situation. *Killinaskully*, however, is lacking somewhat when it comes to subtlety. In the sitcom's first episode, entitled "The German Fillum [sic]", Dieter and his German film partner, Hans, come to the village as part of their work on an earnest documentary that will deal anthropologically with Ireland and "how joining the EU has made a difference to people's lives" (Dieter subsequently decides to stay in Killinaskully and to give up filmmaking, becoming infatuated with a local woman). Their contact and source of information in the village is someone called Willie Power and they tell the villagers continuously: "We are looking for Willie". Dieter, whose surname "Langer" is recognizable to Irish people as a Cork slang word for penis, believes that his and Hans' difficulty in finding Willie "buggars belief". While Pat Shortt has garnered critical and widespread respect for some of his comedic and acting activities, not least for his central role in Lenny Abrahamson's critically acclaimed 2007 movie *Garage*, *Killinaskully* is undoubtedly, however, not his most nuanced work.

Germans in Irish Comedy Sketch Shows
With the banking collapse of 2008 Irish collective self-confidence suffered a setback, while it was fractured completely in 2010 when the Irish state effectively handed over sovereignty to the European Central Bank, the IMF and the European Commission after its application to the European Central Bank's bailout fund. The

'troika' was often abbreviated in the Irish media to 'Frankfurt' and German politicians now acquired an everyday relevance that would have been unthinkable a short time previously. The Irish state was now seen, at least by some elements in the media, as controlled by the German state, with certain commentators writing of Germany in an authoritarian fashion; for example of "German imperialism" (Fanning 2010) and "our European masters" (Ross 2010).

Irish comedy has also begun to reflect these discourses, with German characters now having a distinct presence and acquiring a political relevance missing from earlier depictions within Irish television drama. Thus, we have had Angela Merkel dressed in a brown shirt in *Anglo: The Musical*, which ran in Dublin in late 2012 and early 2013, as well as Angela Merkel as an Alsatian-wielding Nazi in the RTE radio comedy programme *Green Tea*. The *Irish Times* television critic Shane Hegarty (2012) has rightly criticized "such lazy stereotyping", especially within "a country that avoided the Second World War and a subsequently crippling obsession with that conflict".

Various comedians have mercilessly satirized the Irish 'sovereignty situation'. The RTE comedy sketch show, *The Savage Eye*, fronted by former 'street comedian' and 'comedy busker' David McSavage, broadcast a sketch in 2011[3] in which a number of Irish politicians nonchalantly explain the situation, in a mock press conference, thus: "Sure, all we've done is given the Germans the keys to the car, and sure aren't we still sittin in the back looking around. And if we don't like it, we can hop out". The politicians then proceed to rise for the singing of the 'national anthem': The words of Irish anthem 'Amhrán na bhFiann' (The Soldier's Song) sung to Joseph Haydn's melody for 'Das Deutschlandlied'! While the idea of German state dominance over the Irish state is present here, the sketch is also a bitingly critical depiction of the Irish political elite, represented as incompetent and child-like and unable to maintain their own 'vehicle'.[4]

---

[3] See http://www.youtube.com/watch?v=7jedoqmoEb8 (8 April 2013).
[4] Ironically David McSavage, whose real name is David Andrews, comes from a

The comedian Barry Murphy has regularly played German characters within his stand-up routines and in sketches on Irish television, initially as a part of the highly popular post-football *Après Match*[5] sketch series, as well as on the TV programme *Irish Pictorial Weekly*. Indeed, the ubiquity of Germans to everyday life in Ireland is to be seen here as Murphy, undoubtedly one of the most popular and sophisticated of Irish comedians, has actually produced quite an array of German characters. Some of Murphy's Germans are based simply on fish-out-of-water linguistic situations, or linguistic idiosyncrasies. His regular character from his stand-up routines Mikael Shüßter [sic], usually dressed in a waistcoat and with long and strangely ruffled hair, reads his poems while speaking in a thick German accent and intermixes 'direct translations' from German, such as "an outlandish malfunction", with distinct, and often not quite correctly executed, Hiberno-English phrases.[6] The *Après Match* sketches initially solely poked fun at Irish football analysts, although they later widened their remit. Barry Murphy has also played a version of Dietmar Hamann, the former German football international, who played for Liverpool for many years and who now also works as a football analyst for Irish and British television. Gently parodying the real Dietmar Hamann, Murphy's Dietmar speaks in an unusual mix of German-accented English and scouse, the Liverpudlian dialect.[7]

Murphy's routines are devoid of lazy Nazi stereotyping, but undoubtedly poke fun at a stereotype of the ridiculous, po-faced and patronizing German *Besserwisser*. The foremost purpose of these German characters, however, is to satirize the situation in Ireland through the use of a supposed 'outside perspective'. This is seen

---

middle-class south Dublin family ingrained in the higher echelons of Fianna Fáil, the political party in government, with the Green party, during the 'bailout' of 2010.

[5] Barry Murphy has performed post-match sketches on RTE television since 1994, but the sketches only formally received the moniker *Après Match*, in conjunction with fellow performers Ristéard Cooper and Gary Cooke, at the 1998 World Cup in France.

[6] For a short recording featuring this character see here: http://www.youtube.com/watch?v=OMfPa0oP96Y (8 January 2014).

[7] See http://www.youtube.com/watch?v=MC8NmygIKsg (8 January 2014).

superbly in a sketch prior to the Irish general election in February 2011.[8] Speaking in a 'German' reminiscent of Chaplin's *The Great Dictator* with English subtitles, Murphy presents a short news bulletin for German television. The news topic is the situation in Ireland and the Irish election (in Murphy's 'German' "Pixie-Head" or sometimes "Pixie-Head Fuck" is the word for Irish!), which will be fought between "Fin Kompetent" (shown in the colours of the Fine Gael party) and "Korrüpt Finn" (shown in the colours of the Fianna Fáil party), while the land of a hundred thousand welcomes[9] now owes 90 billion euro: minus 90,000 euro a welcome! A biting approach to contemporary Irish politics is also evident via a reference to then Fianna Fáil Senator Ivor Callely, during this period mired in a bizarre corruption controversy: In Murphy's 'German' the term "eine kleine Callely" is used and translated in the subtitles as a "small pool of sick"!

Murphy also has a menacing 'Angela Merkel' character that has made numerous appearances within the past few years. A Murphy sketch with 'Angela Merkel' entitled "A State of the Nation Address from your Leader", was screened as part of *Après Match* in June 2012 following a European Football Championship game.[10] Murphy's Merkel appears as an absurdly over the top Blofeld-type James Bond villain stroking a white cat, who makes menacing remarks such as: "Reality costs – and someone has to pay – you". Murphy links this routine, however, to earlier corrupt Irish politicians when directly citing a famous statement by 1980s Fianna Fáil Taoiseach Charles Haughey, regarding the Irish citizens' need to be financially prudent (while he, of course, lived a corruptly financed extravagant lifestyle in a Georgian mansion, outside of Dublin). Murphy's Merkel, as did Haughey, tells the viewers that "it's time to tighten the belt", adding "or in your case string".

---

[8] See http://www.youtube.com/watch?v=Bdme0kdu5ak (19 February 2013).
[9] This is a reference to the Irish term céad míle fáilte; a hundred thousand welcomes. This term has become a cliché of the Irish tourist industry, with Ireland being labelled the land of a hundred thousand welcomes.
[10] See http://www.youtube.com/watch?v=olD8Nv7C8qs (19 February 2013).

In late 2012 Murphy appeared on the Irish Friday night chat show *The Late Late Show*, consistently one of the most viewed television programmes on Irish television, in character as the German "ECB economist" Prof. Dr. Günther Gruhn.[11] Murphy parodies the figure of the arrogant, somewhat ridiculous German professor – the representation of this stereotype actually has, as Fischer (2000: 331-332) has shown, quite a precedent in Irish literature, ranging from the work of novelist Canon Sheehan, dramatist Denis Johnston to the aforementioned Flann O'Brien. Murphy uses Günther Gruhn to comment on the present harsh economic situation in Ireland (he arrives with his coat on as "I didn't think there'd be any heating"), the changing power positions in the German-Irish relationship ("I'm aware you don't speak German – yet", "We plan ultimately to turn the place [Ireland] into a massive golf course – with Athlone as the first hole"), as well as the backwardness of Ireland (he visited Sligo "for the train arriving on time festival").

Murphy uses the character to also make a number of highly serious, and indeed darkly funny, remarks. Gruhn comments on the corrupt culture of payments he had earlier experienced on a trip to Ireland ("With all the brown envelopes: 'How are you doing? How's your sister, have one of them'"), while he also states that the Germans have "been celebrating since 2008, since you signed the bank guarantee". Murphy here touches on the debate that has raged in Ireland regarding the nationalizing of Irish bank debts; formerly loans from, among others, German banks to Irish banks. The Irish taxpayer has taken on the responsibility for these debts, a situation that some commentators have seen as an unfair adjustment of burden between "those who lent unwisely and those who borrowed foolishly" (Whelan 2011: 289), and which has only very recently received attention within the German media (cf. Bittner & Scally 2013).

Murphy's "Günther Gruhn" routine is ultimately, however, actually quite pro-EU and cannot really be characterized as anti-German. He finishes his performance as Gruhn with quite a long analogy in

---

[11] See http://www.youtube.com/watch?v=GEJaJL_Huh0 (15 March 2014).

which the Euro Zone is described as a "train driving into the future – towards China". Germany is driving the train, Ireland stinks of alcohol and cigarettes and is looking for its seat, while England "is the fellow with the trolley, his own micro-economy, moving along thinking he is not going to the same place as the train – but he is". Greece is "hanging onto the back of the train, in the nip, his mickey in one hand and an ice cream in the other". Germany ultimately goes to the back of the train and tells Greece, in a paternal yet agreeable manner: "Come on Greece, get on the train, we need you, you're better off on the train" (Ireland then proceeds to steal all of the egg sandwiches from England's trolley!). Thus, Murphy's Günther Gruhn character, although humorously arrogant and undoubtedly ridiculous, is also sympathetic and likeable and indeed quite a distance from aggressive Nazi stereotypes.

Conclusion – Holding One's Stereotypes Lightly

While the Euro crisis has progressed, the continent has, to a certain extent at least, been reduced to a popular media battlefield in which overblown stereotypes often function as a type of blunt cultural weapon, from caricatures of the 'lazy Greeks' to the Germans, and principally Angela Merkel, as Nazis. Within this atmosphere it is hoped that people reading and viewing representations of stereotypes "hold them lightly" and adjust them accordingly, to paraphrase Walter Lippmann. It is also hoped that cultural creators continue to utilize outlandish stereotypes, which no thinking person could really take seriously, to make, however, political points of the utmost seriousness.

Sources

Primary Sources

Après Match (1998-), Ireland: Radio Telefís Éireann.

Caught in a Free State (1983), dir. Peter Ormrod, wr. Brian Lynch, Ireland – UK: Radio Telefís Éireann & Channel 4.

Glenroe (1983-2001), dir. Alan Robinson, John Lynch *et al.*, wr. Sean McCarthy *et al.*, Ireland: Radio Telefís Éireann.

Irish Pictorial Weekly (2012-), dir. Maurice Linnane, wr. Barry Murphy *et al.*, Ireland: Blinder Films.

Kaisleann Klaus (2003), Ireland: Magna Films.

Killinaskully (2003-2008), dir. James Finlan & Eugene O'Connor, wr. Pat Shortt, Mike Finn *et al.*, Ireland: Short Comedy Theatre Company.

The Savage Eye (2009-2012), dir. Kieron J. Walsh & Damien O'Donnell, wr. David McSavage, Patrick McDonnell *et al.*, Ireland: Blinder Films.

Secondary Sources

Ardagh, John (1995), *Ireland and the Irish*, London: Penguin.

Barton, Ruth (2004), *Irish National Cinema*, London – New York: Routledge.

Bittner, Jochen & Derek Scally (2013), "Die Spieler und die Dealer", *Die Zeit*, 27 March, http://www.zeit.de/2013/14/irland-bankenrettung-euro-krise (14 March 2014).

Boland, John (2006), "Awful sitcom tops on the box…but do not adjust your mind, there's a fault in reality", *Irish Independent*, 5 January, http://www.independent.ie/woman/celeb-news/awful-sitcom-tops-on-the-box-but-do-not-adjust-your-mind-theres-a-fault-in-reality-26402465.html (14 March 2014).

Brown, Terence (2004), *Ireland: A Social and Cultural History*, London: Harper.

Dyer, Richard (1993), *The Matter of Images – Essays on Representations*, London – New York: Routledge.

Fanning, Aengus (2010), "Throw Off the Shackles of German Imperialism and Regain Our Pride", *Sunday Independent (Ireland)*, 5 December, http://www.independent.ie/opinion/analysis/throw-off-the-shackles-of-german-imperialism-and-regain-our-pride-26603524.html (15 March 2014).

Fischer, Joachim (2000), *Das Deutschlandbild der Iren*, Heidelberg: Winter.

Fischer, Joachim (2012), "The Goethe-Institut in Dublin and its Impact on Irish Culture", in Joachim Fischer & Rolf Stehle, eds., *Contemporary German-Irish Cultural Relations in a European Perspective*, Trier: Wissenschaftlicher Verlag, 127-148.

Hegarty, Shane (2012), "Irish comedians don't need to mention the war", *Irish Times*, 22 December, http://streetfoodlocator.com/blog/2012/12/22/irish-comedians-dont-need-to-mention-the-war/ (15 March 2014).

Lippmann, Walter (1998), *Public Opinion*, New Brunswick – London: Transaction.

McDonagh, Rosaleen (2013), "Authenticity Penetrates the Clichés", *Village*, 1 August, http://www.villagemagazine.ie/index.php/2013/08/authenticity-penetrates-the-cliches/ (15 March 2014).

Myles na gCopaleen (1992), *An Béal Bocht*, Cork: Mercier Press.

O'Toole, Fintan (2011), "A Very Irish Box of Tricks", *Irish Times*, 31 December, http://www.irishtimes.com/culture/media/a-very-irish-box-of-tricks-1.17302 (15 March 2014).

Ross, Shane (2010), "Bankers Who Peddled the Poison", *Sunday Independent*, 5 December, http://www.shaneross.ie/bankers-who-peddled-the-poison/ (15 March 2014).

Sheehan, Helena (2004), *Irish Television Drama: A Society and its Stories* (First Edition 1987), Dublin: RTE, available at: doras.dcu.ie/4627/1/Irish_TV_Drama_by_Helena_Sheehan_(doras).pdf (14 March 2014).

Todorov, Tzvetan (1977), *The Poetics of Prose*, Ithaca: Cornell University Press.

Whelan, Richard (2011), "'Merkel's Folly': Germany Economic Neo-Colonialism", *Studies*, 100, 281-295.

Rita Singer (Bangor und Aberystwyth)[*]
„Vielen Dank im Voraus, meidet die Menschen und bleibt gesund", oder: Die hohe Kunst der universitären E-Mail-Korrespondenz

Die Autorin saß im Oktober 2003 das erste Mal Freitag früh, 7:15 Uhr, in einer Vorlesung von Joachim Schwend und hörte über das Lautsprechersystem des Hörsaals den denkwürdigen Satz: „Ich mag ja den Charles!" Fünf Jahre später drehte sie den Spieß um mit der Aussage: „Ich mag ja Wales!" und durfte sich glücklich schätzen, unter Joachim Schwends Betreuung zu anglo-walisischen Identitäten im 19. Jahrhundert promovieren zu dürfen. Die Unzahl an E-Mails, die zwischen der ehemaligen, schreibeifrigen Doktorandin und ihrem korrekturwilligen Doktorvater ausgetauscht wurden, bezeugt das Maß an Unterstützung, Vertrauen und Freundschaft, das in diesen Jahren entstanden ist. Die folgenden E-Mails wurden zum Teil an der Universität Leipzig zwischen Studierenden und Lehrpersonal ausgetauscht, und zum Teil sind sie frei erfunden, wurden zu Illustrationszwecken jedoch dem typischen Sprachduktus des in dieser Festschrift Befeierten angepasst – eines Meisters der E-Mail-Korrespondenz.

Die Universität Leipzig rühmt sich ja, aus Traditionen Grenzen zu überschreiten. Eine solche Grenze im Sinne der Kommunikationskultur wurde 1991 mit dem Einführen der E-Mail überschritten.

---

[*] Derbyniodd Rita Singer ei gradd M.A. mewn Astudiaethau Prydeinig ac Almaeneg fel Iaith Dramor o Brifysgol Leipzig (2003-7). Yn ei thraethawd doethuriaeth 'Re-inventing the Gwerin: Anglo-Welsh Identities in Fiction and Non-Fiction, 1847-1914' (dyfarnwyd yn 2013) mae'n olrhain sut mae llenorion o Gymru yn llenwi'r cysyniad o'r 'werin' â gwerthoedd dosbarth canol Seisnig. Ariannwyd y prosiect gan y *German National Academic Foundation* (2009-12). Mae hi'n awdur erthyglau ar ddulliau naratif yn ymwneud â 'rhyngoldeb' (*inbetweenness*) cymdeithasol a diwylliannol yn *The Maid of Sker* (1872) gan Richard Doddridge Blackmore a *The Rebecca Rioter* (1880), nofel gymdeithasol Amy Dillwyn. Ar hyn o bryd mae ei diddordebau ymchwil yn cynnwys llenyddiaeth cyfrwng Saesneg o Gymru, Prydeindod preifat mewn llythyrau a dyddiaduron (yn arbennig o'r bedwaredd ganrif ar bymtheg a dechrau'r ugeinfed ganrif), astudiaethau ffilm mewn perthynas â sinema Brydeinig, a delweddau yn ymwneud â gofod a hunaniaethau cenedlaethol sy'n mynd benben â'i gilydd.

Seitdem pflegen nicht nur die Mitarbeiter der Universität einen regen Nachrichtenaustausch untereinander, sondern Leipziger Studierende haben ebenfalls die Möglichkeit, auch außerhalb der Sprechzeiten mit dem Lehrpersonal in Kontakt zu treten. Zwar lassen sich nicht alle Probleme per Knopfdruck und Dateianhang beheben, und es stapeln sich mitunter noch immer viele Studierende mit der Bitte um eine Unterschrift hier und einen Stempel dort vor den Bürotüren der Lehrenden, aber dennoch ist die E-Mail ein immer wieder gern verwendetes Kommunikationsmittel. Welche der im Folgenden zu illustratorischen Zwecken präsentierten E-Mails der Leipziger Anglistik echt und welche erfunden sind, dies herauszufinden obliegt der geneigten Leserschaft, da Dichtung und Wahrheit bekanntermaßen sowieso viel zu nah beieinander liegen und eine schöne „structure of feeling" allemal mehr wert ist als eine nackte Tatsache.

Die gepflegte digitale Kommunikation beginnt bereits mit dem Verfassen kernig formulierter Betreffzeilen, die dem Empfänger den noch unbekannten Inhalt schmackhaft machen wollen. Der Betreff soll also wie eine gekonnte Werbeanzeige Lust auf mehr machen. Nur kommt es selten im Umgang zwischen Studierenden und Dozenten zu Situationen, in denen potenziell der Eindruck einer Verkaufsofferte entstehen könnte, handelt es sich doch im Gegenteil um vorkapitalistische Tauschhändel nach dem Motto, „Tausche fertige Hausarbeit gegen Unterschrift". Dahingegen bietet die institutsinterne Kommunikation keinen Anlass zur Sorge bezüglich unmoralisch erscheinender Geschäftsangebote. Und dennoch tauchen zwischen Betreffen wie „Learning Agreement" oder „Hochschuldidaktische Workshops" gelegentlich E-Mails im Posteingang auf, die schlichtweg rätselhaft erscheinen oder die Empfänger in Alarmbereitschaft versetzen. Zu Ersterem gehört „wichtig – Türen!" oder „blue binder", zum letzteren „Einbruch" oder „Totengedenken, noch was zum Grabstein". Zugegeben, solche kuriosen Überschriften tauchen tendenziell eher zwischen Kollegen auf, denn Studierende haben ein untrügliches Gespür für knappe und präzis formulierte Betreffzeilen.

Absender: Katzenhirsch@generische-email.de
Empfänger: [XXXXX]
Datum: 27.01.2013, 22:39:45 Uhr
Betreff: aaaargh! zu spät!?
Guten Abend, lieber Professor [XXXXX]!
ob der Tatsache, dass ich an nächstmontaglicher Vorführung des Mittsommernachtstraumes vorlesungsbedingt leider nicht teilnehmen werde können, wollte ich Sie hiermit darum bitten, den Film am Mittwoch mitzubringen.
Dankeschön!

Absender: [XXXXX]
Empfänger: Katzenhirsch@generische-email.de
Datum: 28.01.2013, 09:23:13 Uhr
Betreff: Re: aaaargh! zu spät!?
Guten Morgen,
in der Vorlesung heute morgen wurde kein Sommernachtstraum gezeigt, dafür aber schöne Bilder vom Völkerschlachtdenkmal in Leipzig. Kennen Sie das? Passte hervorragend zum Thema heute früh: Erinnerungskultur. Aber das haben Sie vielleicht vergessen, wie Ihre Anwesenheit in der Vorlesung. Oder Ihren Namen in Ihrer Email. Oder dass mein Name ohne t geschrieben wird. Aber das kann schon mal passieren.
Die Veranstaltung mit dem Sommernachtstraum ist übrigens beim Kollegen [YYYYY].
Mit freundlichen Grüßen

Man könnte sogar behaupten, dass die E-Mail die Kommunikation gerade zwischen Wissenschaftlern revolutioniert hat. Wo noch vor nicht allzu langer Zeit Antworten auf Postsendungen ans andere Ende der Welt wochenlang auf sich warten ließen, so erlaubt die E-Mail mittlerweile einen geradezu blitzartigen Austausch von Informationen.

Absender: [YYYYY]
Empfänger: Institutsverteiler
Datum: 29.01.2013, 19:07:57 Uhr
Betreff: Welcher Film?
Dear all,
wer von euch ist das mit dem Screening für den Sommernachtstraum? Das war heute nicht die erste Studentin, die zu mir kam und den Film haben wollte. It's not funny!
Liebe Grüße

Absender: [ZZZZZ]
Empfänger: [XXXXX], [YYYY]
Datum: 29.01.2013, 19:16:22 Uhr
Betreff: Re: Welcher Film?
Lieber [XXXXX], lieber [YYYY],
der Buschfunk unter den Studies hat mal wieder zugeschlagen. Irgendwie kam die Nachricht nicht ganz an, dass das Screening am Montag nicht für die Literaturvorlesung war, sondern für mein Seminar heute. Sorry for all the confusion.
Liebe Grüße

Der hohe Beliebtheitsgrad bei allen Akteuren im universitären Bereich lässt sich also an der Zeit messen, die man jeden Tag mit dem Erledigen der Korrespondenz verbringt. Da ist man schon fast wieder froh, nicht mehr mit Feder und Tintenfässchen am Schreibtisch zu sitzen, denn nicht wenige E-Mail-Postfächer füllen sich jeden Tag aufs Neue bis zum Bersten. Da wundert es auch nicht, dass hin und wieder einige der Nachrichten unbeantwortet bleiben, weil sie schlichtweg übersehen werden. Manchmal allerdings hat das wiederum Methode.

Absender: Schneewittchen@Epost.de
Empfänger: [YYYY]
Datum: 10.02.2013, 10:29:41 Uhr
Betreff: Klausur!
Lieber Professor [YYYY],
ich wollte mal nachfragen, wann die Noten für die Klausur von vor zwei Wochen bekannt gegeben werden. Falls Sie meine Matrikelnummer brauchen, sie ist 1001001.
Mit freundlichen Grüßen
[XXXXX]

Absender: Schneewittchen@Epost.de
Empfänger: [ZZZZZ]
Datum: 10.02.2013, 12:12:33 Uhr
Betreff: Fwd: Klausur!
Lieber Frau [ZZZZZ],
ich habe schon bei Professor [YYYY] nachgefragt, aber noch keine Antwort erhalten. Ab wann können wir mit den Noten für die Klausur von vor zwei Wochen bekannt gegeben werden? Falls Sie meine Matrikelnummer brauchen, sie ist 1001001.
Mit freundlichen Grüßen
[XXXXX]

Copy-Paste, das digitale Pendant zum zerknüllten Blaupause-Papier, ist also nicht wirklich eine Errungenschaft. Besonders nicht, wenn's schnell gehen soll.

Der größte Vorteil der E-Mail-Korrespondenz liegt zweifelsohne in der Unabhängigkeit von den Öffnungszeiten der Post oder der Präsenz der Empfänger an ihrem Arbeitsplatz. Dadurch eröffnen sich allen Schreibenden vollkommen neue Möglichkeiten zu jeder Tages- und Nachtzeit, an sieben Tagen der Woche ihrem Informationsaustauschdrang Luft zu verschaffen. In aller Regel äußert sich dies im Zeitstempel, der in jeder E-Mail enthalten ist und dementsprechend ausreichend Auskunft gibt. So manchen Verfassern reicht dies jedoch nicht aus, und so klingt die Grußformel, als begegne man sich soeben unerwartet auf der Straße.

> **Absender: phil##zze@uni-leipzig.de**
> **Empfänger: [XXXXX]**
> **Datum: 27.01.2013, 23:43:03 Uhr**
> **Betreff: Handout**
> Guten Abend!
> Anbei wie versprochen noch heute Abend unser Handout für morgen.
> Grüße
> [YYYYY]

Aber nicht immer kommt es auf die Einhaltung der tagesaktuellen Begrüßung an, sondern auf den richtigen Ton zwischen freundlicher Distanz und vertrauter Nähe. Höflichkeit ist also das A und O. Und weil es praktisch unmöglich ist, zu höflich zu sein, so kann es manchmal passieren, dass die Empfänger in den Professorenstand erhoben werden während sie noch dabei sind, die Doktorwürde zu erlangen. Sicher ist sicher! Unter Akademikerkollegen jedoch bleibt es demokratisch, denn durch ein „Dear all" vermeidet man gekonnt die Auflistung der zahlreichen, über die Jahre hinweg gesammelten akademischen Grade der angesprochenen Kollegenschaft.

Während die Adresse, die Betreffzeile und die Anrede den Schreibern die Form und den Inhalt mehr oder weniger diktieren, lässt der Nachrichtenteil einen gewissen Freistil zu. Um der Themenschwere und Ernsthaftigkeit solcher Nachrichten ein wenig die Schärfe zu nehmen, bietet sich die Strategie „schriftlicher Small-Talk mit ein bisschen Meta" an.

Absender: kawai_warumoto@nocheinegenerischeEmail.de
Empfänger: [XXXXX]
Datum: 22.03.2013, 20:41:12 Uhr
Betreff: Handout
Liebe Frau [XXXXX]
Im Zug haben Sie erzählt [...], dass Sie eine Freundin haben, die sich jetzt als Tortendesignerin selbstständig macht. Da wollte ich fragen, ob sie eine Internetseite oder Ähnliches hat? :) Nur aus reinem Interesse am Business und so und weil ich selber manchmal solche Torten mache. [...] Ja, und weil ich gerade in meiner schriftlichen Plauderphase bin, dachte ich, ich schicke Ihnen auch noch den Link zu meinem Blog. Ich hoffe, ich breche damit keine unausgesprochenen Taboos, indem ich so persönlich werde und so. :)
Liebste Grüße

Zugegebenermaßen bilden solche mal mehr, mal weniger charmanten E-Mails im Austausch zwischen Studierenden und dem akademischen Lehrkörper eher die verschwindende Minderheit. Auf Verwaltungsebene im Austausch trockener Informationen bilden sie jedoch eine willkommene Abwechslung zwischen all den trockenen Verwaltungsrichtlinien und Erinnerungsrundschreiben an ablaufende Termine, verlorene Protokollen und auszufüllende Formulare. Kurzum, zwischen dem ganzen digitalen Papierverkehr erinnern diese E-Mails die Adressaten daran, dass am anderen Ende des universitären Intranets noch Menschen sitzen. So ist zum Beispiel das Einführen neuer Verwaltungsrichtlinien nicht immer schlüssig und hat häufig die lästige Angewohnheit, in Koexistenz mit kurzfristigen Terminen zu leben, die durch Vermittlungsgespräche zwischen den Gesandten der Nationen Verwaltanien und den Vereinigten Staaten von Forscherei gemanagt werden müssen.

Absender: [XXXXX]
Empfänger: Institutsverteiler
Datum: 15.02.2013, 12:20:34 Uhr
Betreff: Handout
Hallo,
unten steht eine Mail in der mich [YYYYY] an etwas erinnert, was ich schon wieder vergessen hatte und jetzt ist es zu spät, außerdem halte ich es nicht mehr für so eine gute Idee. Ihr versteht jetzt kein Wort? In Ordnung, so geht es mir ständig. Aber ich werde versuchen, Klarheit zu schaffen [...].

Nach dem Versuch einer Rekapitulation vergangener Ereignisse in ihrer richtigen Reihenfolge konstatiert die verfassende Person mit salomonischer Weisheit: „Alles klar? Nein? Egal, Wissen ist Macht, ich weiß nix, macht nix." In aller Regel sind solche Erinnerungsmails allerdings von durchschlagendem Erfolg gekrönt, da sie eine wichtige Ergänzung zum Sitzungsprotokoll darstellen, dessen Inhalt meist bereits nach wenigen Tagen in Vergessenheit geraten ist, und man jetzt die Gelegenheit erhält, schnell wieder in den eigenen vier Bürowänden danach zu suchen und es vor dem nächsten Planungstreffen noch einmal zu lesen.

Zwar ist der Informationsaustausch zwischen Verwaltanien und der Forscherei durchaus essenziell in der universitären Selbstverwaltung, aber es darf dabei auch nicht vergessen werden, dass sich hier in erster Linie Gleichgesinnte begegnen und im steten Austausch von Wissen befinden. Aber wie auch im interkulturellen Austausch zwischen den höheren Ebenen der Verwaltung und den Niederungen der Feldforschung ist dies mal mehr und mal weniger von Erfolg gekrönt, vor allem in Anbetracht des Zugangs zur Fachliteratur. Hier können sich spontan ungeahnte Hindernisse auftun, vor allem, wenn seit Wochen ein bestimmtes Buch in der Bibliothek nicht auffindbar ist, obwohl es im Katalog als präsent gelistet ist. Dies kommt praktisch dem Entwenden der Kronjuwelen aus dem Londoner Tower gleich. Also muss Klarheit über wichtige Besitzverhältnisse geschaffen werden, wie der folgende Konversationsverlauf zeigt.

Absender: [XXXXX]
Empfänger: [YYYYY]
Datum: 14.02.2013, 07:49:03 Uhr
Betreff: Vermisst
Liebe [YYYYY]
Die [Publikation] kenne ich, die ist aus der UB verschwunden, hast du sie geklaut? Ich sags nicht weiter, aber leih sie mir mal aus.
Beste Grüße

Absender: [YYYYY]
Empfänger: [XXXXX]
Datum: 15.02.2013, 11:24:41 Uhr
Betreff: Re: Vermisst

Hallo [XXXXX],
Ich besitze das Buch (nicht gestohlen, selbst gekauft!), kann ich dir mal geben, aber musst du nicht unbedingt lesen.
Liebe Grüße

Neben solchen reibungslosen Abläufen in der elektrotechnisch gestützten Kommunikation kann es aber auch gelegentlich passieren, dass Sand ins digitale Getriebe kommt. Denn obwohl sich in den letzten Jahren der Forschungszweig „Digital Humanities" erfolgreich etabliert hat, ist es nicht so, dass alle Geisteswissenschaftler immer und überall gegen die Tücken der Informationstechnik gefeit sind. Manchmal liegt dies an Betriebsprogrammen, die sich spontan entscheiden, wie Rechts- und Linksverkehr, nicht miteinander kompatibel zu sein.

Absender: [XXXXX]
Empfänger: [YYYYY], [ZZZZZ]
Datum: 18.02.2013, 16:48:41 Uhr
Betreff: Dissertation
Liebe [YYYYY], liebe [ZZZZZ],
ich wollte euch mal einen ausführlicheren Kommentar zu euren Beschreibungen der Dissertation zukommen lassen [...], habe mich auch hingesetzt und [...] meine Kommentare dazu aufgeschrieben. Allerdings habe ich das zu Hause auf meinem neuen Notebook, Word 2007, gemacht. Als ich den Text hier ausdrucken wollte, konnte der hiesige PC das nicht lesen. In der Regel kann er das. Also habe ich einen zweiten Versuch gemacht, aber dann habe ich die Datei nicht mehr gefunden. Entweder habe ich die gelöscht, oder der Computer hat sie gefressen, oder Word 2007 hat sie irgendwie irgendwo abgelegt, wo ich sie nicht mehr finde, keine Ahnung.

Und manchmal liegt es nicht an der Arbeitsverweigerung der Technik, sondern daran, dass ein Rechner unverhofft einen Virus ans ganze Netzwerk verteilt und am Ende gar nichts mehr geht: „Die erste Mail an alle kam zurück ... vermutlich liegt es an den Viren, die ich hier verbreite. Noch ein Versuch: Dear all".

Und so wie es mit allen Dingen ist, kommt auch die E-Mail (und dieser Exkurs in das dunkle Herz der intra-akademischen Kommunikationskultur) irgendwann zu einem Ende. Zwischen „Mit freundlichem Gruße und auf bald" und „Machs gut" liegen also nicht nur

Höflichkeit und Stilebenen, sondern auch jahrelange Korrespondenz in den verwinkelten Korridoren des Geisteswissenschaftlichen Zentrums in Leipzig. In diesem Sinne, „Vielen Dank im Voraus, meidet die Menschen und bleibt gesund".

Hans-Walter Schmidt-Hannisa (Galway)*
Irish Zen

Für Joachim

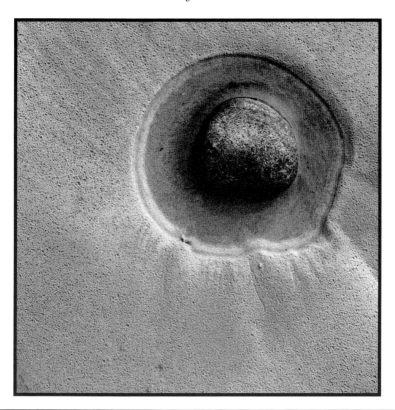

---

* Hans-Walter Schmidt-Hannisa studierte Germanistik und Philosophie in Bamberg und Freiburg i.Br. Er promovierte 1989 mit einer Arbeit zu Clemens Brentano. Im Jahr 2000 habilitierte er sich an der Universität Bayreuth über *Traumaufzeichnungen und Traumtheorien in Pietismus, Aufklärung und Romantik*. Er lehrte an den Universitäten Bayreuth, Würzburg, Keimyung/ Taegu (Südkorea) und Cork (Irland). Seit 2005 ist er Professor of German und Head of Department an der National University of Ireland, Galway. Forschungsschwerpunkte: Aufklärung und Romantik; Literatur und Traum; Geschichte des Lesens und der Lesekulturen, Literatur- und Kulturgeschichte des Geldes. Seit 2011 ist er Honorarkonsul der Bundesrepublik Deutschland in Galway. Fotogalerie im Internet: https://www.flickr.com/photos/23319022@N04/ Erste Fotoausstellungen sind in Planung.

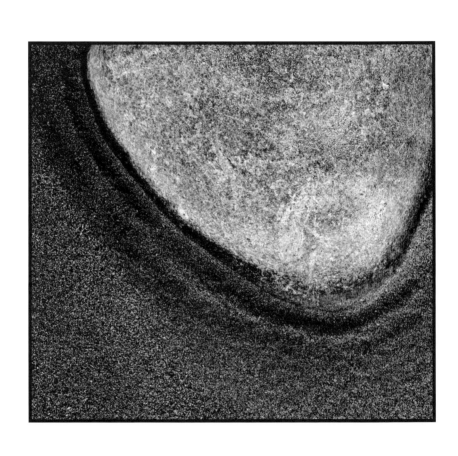

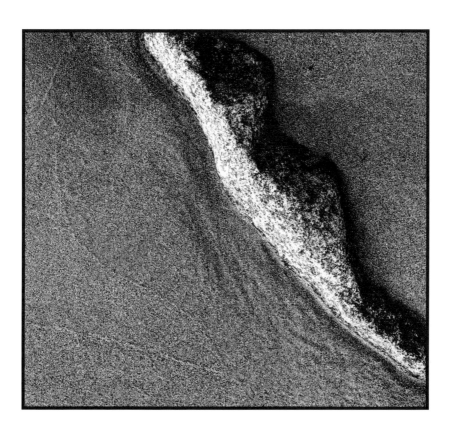

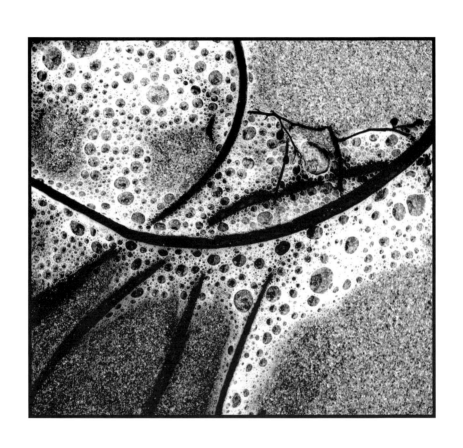

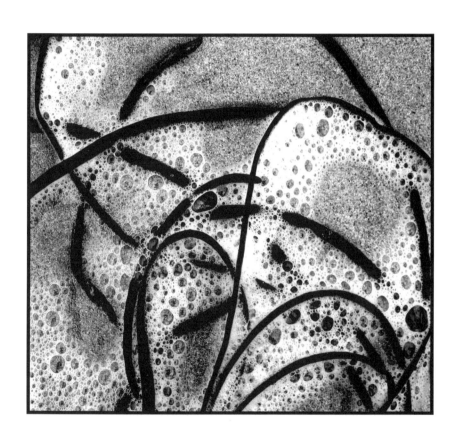

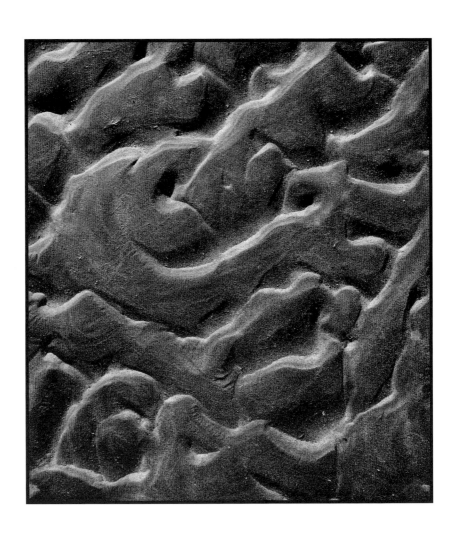

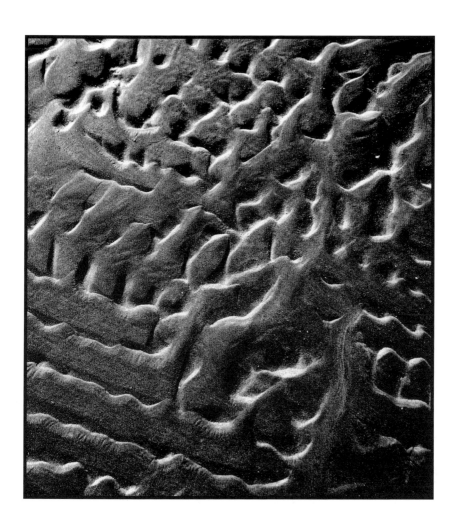

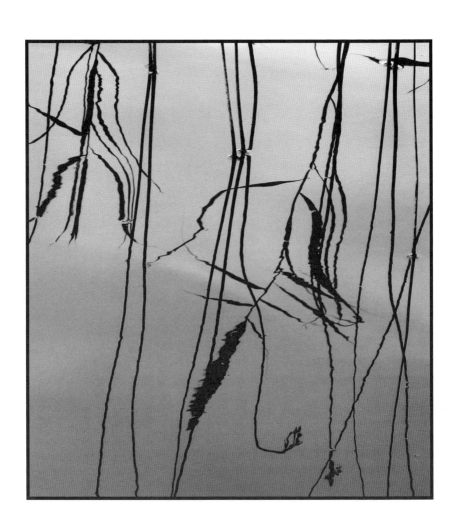

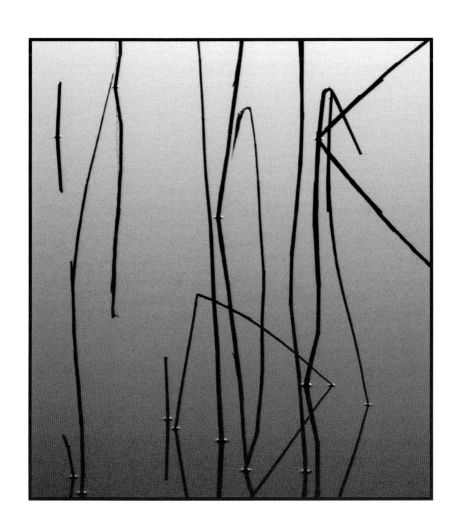

Diachrone Kulturkontakte

The Past and the Present

Jürgen Kramer (Dortmund)*
Von den Möglichkeiten und Grenzen kultureller Einflüsse – Am Beispiel des Brandes von London 1666 und seinen städtebaulichen Folgen

Ich habe Jochen Schwend zum ersten Mal gesehen, als wir beide im Winter 1992/3 für die damalige C3-Stelle „Kulturstudien Großbritanniens" in Leipzig „vorgesungen" haben. Als ich im Laufe des Jahres 1993 den Ruf erhielt und bei den Verhandlungen u.a. erfuhr, dass Jochen bereits seit 1992 im Bereich „Kulturstudien Großbritanniens" als Wissenschaftlicher Mitarbeiter tätig war und dies auch weiter sein würde, befürchtete ich, dass unser Konkurrieren um die Hochschullehrerstelle eine vertrauensvolle Zusammenarbeit beim Auf- und Ausbau des Studienbereichs behindern und erschweren könnte. Wie sich schnell herausstellte, waren diese Befürchtungen völlig unbegründet. Jochen war nicht nur ein ausgesprochen loyaler Mitarbeiter, sondern er hat auch mit seinen inhaltlichen Schwerpunkten (insbesondere in den Bereichen „Geschichte Großbritanniens", „Regionalisierung der britischen Inseln", „Großbritannien und Europa") zur Herausbildung des spezifischen Leipziger Profils beigetragen. Ich bin Leipzig 1997 „untreu" geworden, aber Jochen hat zum Glück für das Institut, seine Mitarbeiter und Studenten die Stellung gehalten: wie immer ideenreich, kompetent und zuverlässig. Aus dem „Vorgänger" wurde der „Nachfolger" – welch' eine gute Lösung! Unser Kontakt – über das Journal, *die Gesellschaft oder beim Gutachten – war seitdem beständig. Für mich war es ein besonderer Glücksfall, dass Jochen einer der anonymen Gegenleser von Routledge war, der meinen Band* Britain and Ireland *sorgfältig gelesen und kenntnisreich kommentiert hat. Natürlich hat er mir sein Wirken – mit der ihm eigenen Diskretion – erst nach Erscheinen des Buches mitgeteilt. Ich hoffe auf seine ungebrochene Schaffenskraft: ad multos annos.*

---

* Jürgen Kramer ist Professor Emeritus für Anglistische Kulturwissenschaft an der Universität Dortmund. Forschungsschwerpunkte: die Geschichte der British Isles und des British Empire, das Meer als kulturelles Konstrukt, der transatlantische Sklavenhandel, die Literatur des Pazifik, Erinnerungskultur(en), antikolonialer Widerstand, Joseph Conrad und Robert Louis Stevenson. Veröffentlichungen: *Cultural and Intercultural Studies* (1990), *British Cultural Studies* (1997), *Britain and Ireland. A Concise History* (2007) und *Taking Stock* (2011); von 1994 bis 2006 war er Mitherausgeber des *Journal for the Study of British Cultures*.

Die Fragestellung
1616 markierte den Beginn der sog. *classical architecture* in Großbritannien: In diesem Jahr erhielt Inigo Jones (1573-1652) den Auftrag, das *Queen's House* in Greenwich nach ‚klassischen' Vorbildern – wie sie von Leon Battista Alberti (1404-72), Sebastiano Serlio (1475-1554), Andrea Palladio (1508-80) u.a. wiederentdeckt und entwickelt worden waren – zu planen und zu bauen (1616-19; 1635-38). Wenig später schon errichtete er – ebenfalls im Auftrag von James I – nach gleichen Prinzipien das *Banquet House* (1619-22) als Ergänzung und Krönung des *Whitehall Palace*. Man könnte sagen: Die Architektur der italienischen Renaissance war in Großbritannien angekommen. Ziel dieser Bauten, deren Stil *magnificence* mit *decorum* auf beeindruckende, aber unaufdringliche Weise verband, war zweifellos, die Bauherren in ihrer Rolle als Herrscher zu bestätigen und den Betrachtern die entsprechende Bewunderung und Ehrfurcht einzuflößen (vgl. Newman 1994). Etwas später, in den 1630er Jahren, wurden im Westen außerhalb der Stadtmauern der *City of London* – ebenfalls nach italienischen, aber auch nach französischen Vorbildern – öffentliche Plätze (Covent Garden, Lincoln's Inn Fields) angelegt, die als standesgemäße Wohnquartiere für die sozialen Eliten und als Vorbilder für die vielen weiteren *squares* dienten, die ein bestimmender Faktor des Londoner Stadtbildes werden sollten. Der folgende Bürgerkrieg und das Protektorat stoppten diesen – vielfach begrüßten und bewunderten – Prozess der Kulturaneignung, der erst mit der Restauration wieder in Gang kam. Umso erstaunlicher ist es, dass der ‚große Brand' der *City* (1666) nicht genutzt wurde, um auf den Trümmern eine neue Stadt nach eben diesem klassischen Vorbild zu errichten. Einhundert Jahre nach der Katastrophe kritisierte der Architekt und Bauingenieur John Gwynn den erfolgten Wiederaufbau und beklagte eindringlich den allgemeinen „failure of urban grandeur" (Porter 1996: 124):

> Such a vast city as London ought to have had at least three capital streets which should have run through the whole, and at convenient distances have been intersected by other capital streets at right angles, by which means all the interior streets would have an easy and convenient communication with them. (Zit. in Porter 1996: 124)

Die öffentlichen Gebäude (so provozierte er seine Leser weiter) hinterließen keine bleibenden Eindrücke, kirchliche Architektur existiere kaum,[1] die königlichen Paläste seien ärmlich, die Straßen relativ schmal, verwinkelt und in schlechtem Zustand. London sei zwar bekannt wegen seines Reichtums und seiner höflichen Umgangsformen, diese stünden aber in seltsamem Gegensatz zu dem Bild, das die Stadt von sich gäbe. Vergleicht man einen Stadtplan aus der Zeit vor dem Feuer mit den Plänen, die unmittelbar nach der Katastrophe vorgelegt wurden, so ist man geneigt, Gwynn Recht zu geben, weil das, was seinerzeit theoretisch denkbar war, aber nicht realisiert wurde, beeindruckend ist. Die Frage ist: Warum wurden diese Pläne nicht realisiert?

Die Vorgeschichte
Zwischen 1600 und 1700 entwickelte sich London mit rund 200.000 Einwohnern von der drittgrößten Stadt Europas nach Neapel (281.000) und Paris (220.000) zu dessen größter mit nunmehr 575.000 Einwohnern. Diese Expansion erfolgte trotz der Maßnahmen ihrer Herrscher und Verwalter, die im 16. und auch in den ersten Dekaden des 17. Jahrhunderts versuchten, das Wachstum der Stadt einzuschränken – vor allem deshalb, weil es ihnen nicht leicht fiel, (a) die steigende Anzahl der Menschen angemessen zu regieren, zu beschäftigen und menschenwürdig unterzubringen sowie (b) die – mehr oder weniger ‚wild' boomende – Bauwirtschaft in geordnete Bahnen zu lenken (vgl. Brett-James 1935: 67-126).

Zentral für die Schwierigkeiten, diese Probleme in den Griff zu bekommen, war die Tatsache, dass ‚London' keine einheitliche Stadt war und von daher keine einheitliche Verwaltung besaß; ein Versuch, die *suburbs* einzugemeinden, scheiterte 1636 (vgl. Bucholz & Ward 2012: 122). Im Grunde bestand die Stadt um 1600 aus drei Teilen: „government and service industries were based to the west of the *City*, financial services were located in the *City* itself, and manufacturing spread out to the east" (Clout 1999: 65). Diese

---

[1] Dies ist sicherlich eine schamlose Übertreibung: Von den 87 durch das Feuer zerstörten Kirchen wurden 51 wieder neu errichtet – nahezu alle nach Wrens Plänen bzw. unter seiner Aufsicht (vgl. Summerson 1993: 191-202)

Unterteilung ist deshalb wichtig, weil sie sich zum einen im 17. Jahrhundert verfestigen und auch in den kommenden Jahrhunderten erhalten sollte und zum anderen der Anstieg der Bevölkerung im Bereich der *City* relativ gering, in den beiden anderen Bereichen dagegen sehr groß war, sodass im letzten Drittel des 17. Jahrhunderts die Bevölkerungszahl der *City* weniger als die Hälfte der Gesamtbevölkerung Londons ausmachte (vgl. Boulton 2000: 317). Dass die Bevölkerung vor allem außerhalb der *City* wuchs, war nicht zuletzt der Tatsache geschuldet, dass die Ländereien der 1536 aufgelösten Klöster mittlerweile verschenkt bzw. verkauft worden waren und schrittweise zu Bauland umgewandelt wurden.

Um 1630 wurde auch von den Gegnern der Expansion akzeptiert, dass London wachsen würde:[2] Jetzt ging es darum, Maßstäbe und Regeln festzulegen, nach denen die noch nicht bebauten Teile der Stadt bebaut und nach welchen Kriterien die neuen Häuser konstruiert werden sollten. Die erste Regel hatte James I bereits 1615 verkündet: *from sticks to bricks*: vom Holz zum Stein (bzw. zum Ziegel):

> As is said of the first emperor of Rome, that he had found the city of Rome of brick and left it of marble, so Wee, whom God hath honoured to be the first of Britaine, might be able to say in same proportion, that we had found our Citie and suburbs of London of stickes, and left them of bricke, being a material farre more durable, safe from fire and beautiful and magnificent. (Zit. in Brett-James 1935: 90)

Vorschriften wie diese waren nicht unproblematisch: Zum einen war ihre Reichweite nicht ohne weiteres klar und bedurfte immer wieder der Klarstellung. Zunächst ging es um die *City* selbst und dann um Gebäude im Umkreis von einer, zwei, fünf und schließlich sieben Meilen außerhalb der Stadttore; unter Cromwell (in der Mitte des Jahrhunderts) wurde die Reichweite auf zehn Meilen festgelegt. Zum anderen wurden immer wieder Ausnahmen beantragt und gegen eine Gebühr, die die Kassen des Königs füllte,

---

[2] Man hat errechnet, dass der Nettozuwachs der Bevölkerung Londons zwischen 1650 und 1750 bei 8.000 Personen pro Jahr lag (vgl. Stone 1980: 171).

genehmigt. Charles I verfolgte die gleiche Politik, nutzte allerdings die Ausnahmeregelungen noch mehr als sein Vater, um seine Kassen für nationale und internationale kriegerische Konflikte zu füllen. Andererseits begann in den 1630er Jahren auch die Bebauung des Gebiets zwischen der *City* und Westminster, des sog. *West End* (vgl. Bucholz & Ward 2012: 57, 153-154, 345-353), die – wie zuvor bei den königlichen Aufträgen – weitgehend kontinentalen Vorbildern folgte. So orientierten sich beispielsweise die Anlage und Bebauung der Piazza von Covent Garden an der Piazza von Livorno und der Place Royale (Place des Vosges) in Paris.

Bevor dieser Prozess architektonischer Kulturaneignung sich jedoch entfalten konnte, bremsten drei folgenreiche Ereignisse alle städtebaulichen Unternehmungen aus: Zunächst führte der sog. Bürgerkrieg (Beginn 1642) dazu, dass die Londoner, die mehrheitlich gegen den König und seine Fraktion standen, zur Verteidigung der Stadt eine elf Meilen lange Befestigungsanlage bauten (vgl. Clout 1999: 66-67), die Material und Zeit kostete. Sodann wurde die Stadt im Jahre 1665 zum vierten Mal im 17. Jahrhundert (nach 1603, 1625 und 1636) von der Pest heimgesucht, die 70.000 Opfer forderte – mehr als bei den drei vorhergehenden Ausbrüchen zusammengenommen (vgl. ibid.: 67). Ein Jahr später schließlich vernichtete ein Großbrand Anfang September etwa 4/5 der *City*. Zwar waren 'nur' acht Tote zu beklagen, aber zehntausende – die Schätzungen schwanken zwischen 65.000 und 80.000 (vgl. Porter 2009: 54-55) – waren obdachlos (vgl. Barker & Jackson 1990: 33).[3]

Das Feuer von 1666 und seine Folgen
Das Feuer brach an einem frühen Sonntagmorgen (2. September), in einer Bäckerei in der Pudding Lane (nahe der London Bridge) aus. Es handelte sich nicht, wie seinerzeit vermutet wurde, um einen holländischen, französischen oder gar katholischen Anschlag, son-

---

[3] Diese Zahlen, die jahrelang Konsens waren, werden mittlerweile in Frage gestellt (vgl. Museum of London 2007, Milne 1990, Porter 1996): Zum einen ist die Zahl der angeblich zerstörten Häuser nicht nachprüfbar (sie findet sich nur auf dem Gedenk-Monument), zum anderen spricht alle Erfahrung mit großen Stadtbränden gegen den geringen und für einen größeren Verlust an Menschenleben. Letzterer wird allerdings in keinem Augen- bzw. Zeitzeugenbericht erwähnt.

dern war aller Wahrscheinlichkeit nach ein Produkt der Unachtsamkeit. Ein starker Ostwind, der sich erst am Dienstagabend legte, trieb das Feuer vor sich her nach Westen, sodass die letzten Flammen erst am Freitag (7. September) gelöscht werden konnten. Insgesamt wurden ca. 13.000 Häuser, 87 Kirchen und 52 Firmenkontore zerstört; der Gesamtverlust wurde auf £10.000.000 geschätzt – und das zu einer Zeit, in der die *City* über jährliche Einkünfte von £12.000 verfügen konnte (vgl. Clout 1999: 68; Barker & Jackson 1990: 32-35; Bell 1994: 223-224).

Neben dem Wind waren vor allem die Bauweise der Häuser, der Zustand der Straßen, aber auch das zögerliche Verhalten der Hausbesitzer sowie die verspäteten Reaktionen der Verantwortlichen für das Ausmaß der Katastrophe verantwortlich. Vor dem Brand war die Londoner *City* im Grunde immer noch eine „mittelalterliche" Stadt, in der zu viele Gebäude mit Holz gebaut waren, die einem Feuer schneller zum Opfer werden konnten als Steinbauten. Zudem standen diese Häuser überwiegend zu dicht beieinander und waren – trotz der vorangegangenen Bevölkerungsverluste (durch Bürgerkrieg und Pest) – mehr als überbelegt. Um zusätzlichen Raum zu schaffen, waren oft die oberen Geschosse über die Hausgrenze des Erdgeschosses vorgebaut worden, sodass sie in die eh schon schmalen Gassen und Straßen hineinragten und generell den stetig zunehmenden Fuhrwerkverkehr, im konkreten Fall des Feuers jedoch vor allem die nötigen Löscharbeiten behinderten. Die Häuser waren auf Grund ihrer Holzanteile (und einer vorangegangenen Trockenperiode) nicht nur leicht entzündbar – in ihnen lagerten auch mehrheitlich leicht brennbare Waren. Zwar wurde versucht, durch das Einreißen und die Sprengung von ganzen Häuserzeilen Raum zu schaffen und das Überspringen der Flammen zu verhindern, aber viele Hausbesitzer zögerten zu lange mit ihrer Zustimmung, um dieser Maßnahme zum Erfolg zu verhelfen; der Bürgermeister seinerseits zögerte zu lange, die erforderlichen Maßnahmen durchzusetzen, weil er für den Wiederaufbau verantwortlich war.

Unmittelbar nach dem Ende des Brandes waren sich der König, seine Ratgeber wie auch die Stadtverwaltung einig, dass es für die abgebrannte Stadt eine neue Anlage geben müsse. Entsprechend schnell wurden bereits am 11. September von Christopher Wren (Abb.1), am 13. September von John Evelyn (Abb. 2) und am 19. September von Robert Hooke (Abb. 3) Entwürfe vorgelegt. Es folgten ein weiterer von dem Stadtvermesser Peter Mills (nicht überliefert), drei einander sehr ähnliche Entwürfe des Kartographen Richard Newcourt (Abb. 4) und einer von Captain Valentine Knight (vgl. Reddaway 1951: 53; Barker & Jackson 1990: 36-37; Brett-James 1935: 298-305). Insbesondere die Pläne von Wren, Evelyn, Newcourt und Hooke verdienen Beachtung, weil sie tatsächlich der *City* ein völlig neues Gesicht gegeben hätten.

In Wrens und Evelyns Plänen sind die kontinentalen Vorbilder leicht erkennbar (vgl. zum Folgenden Barker & Jackson 1990: 36-37). Wren hatte gerade acht Monate in Paris verbracht und dort sowohl die klassischen Gebäude als auch die Straßenführung studiert. Er schlug für den Neubau der *City* entsprechend eine geradlinige Straßenführung vor, die einerseits bestimmte Sichtachsen auf relevante Gebäude (wie Kirchen und die Royal Exchange) eröffnen, andererseits durch markante Plätze (achteckige *piazzas* und viereckige *squares*) mit repräsentativen Wohnhäusern unterbrochen werden sollten. Vor allem plante Wren eine völlig neue Konstruktion und Bebauung des Themseufers, die den Warenumschlag erleichtern und beschleunigen sollte. Evelyns Vorstellungen weisen eine gewisse Ähnlichkeit mit Wrens auf. So spielten auch bei ihm die Plätze nach italienischem Vorbild eine zentrale Rolle, die er noch schematischer als Wren verteilte und auch – besonders am nördlichen Zugang zur London Bridge – größer anlegte. Auch er wollte das Themseufer neu konzipieren – allerdings weniger im Hinblick auf den Handel als auf die ansehnlichen Plätze, die denjenigen, die sich ihnen auf der Themse näherten, ins Auge fallen sollten. Wrens und Evelyns Vorstellungen stimmen in ihrer Auffassung vom Raum und den im Raum gezielt repräsentativ angeordneten Gebäuden weitgehend überein: Für sie geht es um den öffentlich zur Schau gestellten Glanz der Metropole.[4] Wie bereits oben angedeutet, war diese Bauweise – was die Anlage einzelner Plätze anbelangt – in Ansätzen

---

[4] Bei Whitfield (2006: 67) gibt es unter dem Titel „The London that Wren Never Saw" eine Abbildung, die versucht, Wrens Plan räumlich umzusetzen.

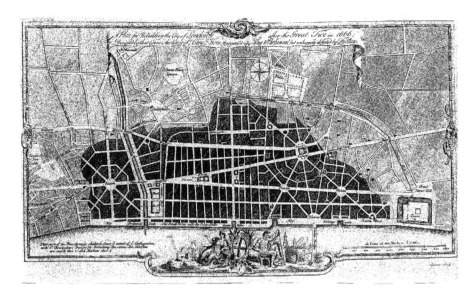

Abb. 1: Christopher Wrens Plan für den Wiederaufbau Londons 1666 (Reps 1965: 16).

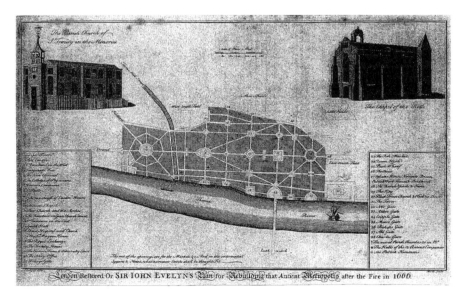

Abb. 2: John Evelyns Plan für den Wiederaufbau Londons 1666 (Reps 1965: 17).

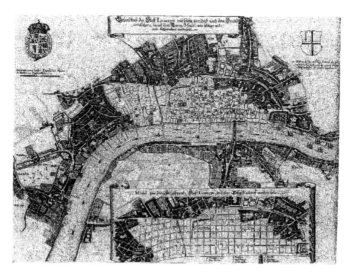

Abb. 3: Das Ausmaß des Feuers von 1666 und Robert Hookes Vorschlag für den Wiederaufbau (Reps 1965: 18).

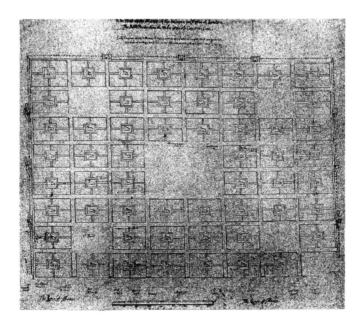

Abb. 4: Richard Neucourts Plan für den Wiederaufbau Londons 1666 (Reps 1965: 164).

im westlichen Stadtgebiet in den 1630er Jahren begonnen, aber bisher noch nicht weiter geführt worden. Richard Newcourts Idee war sicherlich die radikalste:

> The whole area was divided into sixty-four or forty-eight square blocks, each separated from its neighbour by a wide road, and similarly separated from the City wall, which was to be rebuilt to make an exact parallelogram. The space left bare by the irregular winding of the Thames to be empty so as to form an important and useful open space. There were to be either eight blocks from east to west and eight from north to south, or only six from north to south. Each block was to consist of four L-shaped groups of buildings massed round a central open space, separated from it by a wide path. In the central open space was to be erected a church surrounded by a churchyard. This would give either sixty-four or forty-eight churches, each with appropriate room for burials. In the centre of the whole series of blocks was to be a large open space, equal to four squares, and east of this one space for St. Paul's and one presumably for the Bank. (Brett-James 1935: 299)

So unwirksam diese – wie auch Robert Hookes ganz ähnliche – Vorstellungen bei der Neuplanung der Londoner *City* waren, so wirksam waren sie bei späteren Städteplanungen beispielsweise in den USA (vgl. Reps 1965).

Der Karte von John Ogilby und William Morgan aus dem Jahre 1676 (London Topographical Society 1992), die als „the first truly accurate map of London" (Barker & Jackson 1990: 38) gilt, kann man sehr gut entnehmen, wie die Anfang 1667 gefassten Pläne schließlich umgesetzt worden sind.

> The solution adopted evolved over the autumn of 1666, and was as imaginative as it was pragmatic. It was generally agreed that the superstructure of the new City should not be a direct replication of the old. Timber building would therefore be banned in favour of brick: the old streets and lanes would be paved and widened, and obstructions such as market buildings and conduits would be moved out of the roadways. [...] The new town was to be built on the old plan, but with hygiene and access much improved, the risk of major fire decreased, and without major dislocation to the complex pattern of private ownership. (Milne 1990: 80, 82)

Zur Vorbereitung und Aufsicht bei der Durchführung dieses Plans wurde eine Kommission gebildet, in die der König und die Stadt je drei Vertreter schickten (Wren, May, Pratt; Hooke, Jarman, Mills). Im Februar 1667 verabschiedete das Parlament zwei Gesetze. Das erste etablierte den sog. *Fire Court*, der widerstreitende Besitzansprüche klären musste. Diese Institution, deren Arbeit auf ein Jahr veranschlagt war, war bis 1676 tätig – eine Tatsache, die auf die Komplexität der Eigentumsverhältnisse verweist und die Möglichkeiten einer radikaleren Neuorientierung einmal mehr in Frage stellt. Das zweite Gesetz „represents the most comprehensive development plan the City had ever seen" (Milne 1990: 116). Für die neuen Häuser wurden vier Klassen oder Typen konzipiert, deren Struktur (Stockwerke) und Baumaterialien genau festgelegt wurden. Die Straßen wurden – i.d.R. nach ihrer Verkehrsfrequenz – als Durchgangsstraßen (*thoroughfares*), Straßen (*streets*), Sträßchen (*lanes*) und Gassen (*alleys*) definiert und in ihrer Mindestweite bestimmt. Insgesamt profitierten ca. 150 Straßen unterschiedlicher Größenordnung von dieser Erweiterung. Zudem wurde *eine* neue repräsentative Straße – die heutige King und Queen Street –, die von der Themse zur *Guildhall* führte, gebaut (vgl. ibid.: 82; Barker & Jackson 1990: 41).

Wenngleich also der Wiederaufbau der *City* nicht kontinentalen Vorbildern (Wren, Evelyn) oder zukünftige Entwicklungen antizipierenden Entwürfen (Newcourt, Hooke) folgte (vgl. Porter 2009: 77-83) und dadurch einen – der politischen Position Großbritanniens angemessenen – Schub an städtebaulicher Prachtentfaltung oder dezidierter Modernisierung verhinderte, so ist doch die beißende Kritik der Nachwelt (von Gwynn u.a.) mit Vorsicht zu genießen. An die Stelle von ca. 13.000 abgebrannten Häusern waren 9.000 neue getreten. Die *City* „had been substantially rebuilt with speed, care and skill: the medieval plan had been transformed into an elegant modern city of red brick and white stone" (Milne 1990: 88). Mit der durchaus nicht unüblichen britischen Mischung aus so viel Pragmatismus wie nötig und so viel Phantasie wie möglich gelang der Wiederaufbau der Wohnhäuser in gut sieben Jahren. Die repräsentativen Bauten (Kirchen, Zunfthäuser etc.) brauchten länger; St. Paul's wurde erst 1710 fertiggestellt.

Abschließende Bewertung
Es besteht kein Zweifel, dass in den ersten Dekaden des 17. Jahrhunderts bis etwa 1640 eine rege Rezeption und Anwendung architektonischer Ideen und Verfahren vom Kontinent (Italien, Frankreich) in England zu beobachten ist. Dafür sprechen sowohl die von James I in Auftrag gegebenen Bauten (*Queen's House*, *Banquet House*) als auch die von Vertretern des Adels – wie beispielsweise des Earls von Bedford im Falle von Covent Garden – begonnenen Bebauungen von Londons *West End*. Diese Entwicklungen wurden durch die politischen Kämpfe zwischen 1640 und 1660 unterbrochen und erst danach – vor allem bei der Bebauung freier Flächen und der Gestaltung einzelner großer Häuser – fortgesetzt. Sie sollte in den Entwürfen und Gebäuden der noch von Wren beeinflussten „English Baroque school" (Hawksmoor, Vanbrugh, Archer) und des „Palladian Movement" (Campbell, Burlington, Kent) in der ersten Hälfte des 18. Jahrhunderts zur vollen (und bewunderungswürdigen) Entfaltung kommen.

Beim Brand und Neubau der *City* gab es allerdings eine Reihe von Faktoren, die es nicht (oder doch nur in bescheidenem Maße) erlaubten, den städtebaulichen Prinzipien der *classical architecture* zu folgen. Es waren vor allen Dingen zwei Faktoren rechtlicher und ökonomischer Art, die gegen die grundsätzlichen Neustrukturierungen und für einen pragmatisch am alten Straßenbild orientierten Neuaufbau sprachen: Zum einen mussten „the rights of all the individual property holders" (Milne 1990: 80) respektiert werden. Bei einer Neustrukturierung hätten alle Grundstücke zusammengelegt werden müssen, um die Rechte anschließend neu zu verteilen. Wie lange dies gedauert hätte, kann man sich ausmalen, wenn man bedenkt, dass die Klärung der Rechte für den Neuaufbau auf der Basis der *vor dem Ausbruch des Feuers geltenden* Straßen- und Grundstücke-Struktur neun Jahre dauerte (vgl. Bucholz & Ward 2012: 327). Zum anderen war der Zeitfaktor von großer Bedeutung: Das kommerzielle Leben der Stadt war durch das Feuer zum Erliegen gekommen; die Handwerker und Kaufleute waren – aus der Not der Flucht vor dem Feuer eine Tugend machend – in die Vororte abgewandert. Um ihre Rückkehr zu beschleunigen und um zu verhindern, dass sie sich permanent in den Übergangsquartieren einrichteten, war ein schneller Wiederaufbau dringend nötig.

Hinzu kamen drei grundsätzlichere Erwägungen: Zum einen hatte der britische König – im Vergleich zum Papst oder zum König von Frankreich – wesentlich weniger Geld zur Verfügung (vgl. ibid.: 58, 133, 137). In der Verwendung öffentlicher Gelder war er dem Parlament verantwortlich. Warum sollte er – wo er doch seinen Regierungssitz eh schon außerhalb der *City* hatte – in ihre Prachtentfaltung investieren? Zum anderen hatte Charles II – auch auf Grund der Tatsache, dass er zwar seine Königswürde durch die Restauration von 1660 wiedererlangt hatte, sie aber auch immer wieder wegen seiner religiösen Orientierung zum Katholizismus in Zweifel gezogen wurde – Angst vor Unruhen im Volk. Um sie zu verhindern, setzte er während des Feuers viel Militär in der Stadt und ihrer Umgebung ein und war an einem schnellen Wiederaufbau auch deshalb interessiert, weil er Unzufriedenheit in der Bevölkerung verhindern wollte. Schließlich ist zu bedenken, dass selbst diejenigen, denen die komplexen Eigentumsverhältnisse, die baldige Rückkehr der Handwerker und Kaufleute oder drohende soziale Unruhen gleichgültig sein konnten, sich vor grundsätzlichen, radikalen und u.U. nur mit Gewalt durchsetzbaren Maßnahmen (wie z.B. dem Zusammenlegen und Neuverteilen von Baugrund) scheuten, weil die – negativen – Erfahrungen mit ebensolchen Maßnahmen während des Protektorates erst wenige Jahre zurücklagen.

Quellen

Barker, Felix & Peter Jackson (1990), *The History of London in Maps*, London: Barrie & Jenkins.

Bell, Walter George (1994), *The Great Fire of London in 1666* (Erstauflage 1923), London: Bracken Books.

Boulton, Jeremy (2000), „London 1540-1700", in Peter Clarke, Hrsg., *The Cambridge Urban History of Britain*, Vol. 2, Cambridge: Cambridge University Press, 315-346.

Brett-James, Norman George (1935), *The Growth of Stuart London*, London: Allen & Unwin.

Bucholz, Robert O. & Joseph P. Ward (2012), *London. A Social and Cultural History, 1550-1750*, Cambridge: Cambridge University Press.

Clout, Hugh, Hrsg. (1999), *The Times History of London* (Erstauflage 1991), St. Helens: The Book People Ltd.

London Topographical Society (1992), *The A to Z of Restoration London (The City of London, 1676)*, [London], Publication No. 145.

Milne, Gustav (1990), *The Great Fire of London* (Erstauflage 1986), New Barnet – London: Historical Publications.

Museum of London (2007), „The Great Fire of London: Myths and Realities", http://www.museumoflondon.org.uk/NR/rdonlyres/9B20D80D-FFFF-4156-B8F7-50179CDDE031/0/Session1.pdf (3. September 2013).

Newman, John (1994), „Inigo Jones and the Politics of Architecture", in Kevin Sharpe, Hrsg., *Culture and Politics in Early Stuart England*, Basingstoke: Macmillan, 229-255.

Porter, Roy (1996), *London. A Social History* (Erstauflage 1994), London: Penguin.

Porter, Stephen (2009), *The Great Fire of London* (Erstauflage 1996), Stroud: The History Press.

Rasmussen, Stehen Eiler (1982), *London. The Unique City*, Cambridge, MA – London: MIT Press.

Reddaway, Thomas F. (1951), *The Rebuilding of London After the Great Fire* (Erstauflage 1940), London: Edward Arnold & Co.

Reps, John W. (1965), *The Making of Urban America. A History of City Planning in the United States*, Princeton, NJ: Princeton University Press.

Stone, Lawrence (1980), „The Residential Development of the West End of London in the Seventeenth Century", in Barbara C. Malament, Hrsg., *After the Reformation*, Manchester: Manchester University Press, 167-212.

Summerson, John (1993), *Architecture in Britain 1530 to 1830* (Erstauflage 1953), New Haven, CT – London: Yale University Press.

Whitfield, Peter (2006), *London. A Life in Maps*, London: The British Library.

Anna Saunders (Bangor)*
Memorialising the 'Heldenstadt der DDR'

I have had the pleasure to work with Jochen on several occasions, through various Erasmus teaching exchanges (it is amazing how many students he can summon to a lecture at 7am!) and a conference volume. Our research interests overlap in the fields of memory studies and regional identities, and Jochen has always taken interest in my research on monuments and memorials; indeed, on one of my latest visits to Leipzig, he took me on a fascinating day trip to see both the Kyffhäuserdenkmal *and Werner Tübke's* Panoramabild. *He has also regularly sent newspaper clippings and articles to me on monuments and memory in Leipzig and Saxony, for which I am extremely grateful. The below musings on the contact between past and present cultures in Leipzig are thus a small way of saying 'thank you' to Jochen for his interest, time, generosity and enthusiasm!*

Introduction

Over recent years, Leipzig has been dogged by controversial – yet sometimes half-hearted – discussions over the location, design and meaning of the proposed *Freiheits- und Einheitsdenkmal* for the town. Funded by federal and regional government money, the project is a spin-off from Berlin's national monument competition of the same name, and represents the latest of many projects to mark Leipzig's leading role in the demonstrations of 1989. The desire to commemorate this history appears to have grown dramatically over the past two decades, as Leipzig has become increasingly celebrated and marketed as the birthplace of the 'peaceful revolution'. In 1998, for example, the town authorities and tourist office announced the intention to raise the profile of Leipzig as the "Stadt der Wende", with the aim of attracting more tourists in the tenth anniversary year.

---

* Anna Saunders is Senior Lecturer in German at Bangor University, UK. She is author of *Honecker's Children* (2007) and has co-edited two volumes relating to the subject of collective memory, most recently *Remembering and Rethinking the GDR* (with Debbie Pinfold, 2013). Her research interests include questions of history and memory in eastern Germany, memorialisation in contemporary Germany and the interplay between politics and the built environment; she is currently preparing a monograph on the memorialisation of the GDR.

October 1999 indeed witnessed a wide range of events, concerts, exhibitions and a festival, as well as the opening of the *Zeitgeschichtliches Forum Leipzig*, the unveiling of a plaque outside the "Runde Ecke" and the dedication of the town's first monument to the revolution next to the Nikolaikirche. Ten years later, however, celebrations took place on a much larger scale, with a *Lichtfest* – now an annual tradition – attracting more than 100,000 people. 2009 also witnessed a wide range of exhibitions, concerts and discussions, as well as the unveiling of another monument, the *Demokratieglocke*, on Augustusplatz. Unsurprisingly, the 25th anniversary in 2014 also promises to host a wide range of commemorative events, and such efforts indicate a growing desire in Leipzig to lay claim to its role in recent history and to move away from a tradition of remembrance which is often dominated by Berlin and the fall of the Wall.

The widespread search for more ingrained, cultural forms of memory of 1989 demonstrates the symbolic power of concrete memorial form and the fact that, to quote Brian Ladd (1997: 1), "memories often cleave to the physical settings of events". Moreover, as Andreas Huyssen (1995: 225) highlights, it is precisely in the present age of virtual technologies and high speed communications that the desire for both the "material quality of the object" and a sense of place have seen the rebirth of monuments and museums. However, the growth of a memory culture around 1989 has not always been straightforward: in seeking to cast recent memories in more concrete form, the initiators of memory projects are regularly forced to contend with the varied and often conflicting memories of those who lived through events. The opening of the *Zeitgeschichtliches Forum Leipzig* in 1999, for instance, caused consternation amongst many locals, who felt that the museum's focus on resistance and opposition under the SED dictatorship did not resonate with their own lived experiences of this past, and represented instead a western perspective on the GDR (cf. Berdahl 2008). While conflict between communicative and cultural forms of memory – to use Jan Assmann's terms (1992) – clearly highlights some of the problems with contemporary remembrance of 1989, this essay shows that the fates of recent memorial projects in Leipzig have also been bound up with the process of their evolution. Using the current *Freiheits- und*

Einheitsdenkmal debate as a springboard for the discussion of other monuments to 1989, the essay will reveal a shift in the development of memorial projects over time, and suggest that although collective memory of this period remains strong, recent projects have met with limited acceptance due to their failure to reflect a certain Zeitgeist of 1989.

Leipzig's *Freiheits- und Einheitsdenkmal*: 'so wenig Denkmal wie nötig'?

The proposal for an iconic *Freiheits- und Einheitsdenkmal* in Leipzig would seem to be a natural addition to existing commemorative traditions, and indeed fitting for a town which was ironically dubbed the "Heldenstadt der DDR" in 1989. However, enthusiasm for the project appears to be limited, and many critics have objected to the 'heroic' scale of the project in terms of its monumental proportions (it is to occupy approximately 20,000m^2), its cost (an estimated €6.5 million) and its intended symbolic national status. Leipzig citizens are, perhaps, all too familiar with the heroic and self-celebratory nature of former national monuments, as embodied in the *Völkerschlachtdenkmal* or former socialist realist monuments from the GDR, such as the massive Karl Marx relief which formerly hung on the main university building on Augustusplatz. While the heroic actions of those who demonstrated on 9 October 1989 are not to be doubted, many remain sceptical that the democratic nature of the movement and the spontaneous spirit of 1989 can be represented in such a prescribed and symbolically loaded project. Despite the efforts of the town to engage the local population through workshops, public meetings and online forums, the response has been lukewarm; although approximately half of the 1,002 respondents to a town council survey were reported to be in favour of a monument, surveys carried out at various intervals by the *Leipziger Volkszeitung* revealed much lower levels of enthusiasm (Stadt Leipzig 2011; Krutsch 2009; Orbeck 2011). Even after the announcement of the three finalists in 2012, the designs of which could hardly be described as heroic or monumental, public reaction remained muted and the design of the first prize winners attracted much negative attention in the online forum. As Jens Bisky (2012) commented in the *Süddeutsche Zeitung* on popular responses to the three designs: "Der 'Herbstgarten' ist ein Favorit vieler Leipziger, sein Vorzug klar: so viel Grün wie möglich und so wenig Denkmal wie nötig."

Interestingly, public criticism of the designs was similar to that of the proposed Berlin monument, in which the colourful and playful nature of designs – perhaps in an attempt to get away from traditional monumental aesthetics – was not seen to be appropriate to portray an event of such historical weight. The demands on artists to break away from traditional monumental aesthetics, yet also to reflect the heightened significance of 1989, was clearly a difficult balancing act. Discontent concerned not only aesthetics, however, but also pragmatics: the location on the redeveloped Wilhelm-Leuschner-Platz proved highly controversial, for many felt that it was inauthentic and chosen purely for reasons of town planning; others objected to a lack of transparency in decision-making processes, and the perceived desire of politicians to steamroll the process regardless of popular opinion. As a centrally funded, national project that has been directed from above, it thus appears to conflict with the values that were at the core of the protest movement in 1989: a desire for democracy, mass involvement and local activism.

Leipzig's Iconic Symbol: the *Nikolaisäule*

Popular criticism of the *Freiheits- und Einheitsdenkmal* must be understood against the backdrop of existing monuments to the memory of 1989 in Leipzig, some of which have long since become part of the fabric of the town. The earliest such project was led by the *Kulturstiftung Leipzig*, which launched a competition in 1992 to redevelop the Nikolaikirchhof. The aim of the competition was to develop a communicative urban space which would reflect the events of autumn 1989 through artistic form and generate "ein Spannungsfeld zwischen jahrhundertealter Kulturgeschichte und aktuellen Geschehnissen und Prozessen".[1] From the outset, this was

---

[1] 'Nikolaikirchhof Leipzig. Ausschreibung' (1992), document in files of the *Kulturstiftung Leipzig*. I am particularly grateful to Dr Wolfgang Hocquél for his help in accessing these files.

thus a project which was intended to be as much about the dynamic interplay between the cultures of past and present, as about presenting a specific image of the past. In early 1994, Leipzig artist Andreas Stötzner was awarded first prize for his proposal: to place a replica of one of the eight central pillars inside the Nikolaikirche on the square (Fig.1).

Fig.1: Andreas Stötzner's 'Nikolaisäule', Nikolaikirchhof (Photo Anna Saunders).

Although relatively simple in concept, the idea is particularly striking due to the unusual design of the interior pillars, resulting from Johann Friedrich Carl Dauthe's classical renovation of the Gothic church in the late eighteenth century, inspired by French enlightenment style. The resulting monument, a tall white pillar, with light green palm leaves extending upwards to the sky, thus stands as an eye-catching structure in the square: both familiar and strange at the same time. While Stötzner's idea of a column harks back to traditional monumental form – as seen in the concept of the '*Siegessäule*'

– it refrains from all sense of heroism, instead uniting the cultural history of the town with its more recent political history. Indeed, in bringing the column out of the church, Stötzner reflects the movement of oppositional ideas in 1989 from inside the church onto its streets. The material of the construction also proves symbolic, for it was decided after much debate that the pillar should be constructed out of concrete rather than marble, as originally intended; as Birgit Damrau, the then director of the *Kulturstiftung*, stated, "Nicht wenige von uns glauben, daß Beton dem Anlaß angemessener ist [...]. Denn schließlich waren es einfache Leipziger, die im Herbst 1989 die Kirche verließen und um den Ring zogen." (cit. in Tappert 1998)

While the aesthetics and materials of the design drew on local traditions and reflected the sentiment of 1989, so too did fundraising efforts. Although the town of Leipzig and the *Bund* provided some funds, two thirds of the necessary 260,000 DM were raised through donations from citizens, businesses and organisations, meaning that the completion of the project was delayed until 1999. The fundraising effort was backed by a large number of significant figures from 1989, including conductor Kurt Masur and pastor Christian Führer. Numerous articles in the *Leipziger Volkszeitung* advertised for donations, and Führer even appealed by stating that "Jeder Leipziger, der damals auf dem Ring demonstrierte, sollte sich mit einer persönlichen Spende beteiligen." ("Spender für '89-Kunstwerk gesucht" 1997) The campaign drummed up support from across the town, and the names of all those who donated money were inserted into a copper tube inside the monument. Once funds were secured, the replica, created by sculptor Markus Gläser, was unveiled on 9 October 1999 after peace prayers in the Nikolaikirche, thus at almost exactly the same time that the demonstration began ten years earlier; in this way remembrance took place through repetition, adding weight to the symbolism of the pillar and building ritual memory. The monument has since become an iconic symbol of the city, and has attracted remarkably little criticism; not only does it appear on postcards and tourist brochures of the town, but since 2001 a miniature golden copy of the pillar has been given to winners of the media prize awarded by the *Medienstiftung der Sparkasse Leipzig* for journalists active in fighting for the freedom of the press.

The monument has also come to public attention once again since the proposal for the *Freiheits- und Einheitsdenkmal*, for the latter has prompted several public figures, such as author Erich Loest and cabarettist Bernd-Lutz Lange, to declare their preference for the column and its authentic location over any new project (cf. Loest 2010; Mayer 2010). Numerous comments in online forums and readers' pages of the local paper have echoed such sentiments, declaring the column to be the most appropriate monument for this history, and "das Denkmal schlechthin" ("Einheitsdenkmal bewegt die Leser" 2011). In contrast to the larger national project apparently imposed from above, this more modest structure instead embodies local and democratic traditions which many deem to be a more appropriate symbol of the memory of 1989.

Further Developing the Nikolaikirchhof

The *Nikolaisäule* has been complemented by two further elements on the square, both of which adopt similarly simple and understated symbolism. The idea for the first element originated with Stötzner's design which also featured a fountain on the square, and was inspired by seventeenth-century pictures of a fountain in this location. While the jury was not taken with his specific fountain design, the concept appealed, especially considering that it returned the square to its earlier state. A competition for a fountain was thus launched in 1997; the winning design, however, proved unexpectedly controversial, for it envisaged a long stream of water, starting at the monument and ending in a round basin, thus reflecting the vertical of the pillar on the horizontal of the square. Controversially, a low wall was intended to accompany the flow of water, provoking criticism that the unity of the square would be destroyed and the symbolism of the column lost (cf. Hochstein 1998; Richter 1998). Protest grew against the design, with claims that a 'Mauerbau' on this of all squares was inappropriate (cf. Hochstein 1998),[2] and despite a public forum and efforts to show residents what its outline would look like on the square, protest persisted. With the city due to pick up a bill of 240,000 DM for the project, and in the face of public objections and indecision even amongst the initiators, it was

---

[2] See, for example, readers' letters in *Leipziger Volkszeitung*, 24 June 1998, 21.

decided in early 1999 that the project should be put on hold. As Wolfgang Tiefensee stated, the symbolism of the Nikolaikirchhof was so great that "eine breitere Zustimmung wünschenswert wäre" (cit. in Richter 1999); public support was clearly seen to be central to the project as a whole.

It was not until 2002 that the *Kulturstiftung* launched a further fountain competition, this time together with one for a light installation, both of which were intended to complete the landscaping of the square. As Wolfgang Hocquél of the *Kulturstiftung* stated, the aim was to make "die Nikolaikirche und den Kirchhof als Ausgangspunkt der tief greifenden gesellschaftlichen Veränderungen dauerhaft erlebbar" (cit. in Rosendahl 2003), once again underlining the communicative and dynamic emphasis of the project. The winning design by London architect David Chipperfield proved highly symbolic, for it represents in physical form the idiom 'der Tropfen, der das Fass zum Überlaufen bringt': water brims to the top of a simple cylindrical basin made from Lausitz granite, and seemingly about to overflow, metaphorically represents the political situation in 1989. Much more self-contained than the previous proposal, this design triggered relatively little discussion and has become well integrated into the square. The parallel competition for a light installation was intended to highlight the events of autumn 1989 on the square at night time. The winning design, 'public light_öffentliches licht', by Leipzig artists Tilo Schulz and Kim Wortelkamp, consists of 146 square lamps set into the cobble stones on the square. Between 8pm and 11pm, they become illuminated one by one at a rate of roughly one per minute, representing the gradual amassing of people on the square and at the entrance to the church; at 11pm they disappear, only to return the next evening. In the artists' words, and in keeping with the competition aims, the design "[will] kein Denkmal setzen. Vielmehr soll sich der Prozess, das situative Aufflackern widerspiegeln" (Schulz & Wortelkamp, n.d.). The designs from both competitions were displayed publically in March 2003 and unveiled later the same year; together with Stötzner's column, they work to form a memorial ensemble for the political *Wende* of 1989, highlighting an authentic location in an understated and unheroic fashion. As a gradual process of development which involved community engagement and compromise from the start, and promoted dialogue between the traditions of past and present, this ensemble reflects the organism of the 1989 demonstrations and aims to promote communicative space for the future.

**Questionable Symbols of 1989:
Lacking Democratic Credentials?**
The ensemble around the Nikolaikirche exists in marked contrast not only to the proposed *Freiheits- und Einheitsdenkmal*, but also to other more recent monuments relating to 1989. The *Demokratieglocke* on Augustusplatz, for instance, unveiled on the twentieth anniversary of 9 October in 2009, has been received with notable ambivalence. This is perhaps surprising given its origins, for the project was initiated by a network of eastern German foundries in 2007, who wanted to cast a bell and donate it to Leipzig as a symbol of gratitude for the city's role in 1989 (cf. Klötzer 2007). However, the subsequent competition launched by the *Kulturstiftung Leipzig* for a monument to incorporate such a bell involved little public input, as the funds were already in place. The winning design by Via Lewandowsky, a bronze egg in which the bell is now housed, was thus announced in late 2008 and unveiled only ten months later (Fig.2).

Fig.2: Via Lewandowsky's 'Demokratieglocke',
Augustusplatz (Photo Anna Saunders).

It was this very swiftness and lack of local consultation which proved contentious amongst townspeople, as demonstrated by a large number of readers' letters sent to the *Leipziger Volkszeitung*.[3] Some, for example, lamented that activists from 1989 had not been consulted on the matter, while others suggested that the inscription around the base of the egg, by author Durs Grünbein, should instead have been written by one of Leipzig's own writers.[4] The form of an egg also caused much confusion, for although it is to represent the concept of new beginnings which emerged from the peaceful revolution, as well as an aesthetically harmonic whole following unification, it did little to conjure up images of 1989 in the same way as the ensemble on the Nikolaikirchhof. The bell itself rings every Monday at 6.35pm, the time at which the demonstration began on 9 October 1989, and once every hour between 8am and 8pm at a randomly generated time, representing the fact that a mass movement may start at any moment of the day. However, even this aural symbolism has proven rather abstract, provoking the *Kulturstiftung* to provide the necessary explanations on an information sheet. Having failed to engage the local population during the construction process and through its aesthetics, the project – which began with a gesture of genuine solidarity – thus appears to remain outside any active memory tradition.

The twentieth anniversary of 1989 also provoked several other plans for concrete memory markers. One of the more controversial was American artist Miley Tucker-Frost's design for a monument, which she was moved to design after spending time in Leipzig and learning about the history of the peaceful revolution. Through a figurative design of protesters assembled around candles (later re-worked into a smaller group standing arm-in-arm), the artist hoped to evoke an emotional response amongst viewers. Critics, however, such as the director of the *Galerie für Zeitgenössische Kunst*, Barbara Steiner, claimed that its traditional aesthetics were out of tune with contemporary discussions in the field of art; others dismissed it as "Kitsch"

---

[3] See, for example, *Leipziger Volkszeitung* of 2009, on 5 January, 18; 14 January, 16; 17 January, 18; 7 April, 16.

[4] Readers' letters in *Leipziger Volkszeitung*, 5 January 2009, p. 18.

(Schimke 2008a and 2008b). Criticism was also directed at Mayor Burkhard Jung for initially accepting the small-scale model without the proposal having been discussed in appropriate circles. As with the *Demokratieglocke*, popular discontent focused not only on aesthetics, but significantly also on the lack of public consultation and democratic decision-making. Due to such objections, only a model of the revised design was given to the town on 9 October 2009, despite Tucker-Frost's initial intention to give the full monument to the town in honour of the 20th anniversary; the realisation of a full-scale monument remains uncertain.

Maintaining the Zeitgeist of 1989

The lack of public enthusiasm towards the *Freiheits- und Einheitsdenkmal*, the *Demokratieglocke* and Tucker-Frosts's proposal reflects the fact that – in contrast to the ensemble on the Nikolaikirchhof – these projects have not grown organically from within the community. Somewhat ironically, the fact that they have all been donated as gifts to the town appears to have provoked widespread scepticism and even active resistance. Although the authorities have undertaken numerous activities to include the population in discussions concerning the *Freiheits- und Einheitsdenkmal*, turnout at such events has been low and many continue to see it as a project led from above, in which democratic decision-making processes play little of a role. One may be tempted to conclude that the town is becoming oversaturated with this memory, and suffering from 'monumentitis' with regard to 1989; after all, other concrete memory markers include twenty information pillars erected in 2010 and 2011 at sites of the peaceful revolution, a huge wall painting in memory of the peaceful revolution by artist Michael Fischer-Art, as well as numerous historic monuments, such as the Nikolaikirche and the 'Runde Ecke'. However, high attendance figures at the annual *Lichtfest* and continuing interest in this history through new publications, memoirs and societal activities, such as those organised by the *Stiftung Friedliche Revolution*, would suggest otherwise; memory of this period is clearly far from stagnant. Indeed, there seems to be a common desire to translate communicative memories into longer-lasting cultural forms while this memory is still alive. This process appears, however, to be evident above all in a continuing desire for democratic decision-making, widespread participation and respect for local traditions. While the resulting concrete structures of monuments may not always be able to reflect these values, the processes of planning, debating, fundraising and construction must, it seems, still reflect the democratic Zeitgeist of 1989 in order to resonate broadly amongst the population. In many ways, the contemporary function of these projects is, thus, to serve as an extension of the demonstrations of 1989. Whether or not the future *Freiheits- und Einheitsdenkmal* will – with time – manage to negotiate these demands still remains to be seen.

Sources

Assmann, Jan (1992), *Das kulturelle Gedächtnis: Schrift, Erinnerung und politische Identität in frühen Hochkulturen*, Munich: C.H. Beck.

Berdahl, Daphne (2008), "Re-Presenting the Socialist Modern: Museums and Memory in the Former GDR", in Katherine Pence & Paul Betts, eds., *Socialist Modern: East German Everyday Culture and Politics*, Ann Arbor, MI: University of Michigan Press, 345-366.

Bisky, Jens (2012), "Schaut auf diese Stadt", *Süddeutsche Zeitung*, 19 July, http://www.sueddeutsche.de/reise/einheitsdenkmal-fuer-leipzig-schaut-auf-diese-stadt-1.1416118 (4 September 2013).

"Einheitsdenkmal bewegt die Leser" (2011), *Leipziger Volkszeitung*, 15-16 January, 19.

Hochstein, Christine (1998), "Anhörung im Rathaus: Gestaltung des Nikolaikirchhofes erhitzt die Gemüter", *Leipziger Volkszeitung*, 21 July, 6.

Huyssen, Andreas (1995), *Twilight Memories: Marking Time in a Culture of Amnesia*, New York: Routledge.

Klötzer, Werner (2007), "Info- und Diskussionsmaterial für die Beratung am 13.12.2007", Leipzig, 30 November. Document in files of Kulturstiftung Leipzig.

Krutsch, Peter (2009), "Wir brauchen kein Denkmal", *Leipziger Volkszeitung*, 7 February.

Ladd, Brian (1997), *The Ghosts of Berlin*, Chicago: University of Chicago Press.

Loest, Erich (2010), "Nie waren Genies so wertvoll", *Nordwest-Zeitung, Oldenburger Nachrichten*, 15 January, 14.

Mayer, Thomas (2010), "'Wir sind das Volk'", *Leipziger Volkszeitung*, 22 December, 19.

Orbeck, Matthias (2011), "Anrufer lehnen Denkmal ab", *Leipziger Volkszeitung*, 13 January, 19.

Richter, Andrea (1998), "'Brunnen macht den Platz kaputt'", *Leipziger Volkszeitung*, 19 June, 16.

Richter, Andrea (1999), "OBM legt Brunnen für Nikolaikirchhof auf Eis", *Leipziger Volkszeitung*, 8 February, 11.

Rosendahl, Ingolf (2003), "Dritter Anlauf für Brunnen an St. Nikolai", *Leipziger Volkszeitung*, 1 March, 15.

Schimke, Robert (2008a), "Erinnerung polieren", *Die Tageszeitung*, 16 June, 13.

Schimke, Robert (2008b), "Kulturkompetenz", *Kreuzer*, 1 July, 55.

Schulz, Tilo & Kim Wortelkamp (n.d.), "public light_öffentliches licht", competition entry in files of *Kulturstiftung Leipzig*.

"Spender für '89-Kunstwerk gesucht" (1997), *Leipziger Volkszeitung*, 10 September, 11.

Stadt Leipzig (2011), "Medieninformation", Leipzig, 14 February, 141/mmb (document available at 'Bürgerforum' on 8 March 2011).

Tappert, Andreas (1998), "Heiße Phase bei Neugestaltung des Nikolaikirchhofes beginnt", *Leipziger Volkszeitung*, 6 January, 11.

David Nisters (Leipzig)*
Open Texts and Reanimated Authors: Roland Barthes and Medieval Manuscript Culture

During my time as Prof. Joachim Schwend's student assistant and as a member of the English Department at Leipzig University, I have come to appreciate Jochen's views on many different topics. In fact, this paper was inspired by two of his remarks, namely that he has always enjoyed reading Roland Barthes and that he would prefer any scholarly activity over dealing with medieval topics (although part of his activity as a university lecturer requires him to focus on the Middle Ages in considerable detail). In the following paragraphs, I should like to suggest that Jochen's interest in Barthes' ideas leads directly to some of the most fundamental aspects of medieval culture and shows the connection between past and present.

Introduction

Roland Barthes' theory of textuality has had a considerable impact on literary as well as cultural studies owing to his stress on the instability of textual meaning, the productive character of the reading process and the relatively small importance of the author in the generation of textual significance. Against the background of the history of writing, however, this postmodern textual theory is not merely an abstract concept but can be argued to describe aptly the reality of writing within medieval manuscript culture. In the Middle Ages, thus, the inevitable instability of texts was closely connected to the notion of an empowered readership. On account of the medieval concept of the *auctor*, moreover, vernacular writers typically rejected any claim to being the original creators and ultimately even the persons responsible for their own work. The role of the author, the function of the reader and the status of a piece of writing

---

* Having studied English, Philosophy and Comparative Literature at Leipzig University and at University College Cork (Ireland), David Nisters became a member of Leipzig's English Department in 2009. His research interests encompass the notion of authorship in the later Middle Ages as well as the presentation of vernacular English poetry in fifteenth-century manuscripts and early printed copies.

in the Middle Ages can, therefore, be viewed against the background of Roland Barthes' theory of text and its implications. Before considering this contact between pre-modern and postmodern cultures in depth, however, the importance of texts for studying culture as well as Barthes' textual theory need to be examined in some detail.

The Idea of the Text: Traditional and Postmodern Approaches
Since understanding the way of life of a group of people involves understanding their system of signs, the study of culture is closely connected to semiotic analysis. Thus, a material object, such as a leather boot, might mean one thing to a group of punks yet the same object may mean something else to a group of skinheads. On account of the importance of signs for understanding cultures, therefore, "the investigation of culture has become closely entwined with the study of signification." (Barker 2004: 45) By the same token, investigating cultures has to do with the study of texts since a text can be broadly characterised as any combination of individual signs, such as words, images or colours. The idea of a text as a combination of signs derives from the Latin root of the modern English noun *text*, namely *textus*, that is, a tissue or a connection of elements. On account of the crucial function of signs for identifying and examining the way of life of a group of people, therefore, the text can be seen as a central point of reference for studying culture.

While cultural studies may be viewed as a text-related project on the basis of these considerations, the very notion of text can by no means be considered uncontested. In fact, the term *text* has been used in at least two significantly different ways by scholars. The classical, or traditional, approach "regards *text* as an autonomous, stable, and coherent object with a determinate identity." (Di Leo 1998: 371) According to this traditional notion of textuality, texts consist of a variety of sign-forms with a direct and unchangeable relation to the meanings that are signified by them. As Di Leo states when summarising this traditional notion of the text:

> [A] text is a written message involving two major components: a signifier and a signified. The former, the signifier, manifests itself

in the materiality of the text, that is to say, its letters, words, sentences, and so on. The latter, the signified, is a univocal and definitive meaning – a meaning that is positively closed to multiple meanings. (Ibid.)

Against this traditional view on textuality, twentieth-century scholars have established a contrasting theory of textuality. Most notably, Roland Barthes takes the text to be "the very theatre of a production where the producer and reader of the text meet: the text 'works', at each moment and from whatever side one takes it." (1990: 36) Consequently, it cannot be seen as an object with an unchanging and definite meaning but as "a polysemic space where the paths of several possible meanings intersect" (ibid.: 37) and "a mobile play of signifiers, with no possible reference to one or several fixed signifieds" (ibid.). Among other things, this view fosters an awareness for contrasting readings of one and the same combination of signifiers in different times or cultural contexts.

By the same token, postmodern textual theory assigns a decisive function to readers where the generation of meaning is concerned. In postmodern textual theory, thus, meaning is usually regarded as being produced not so much by the author of a work than by its readers. As Barthes holds:

> Not only does the theory of the text extend to infinity the freedoms of reading (authorising us to read works of the past with an entirely modern gaze, so that it is legitimate, for example, to read Sophocles' 'Oedipus' by pouring Freud's Oedipus back into it, or to read Flaubert on the basis of Proust), but it also insists strongly on the (productive) equivalence of writing and reading. […] Full reading […] is the kind in which the reader is nothing less than the one who desires to write, to give himself up to an erotic practice of language. (1990: 42)

Rather than discovering authorial intention, then, readers create a text as a meaningful unit in the process of dealing with a work, such as a novel or a picture. As a consequence, a text cannot be seen as a carrier of fixed truth but must be regarded as the open process of assigning a large variety of meanings to a work.

The rejection of the idea that a text is an author-centred agent of truth has, moreover, typically been combined with an emphasis on the non-originality of writing. By way of evoking the meaning of Latin *textus*, therefore, several writers have characterised the text as a tissue of pre-existing elements rather than the original invention of an author. Roland Barthes, in fact, links the idea of non-originality to the notion of the text as 'a polysemic space' when he writes:

> We know now that the text is not a line of words releasing a single 'theological' meaning (the 'message' of the Author-God) but a multi-dimensional space in which a variety of writings, none of them original, blend and clash. The text is a tissue of quotations drawn from innumerable centres of culture. […] [T]he writer can only imitate a gesture that is always anterior, never original. His only power is to mix writings, to counter the ones with the others, in such a way as never to rest on any of them. (1988: 170)

Hence, postmodern textual theory, as put forward by Barthes, produces a stark contrast to the traditional understanding of the text as a combination of signs with a definite meaning. According to the postmodern outlook, any text is open, its meaning is produced by its readers and the author is dead. Although this position has frequently been associated with relatively recent periods of Western cultural history, traces of postmodern textual theory can already be found in pre-modern cultural contexts.

Medieval Textual Culture: Writers, Readers and Manuscripts
During the last couple of decades, as a matter of fact, scholars have often drawn on the textual culture of the Middle Ages as a setting for approaches to writing and reading that closely resemble postmodern textual theory. Similar to Barthes, these scholars have put a strong emphasis on the instability of texts within medieval cultures by means of referring to the concept of *mouvance*. This concept is discussed by Paul Zumthor in his *Essai de Poétique Médiévale* (1972), published in English under the title *Toward a Medieval Poetics*, when he comments on the textual differences among manuscript-copies of one and the same work, such as scribal practices "by which considerable stretches of text may be added, suppressed, modified, or transposed" (1992: 46). Zumthor, in effect, claims that the array

of possible variants "could not but conspire to prevent the early formation of the idea of the work as something complete in itself." (ibid.) As a result, the medieval text cannot be regarded as an unchangeable combination of signifiers with a definite meaning. In fact, the existence of textual variation in medieval manuscripts fosters the idea of the medieval work as being not so much "complete in itself than the text still in the process of creation; not an essence, but something coming into being; rather a constantly renewed attempt to get at meaning than a meaning finally fixed" (ibid.: 48). The instability of texts within medieval manuscript culture can, therefore, serve as a historical illustration of Roland Barthes' theory of the open text.

Textual variations in medieval manuscripts may, indeed, be considered an example of what Barthes calls 'the (productive) equivalence of writing and reading'. Thus, the existence of textual variation in different manuscripts reflects the contrasting readings of medieval scribes. Two versions of Chaucer's Nun's Priest's Tale in Oxford, Bodleian Library MSS Bodley 414 and Hatton donati 1 can be cited to illustrate this point. A large section of the earlier part of the Nun's Priest's Tale is about the dream of the cockerel Chauntecleer, the hen Pertelote and their discussion about the truthfulness of dreams. Chauntecleer's account of his own dream reveals its nightmarish quality since he is pursued by a fox in his vision, yet the description of the animal differs considerably in the two manuscript-versions of the tale. In MS Bodley 414, Chauntecleer holds that the fox "was like an hounde & wold haue made arrest / upon my bodi and wold haue had me dede" (fol. 173v) while in the corresponding passage in MS Hatton donati 1, the fox "was like an hounde and wold haue made a reste / upon my body and wold haue had no drede" (fol. 218r). Insofar as these two versions reflect contrasting interpretations of the tale by at least two different scribes, the work of these scribes allows for viewing Chaucer's text as a 'polysemic space'. In fact, the description of the fox as wanting the cockerel to be dead in MS Bodley 414 (cf. Fig.1) is as meaningful as the corresponding passage in MS Hatton donati 1 (cf. Fig.2), where the fox is charac-

Fig.1: Oxford, Bodleian Library MS. Bodl. 414, fol. 173v. Reproduced with permission of The Bodleian Libraries, The University of Oxford.

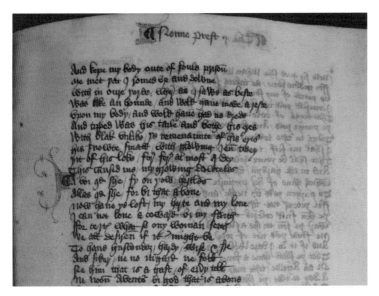

Fig.2: Oxford, Bodleian Library MS. Hatton donat. 1, fol. 218r. Reproduced with permission of The Bodleian Libraries, The University of Oxford.

terised as a fearless animal, and none of them can simply be taken to be more appropriate than the other.

The different versions of Chaucer's Nun's Priest's Tale in the two Bodleian manuscripts, thus, exemplify in how far medieval texts could be open to different meanings. This fundamental textual instability was recognised by medieval writers as a problem since the value of a text strongly depended on its function as an agent of truth. If a work was subject to unforeseeable and unavoidable changes, however, its truth could not be guaranteed by the writer. In order to tackle this difficulty, medieval writers frequently presented their work as incomplete and invited their readers to change and improve it. As Jocelyn Wogan-Browne and her fellow-editors state:

> So persistent is this concern with truth that vernacular writers routinely submit their works to their readers for improvement (or at least make this rhetorical gesture), envisaging the search for truth as a collaborative project that does not end with the completion of a text but simply moves into a new phase. (Wogan-Browne *et al.* 1999: 13)

In the prologue to his early fifteenth-century translation of Boethius' *De Consolatione Philosophiae*, for example, John Walton states his "[i]nsuffishaunce of connyng and wytte" (1999: 35, line 1) in producing the translation and bids his patron "[t]hat be youre help hit may amendyd be." (ibid., line 8) John Lydgate's prologue to the *Troy Book* ends on a similar note since the speaker concludes by "[p]reynge to alle that shall it [that is, the *Troy Book*] rede or se, / Wher as I erre for to amenden me, [...] / Commyttyng al to her correccioun" (1999b: 48, lines 209-211). Hence, the instability of medieval texts is to be understood as having fostered the notion of an empowered readership.

The reluctance of Middle English writers to present themselves as the persons responsible for their works was, however, not exclusively grounded in the inevitable instability of any piece of writing. As a matter of fact, their reluctance also concerned the medieval concept of authority itself in that the terms *auctor* and *auctoritas* were generally reserved for writers of former times. As Alastair Minnis explains in his study *Medieval Theory of Authorship*: "No 'modern' writer could decently be called an *auctor* in a period in which men saw themselves as dwarfs standing on the shoulders of giants, i.e. the 'ancients'. [...] [I]t would seem that the only good *auctor* was a dead one." (2010: 12) As a result, vernacular writers typically rejected the status of an *auctor* and frequently portrayed themselves as mere translators or compilers. When the god Cupid accuses Chaucer of having depicted love too negatively in the G-prologue to the *Legend of Good Women*,[1] for example, the character Alceste presents Chaucer as an ignorant translator for the sake of defending him. According to Alceste, "for that this man is nyce [that is, foolish], / He may translate a thyng in no malyce" (1988a: 598, lines 340-341). In San Marino, Huntington Library MS Ellesmere 26.C.9, moreover, the Retraction at the end of Chaucer's Parson's Tale is supplemented by the colophon "Here is ended the book of the tales of Caunterbury compiled by Geoffrey Chaucer of whos soule Iesu Christ haue mercy Amen" (fol. 232v). These presentations of the 'modern' vernacular writer Chaucer as a compiler and translator rather than an *auctor* foster the idea that genuine authorship presupposed a writer's death.

In addition, the predominant function of dead *auctores* in medieval literary cultures was to assign value to a piece of writing in that they were referred to for the sake of presenting it as a 'tissue of quotations'. Citing an esteemed *auctor* as the source of their work, hence, provided medieval writers with a means to guarantee the esteem of their own text. If a text was based on authoritative works, then this text had to be seen as authoritative as well on account of its adoption of the *auctores*. Alceste's defense of Chaucer in terms of his ignorance in the G-prologue to *The Legend of Good Women* can be read against the same intellectual background since it "assumes a model of textual production in which writers gain authority less by

---

[1] There are two versions of Chaucer's prologue to the *Legend of Good Women*, referred to as F and G respectively. The so-called 'F-prologue' is named after Oxford, Bodleian Library MS Fairfax 16, but can also be found in other manuscripts. The so-called 'G-prologue' only survives in Cambridge, University Library MS Gg.4.27.

their originality than by their contribution to an ongoing tradition" (Wogan-Browne *et al.* 1999: 5). As a result of the reluctance of medieval writers to understand themselves as original creators, these writers frequently included references to real or invented sources into their works. Thus, Chaucer mentions the real *auctores* Homer, Dares Phrygius and Dictys Cretensis in the first book of *Troilus and Criseyde* as a recommendation for further reading on the Trojan War (cf. 1988b: 475, lines 145-147). Yet, he also refers to a fictitious source when he claims to have followed "the sentence, / As writ myn auctour called Lollius" (ibid.: 478, lines 393-394). While these passages provide evidence for the need of medieval writers to give credit to their dead *auctores*, however, tendencies to introduce a more vital concept of authorship can be detected in many vernacular English works of the later Middle Ages.

Shortly after his death in 1400, in fact, Geoffrey Chaucer came to be portrayed as the vernacular equivalent of the established ancient *auctores* by many of his followers. In the prologue to his *Siege of Thebes*, John Lydgate assigns authority to Chaucer by describing him as the "[f]loure of poetes thorghout al Breteyne" (1999a: 346, line 40) and adds that he "never shal appallen [that is, fade] in my mynde / But alwey fressh ben in my memoyre" (ibid., lines 44-45). Lydgate's reverence for his predecessor is in line with the widespread late medieval practice of emphasising Chaucer's authoritative status. Fifteenth-century English poets, indeed, "cultivated a relationship of dependence on Chaucer by depicting him as a poet worth citing and imitating, as Chaucer cited and imitated the classical *auctores*, Virgil and Ovid" (Watson 1999: 347). This relationship could, moreover, result in the metaphorical attempt to raise the poet from the dead in the course of commemorating his achievements.

The act of reanimating Chaucer becomes most evident in Thomas Hoccleve's *Regement of Princes*. In the context of comparing him to the Classical *auctores* Cicero, Aristotle and Virgil (cf. 1999: 332, lines 2085-2090), the speaker in Hoccleve's text bemoans Chaucer's death when he states: "Deth, by thy deth, hath harme irreparable / Unto us don" (ibid., lines 2082-2083). By means of addressing Chaucer directly, Hoccleve establishes him as an addressee and, thus, treats him as if he were still alive. This attempt to present Chaucer as being alive is even more striking in a later passage of the *Regement* when the speaker states:

> Althogh his lyfe be queynt, the resemblaunce
> Of him hath in me so fressh lyflynesse
> That to putte other men in remembraunce
> Of his persone I have heere his lyknesse
> Do make, to this ende, in sothfastnesse,
> That thei that have of him lost thought and mynde
> By this peynture may ageyn him fynde. (ibid.: 333, lines 4992-4998)

Hoccleve's emphasis on the 'lyflynesse' of Chaucer's memory hints at the possibility of keeping the poet alive by commemorating him. Moreover, "Hoccleve clearly intends a portrait of Chaucer to stand beside this stanza" (Pearsall 1999: 333), and images of the poet supplement the passage in various manuscript-copies. The combination of written text and painted image further supports the 'lyflynesse' of Chaucer's memory. If he can live on by being remembered, then the insertion of Chaucer's portrait must be considered an instrument of bringing the poet back to life in that it provides readers with a vivid impression of him.

Conclusion

In conclusion, the status of a text in the manuscript culture of the Middle Ages can be analysed against the background of Roland Barthes' postmodern theory of textuality on account of its instability, the opportunity of readers to shape its character as well as to influence textual meaning and its non-originality. The corresponding reluctance of medieval writers to assume the status of authors was intensified by the notion of the *auctor* as a dead writer, and this aspect constitutes a further link to Barthes' approach in that it supplements the postmodern metaphor of the dead author with medieval reality. In contrast to Barthes, however, medieval writers did not embrace textual openness as an opportunity but rather as a threat to the stability of meaning. While vernacular poets of the later Middle Ages, such as Hoccleve and Lydgate, reacted to this situation in a variety of ways, they generally promoted the reconsideration of the established concept of authorship by means of presenting Chaucer as the vernacular equivalent of the Classical *auctores*. In so doing, these writers tried to reanimate Chaucer by virtue of keeping his memory alive. These developments are, then, not only to be seen as important steps towards the more recent idea that a writer does not have to be dead in order to be recognised as an author, but they also provide an important insight into the contact between postmodern and medieval cultures and the way in which the past can be considered part of the present.

Sources
Primary Sources (incl. Manuscripts)

Chaucer, Geoffrey, *The Canterbury Tales*, MS Bodley 414, Bodleian Library, Oxford.

Chaucer, Geoffrey, *The Canterbury Tales*, MS Ellesmere 26.C.9, Huntington Library, San Marino.

Chaucer, Geoffrey, *The Canterbury Tales*, MS Hatton donati 1, Bodleian Library, Oxford.

Chaucer, Geoffrey (1988a), "*The Legend of Good Women*", in Larry D. Benson, ed., *The Riverside Chaucer* (Third Edition), Oxford: Oxford University Press, 587-630.

Chaucer, Geoffrey (1988b), "*Troilus and Criseyde*", in Larry D. Benson, ed., *The Riverside Chaucer* (Third Edition), Oxford: Oxford University Press, 471-585.

Hoccleve, Thomas (1999), "*The Regement of Princes*", in Derek Pearsall, ed., *Chaucer to Spenser. An Anthology of Writing in English, 1375-1575*, Oxford – Malden, Mass.: Blackwell, 322-334.

Lydgate, John (1999a), "*The Siege of Thebes*", in Derek Pearsall, ed., *Chaucer to Spenser. An Anthology of Writing in English, 1375-1575*, Oxford – Malden, Mass.: Blackwell, 345-349.

Lydgate, John (1999b), "*Troy Book*: Prologue (Extract)", in Jocelyn Wogan-Browne *et al.*, eds., *The Idea of the Vernacular. An Anthology of Middle English Literary Theory, 1280-1520*, Exeter: University of Exeter Press, 42-50.

Walton, John (1999), "Translation of Boethius, *Consolation of Philosophy: Prefacio Translatoris*", in Jocelyn Wogan-Browne *et al.*, eds., *The Idea of the Vernacular. An Anthology of Middle English Literary Theory, 1280-1520*, Exeter: University of Exeter Press, 34-38.

Secondary Sources

Barker, Chris (2004), *The SAGE Dictionary of Cultural Studies*, London – Thousand Oaks – New Delhi: SAGE Publications.

Barthes, Roland (1988), "The Death of the Author" (First Edition 1967), transl. Stephen Heath, in David Lodge, ed., *Modern Criticism and Theory. A Reader*, London – New York: Longman, 167-172.

Barthes, Roland (1990), "Theory of the Text" (First Edition 1973), transl. Ian McLeod, in Robert Young, ed., *Untying the Text. A Post-Structuralist Reader*, London – New York: Routledge, 31-47.

Di Leo, Jeffrey R. (1998), "Text", in Michael Kelly, ed., *Encyclopedia of Aesthetics*, Oxford: Oxford University Press, 370-375.

Minnis, Alastair J. (2010), *Medieval Theory of Authorship. Scholastic Literary Attitudes in the Later Middle Ages* (First Edition 1984), Philadelphia: University of Pennsylvania Press.

Pearsall, Derek, ed. (1999), *Chaucer to Spenser. An Anthology of Writing in English, 1375-1575*, Oxford – Malden, Mass.: Blackwell.

Watson, Nicholas (1999), "The Politics of Middle English Writing", in Jocelyn Wogan-Browne *et al.*, eds., *The Idea of the Vernacular. An Anthology of Middle English Literary Theory, 1280-1520*, Exeter: University of Exeter Press, 331-352.

Wogan-Browne, Jocelyn *et al.*, eds. (1999), *The Idea of the Vernacular. An Anthology of Middle English Literary Theory, 1280-1520*, Exeter: University of Exeter Press.

Zumthor, Paul (1992), *Toward a Medieval Poetics* (First Edition 1972), transl. Philip Bennett, Minneapolis – Oxford: University of Minnesota Press.

Christian Todenhagen (Chico, CA)*
What on Earth Was I Thinking?
Linguistics' Role in Re-viewing the Past Reluctantly

Roughly ten years ago, Joachim Schwend, Wolfgang Thiele and I co-edited an anthology on political discourse. In their preface Jochen and Wolfgang – being the good friends they are – pointed out that the publication coincided with my 65th birthday. I am about ten years Jochen's senior in lived experience, and letting him benefit from some of what I have learned in the meantime would certainly be an act of friendship. In my contribution to the discourse anthology, I had used research and concepts with which Jochen, as co-editor, is familiar and which helped me to make rhyme and reason of those gnawing questions which are revolving around major lifetime decisions like career changes or around milestones like anniversaries. Sharing my observations with Jochen leads me to look forward to my future association with a good friend.

Intercultural contacts – delightful as they are – can lead to quite unexpected experiences. A case in point is one observation made by a couple of German friends who visited the United States. They were quite taken by the usefulness of a turn of phrase they had heard in a restaurant: "Could you put these in a doggy bag for me, please?" They were so impressed, indeed, that they used it soon after their return to Germany: "Könnten Sie mir bitte den Rest für unseren Hund einpacken?" Their waiter relayed this message to the chef who confronted them and demanded an apology. My friends – quite confused – obliged, of course, and heartily regretted having voiced their request in the first place. In the U.S., a 'doggie bag' is widely understood to mean "it was so good, we want to take our leftovers

---

* Dr. T. stopped teaching in the English Department of California State University, Chico in 2007. He is now examining the linguistic abilities of his Giant Schnauzer "Hedwig" who – although completely unimpressed with her master's doctorate from the University of Hamburg, Germany – can already distinguish reliably between the different English phonemes in NO and GO. He is also directing his attention to the linguistic inclinations of psychiatrists and psychoanalysts. His university supports him generously in the latter undertaking.

home." The German chef heard the translation as meaning "this dinner tasted like dog food."

Similar examples, resulting in even more rueful feelings, are limitless. One only has to think of those experiences that come under the heading of 'buyer's remorse'. And there are, of course, those intense regrets that affect our relationships with ourselves: What on earth made me do that? – How on earth did I end up here? etc. These regrets suddenly appear in one's thoughts out of nowhere, very often taking one way back in time to the earlier days of one's life, and inviting one to retrace vital past decisions.

The first major problem facing an inquiry into intrapersonal regrets concerns the observation that they reawaken one's memories and, consequently, the question arises as to whether that kind of personal information can at all be reliably retrieved. This subject was intensely discussed by S. Freud und C. G. Jung and revived in the public discourse not too long ago under the heading of 'recovered memory'. Jung approached the issue from a variety of angles and, in one of his publications, voiced a conviction of special relevance here (cf. Jung 1985: 166-168). He stated that if an individual was seeking the cause of an inner conflict in an event from his past life, he was in fact misplacing this conflict and its demands from the present time he was living in. Jung thus shifted the emphasis from the past to the mandate of present circumstances.

Unfortunately, however, Jung was arguing within the specific context of a particular psychiatric inquiry. A wider perspective is needed in our discussion of regrets, and that one may come from the 'linguistic turn' of Wilhelm Dilthey and Jacques Lacan. Dilthey, a hermeneutist, turned to linguistic resources to understand and interpret human behavior and experience. He is perhaps best known – as H. P. Rickman (1979: 148) noted – for widening the concept of *text* to include written records of human life. And if these written words could be authoritatively interpreted, why not spoken words as well and further also instances of nonverbal communication like facial expressions, gestures, and body language in general? They are meaningful in the same manner as words are. Dilthey summarized his thoughts in this statement as translated by Rickman (loc. cit.):

> As words have meaning by which they designate something, or sentences constructed by us, so [...] meaning of the parts of life can be figured out. Meaning is the special kind of relationship which the parts of life have to life as a whole. This meaning we understand as words in a sentence.

Dilthey's linguistic turn appears quite tentative and incipient today in view of the status assigned by J. Lacan to language for describing and understanding the human mind and its working. Lacan, a psychiatrist like Jung, held the conviction that when, for example, a child acquires his language, he does not do it in the manner of adding language to his inventory of usable skills. Rather he inserts himself into his language system to the extent that he becomes part of it as a subject whose mental powers are molded by its systemic constraints and possibilities.[1] Thus Paul Ricoeur (1984: 57) concludes not surprisingly: "If, in fact, human action can be narrated, it is because it is always already articulated by signs, rules and norms. It is already symbolically mediated."

On this basis, linguistics can now be called upon to point to the kind of mental operations which help overcome the problem posed by intrapersonal regrets, and language itself can contribute convenient illustrations of these operations: One of the laws by which meaning is created in language rests on the interplay of two movements. The first meaning generating movement is progressive. The listener to the sentence "Soon after his divorce he met a handsome ..." will have anticipated the word "woman" or a similar signifier and knows already that she is a mature individual, that she dresses in a particular style, that she prefers a tailored suit to a frilly dress, for example, etc. The confirmation comes in part when the speaker continues, "who owned her own consulting business." After the completion of the sentence, the second meaning generating movement will make the

---

[1] The idea of the subject as the effect of the signifier is the foundation of J. Lacan's second creative period, his linguistic one, and central to his Rome report of 1953, "Function and Field of Speech and Language in Psychoanalysis", repr. in Lacan 1977.

listener add this information retrospectively to the signifying complex "woman" in addition to conjectures about her financial status, lifestyle preferences, etc.

In every day speech, retrospective processes like this one operate quite smoothly and, indeed, they have to, or linguistic exchanges would not be possible. On occasion, however, retrospective signification may run into difficulties. For example, when the Hollies sing "He ain't heavy, he's my brother", listeners have to construct a new meaning of "heavy" retrospectively. This is not an easy enterprise for them and they may attempt it at different points in the song's lyrics or not until its completion (cf. for example "The Hollies").

As human subjects are dominated by language and give meaning to their experiences in a manner determined by language, they will have to 're-transcribe' them at certain times retrospectively. Freud wrote more than a hundred years ago "the material present in memory-traces [… is] subjected from time to time to a re-transcription (Umschrift)." And "the successive registrations represent the psychic achievement of successive epochs. At the boundary of two such epochs, a translation of the psychic material must take place." (cited in Mason 1985: 208) Again this process generally operates smoothly and without the awareness of the individual. But at times the mental machinery will grind to a halt and then a question like "Why on earth did I do that?" will emerge. In the case of the restaurant scene above, there, indeed, may be no answer. A person has to accept that he made a mistake and, with his acceptance, his question will become moot. The benefit he might gain from the experience might be that the regret motivates him enough to learn not to find himself in the same situation again.

In the case of intrapersonal regrets, however, there may be an answer to the vexing *wh*-questions beginning with *who*, *where*, *when*, etc. as the following illustration will show (taken from Meltzer 1998: 286-289). Sara, a lawyer, was told at the end of her annual review that she was not going to make partner, although she had been promised so and had worked extremely hard to deserve it. It was implied that she should leave the law firm, but since she had put in six years of her working life, she would be allowed to stay on for another four months. An email from the partners informed her that the extra four months were allowed with the condition that she tell the other associates she was leaving by her own choice. Sara answered by return of email that obviously the partners were worried what their associates would think of promised partnerships which were not forthcoming, and then, in a moment of "blissful vindication", cc-ed the partners' email and her reply to the entire staff. As a consequence, Sara had to vacate her office the very same day. Later – looking back from the present – Sara thought it was a "psycho move" though it had seemed her best option then. For a long time, Sara was too embarrassed to even think about having been fired, let alone discuss it. Only at the insistence of her new colleague, Conrad, did she do so. At the end of her account, Conrad gave her the answer to her question "What made me fire off that email?" which had eluded her so far: "You were looking out for your friends!" A "tiny grin lit her cheeks. 'I am glad you see it like that.'" (ibid.: 289) With the explanation provided by Conrad, Sara's regret had disappeared. She had completed the re-transcription of a past epoch to her satisfaction and could move on unburdened. The example illustrates how difficult the process of dealing with intrapersonal regrets can be. Sara had needed help from a third party and there had been extensive demands on her mental energies. Her tiny smile must have understated her joy because subsequently she allowed herself to be given a first long embrace by Conrad. And that is, after all, understandable since she had learnt that very moment who she was as a human being and had her life restored to its wholeness again.

The term intrapersonal regret seems to apply accurately only to situations in which an individual keeps torturing himself over a past decision in a similar manner to that of Jung's patient who misplaces his problems into the past. He is like the person who hears the line "He ain't heavy, he's my brother", is stuck on the term 'heavy' and cannot make sense of the complete expression. To understand, he must shift his attention to the end of the sentence and assign to 'heavy' its meaning in a manner which Freud called *nachträglich*. In the same way, it is through *Nachträglichkeit* that the human mind gains insight into its personal experiences.

Sources

Dilthey, Wilhelm (1973), *Gesammelte Schriften*, vol. VII (First Edition 1927), Stuttgart – Göttingen: Vandenhoeck & Ruprecht.

Jung, Carl Gustav (1985), *Freud and Psychoanalysis*, transl. R. F. C. Hull, Princeton, N. J.: Princeton University Press.

Lacan, Jacques (1977), "The Function and Field of Speech and Language in Psychoanalysis", in Jacques Lacan, *Ecrits: A Selection*, transl. Alan Sheridan, New York – London: Norton, 30-113.

Mason, Jeffrey (1985), *The Complete Letters of Sigmund Freud to Wilhelm Fliess*, Cambridge, Mass. – London: Harvard University Press.

Meltzer, Brad (1998), *Dead Even*, New York: Rob Weisbach.

Ricoeur, Paul (1984), *Time and Narrative*, vol. 1, transl. Kathleen McLaughlin & David Pellauer, Chicago: Chicago University Press.

Rickman, Hans Peter (1979), *Wilhelm Dilthey: Pioneer of the Human Studies*, Berkeley – Los Angeles – London: University of California Press.

"The Hollies – He Ain't Heavy He's My Brother" (n.d.), Song Meanings, http://songmeanings.com/songs/view/82509/ (4 January 2014).

Thiele, Wolfgang, Joachim Schwend & Christian Todenhagen, eds. (2005), *Political Discourse: Different Media – Different Intentions – New Reflections*, Tübingen: Stauffenburg.

Sabine Coelsch-Foisner (Salzburg)*
Erinnerung an eine Flusswanderung, oder:
Gedanken zum „*Museal Turn*"

Mit Jochen Schwend verbinden mich mehrere kulturwissenschaftliche Tagungen, insbesondere zu den Consumer Cultures *und zu den Erinnerungskulturen. Der vorliegende Text assoziiert wissenschaftliche Perspektiven des Erinnerns mit einer persönlichen Erinnerung. Er handelt von einer gemeinsamen Flusswanderung im Rahmen der* Salzburg Annual Conference 2010 *über kulturelle Infrastrukturen des Erinnerns.*

Über die Salzach hatte sich jener rötlich-silbrige Schimmer gelegt, der an manchen Spätnachmittagen im Herbst die Farben des Himmels spiegelt und ein glänzendes Band in die Landschaft wirft. Wer in solch einer Stimmung den Fluss entlanggeht, merkt kaum, wie die Dämmerung hereinbricht und die Böschungen und umliegenden Waldhügel allmählich dunkel färbt. Ein paar Menschen waren noch mit ihren Hunden unterwegs. Wir gingen den Weg flussaufwärts in Richtung Süden, wo in einem Bildungszentrum außerhalb der Stadt unsere jährliche Salzburger Herbsttagung stattfand: *The Museal Turn / Die museale Wende* – eine Tagung über die Anstrengungen öffentlicher Einrichtungen und privater Lebenswelten, das Vergangene zu bewahren, Vergessenes ans Licht zu befördern, und das kulturelle Gedächtnis lebendig zu halten. Was bedeutet dieses organisierte,

---

* Sabine Coelsch-Foisner ist seit 2005 ordentliche Professorin für Englische Literaturwissenschaft und Kulturtheorie an der Universität Salzburg; 2001 erhielt sie für ihre Habilitation den Kardinal-Innitzer-Preis, 2004 den Kulturpreis des Landes Oberösterreich. Seit 2007 leitet sie den Fachbereich Anglistik und Amerikanistik und war zudem 2004-2010 Leiterin des Interdisziplinären Forschungszentrums Metamorphischer Wandel in den Künsten / IRCM. Seit 2010 leitet sie den interdisziplinären Programmbereich Arts & Aesthetics und gründete gemeinsam mit Künstlern und Kultureinrichtungen die renommierte Programmreihe Atelier Gespräche. Sie ist seit 2010 Vizepräsidentin der Internationalen Gesellschaft für Fantastikforschung sowie Herausgeberin von mehreren internationalen Reihen, darunter *Wissenschaft und Kunst* und hat mehrere nationale und internationale Drittmittelprojekte. Forschungsbereiche sind englische Literatur, Theater, Lyrik, Kultur- und Ästhetiktheorie, Fantastik, kulturelle Infrastrukturen und Literatur und die anderen Künste.

inszenierte Tradieren von Vergangenheit? Erschöpfen sich die Triebfedern des Erinnerns im Bildungsauftrag zivilisierter Gesellschaften, in der Schaffung kollektiver Identitäten und im kulturellen Gewissen als ‚Kompensation' des Verlusts und des Leidens ganzer Generationen und Völker? Wo hat die persönliche Erinnerung ihren Platz? Was vermag sie dem Vergehen entgegenzuhalten?

Es wurde frostig und wir setzten mechanisch einen Fuß vor den anderen, im Blickfeld die dunkler werdenden Konturen des Tennengebirges, wo sich das schimmernde Band des Flusses verlor, davor kahle Stängel und geknickte Gräser am Wegrand, und ab und zu tauchten vor unseren Füßen Klumpen aus nassen, faulenden Blättern auf. Eine andere Form des Erinnerns bemächtigte sich unserer Gedanken, fernab kulturtheoretischer und poetologischer Diskurse. Wir sprachen von Bekannten und Freunden – leidenschaftlichen Sammlern, die getrieben waren vom Drang nach Vollständigkeit, nach einer Vollkommenheit, die es im realen Leben nicht zu erreichen gab. Wir erzählten einander von Erwartungen und Zielen, Erfolgen und Misserfolgen. Wir sprachen über den Fluss der Zeit, den wir in ähnlicher Weise über andere Personen wahrnahmen: in Gestalt unserer Eltern, die versuchten, trotz ihres Alters und beginnender Gebrechen an ihrem gewohnten Leben festzuhalten und den Alltag im eigenen Heim zu bewältigen; in Gestalt von Freunden und Kollegen, deren Leben eine plötzliche Wende genommen hatte. Die Ungewissheit über das, was vielleicht schon morgen uns treffen könnte, begleitete unsere Gedanken am Ende eines Tages zum Ende eines Jahres hin.

Der offizielle Befund eines musealen Schubs in der Gegenwartskultur, den wir im Rahmen unserer Jahrestagung beleuchteten, wurde zur Konfrontation mit der eigenen Geschichte. Fragen nach dem existenziellen Grundbedürfnis, Vergangenes zu bewahren und weiterzugeben mischten sich in die akademischen Diskussionen der vergangenen Tage: Entlastet die forcierte Beschäftigung mit dem Vergangenen bloß den ‚änderungstempobedingten Vertrautheitsschwund' mit unserer Geschichte, wie Hermann Lübbe festhält, oder spannen wir sie als Schirm gegen die eigene Zeitlichkeit – und Verwundbarkeit, als scheinbaren Halt im Strom unaufhaltbarer

Veränderungen? Als wäre das Hier und Jetzt unantastbar, fern des Verfalls jener, deren Spuren wir in Schauwelten als die ‚andere' Geschichte betrachten, um uns zu vergewissern, dass wir – gleichsam aus der Sicht der statisch Betrachtenden, der Unverwundeten, Unverwundbaren – nicht davon betroffen sind. Verleiht die Beschäftigung mit der Geschichte der ‚Anderen' nicht eine trügerische Sicherheit des eigenen Verweilens im Jetzt?

Instinktiv widersetzt sich der Geist den Signalen der Vergänglichkeit, den Spuren unentrinnbarer Veränderungen in der Natur und fragt nach Möglichkeiten des Überdauerns und des Verbleibs geschaffener Welten. Die Geschichte der Kunst und der Literatur ist voll vom Bemühen, Monumente zu errichten. Sammlungen, Denkmälern und Gedächtnisorten haftet der Trost des Beständigen an. Als Orte des Überdauerns schaffen sie gewissermaßen Präzedenzfälle für das *eigene* Überdauern. Im Festhalten am Vermächtnis der Vergangenheit, im Zurschaustellen und in der Verlebendigung dessen, was eben nichts mehr mit dem Leben zu tun hat, manifestiert sich ebenso die Angst vor der Vergänglichkeit wie im monumentalen Gestus des elisabethanischen Sonetts, im absurden Theater, in der Erinnerungspoetik Dylan Thomas oder in Sartres existentialistischen Romanen. Kaum ein englischer Autor wusste den Leser drastischer mit der Vergänglichkeit des Lebens in einem auf die Moderne vorgreifenden gottlosen Universum zu konfrontieren als Thomas Hardy. Einer kosmischen Gleichgültigkeit ausgesetzt, erfahren seine Charaktere ihre Existenz lediglich als Zufall in Zeit und Raum. Ihr Schicksal ist deshalb so trostlos, weil ihnen in einer auf Beliebigkeit beruhenden Welt jegliche Hoffnung verwehrt ist, je in einem Jetzt verweilen zu können. Stattdessen befindet sich jede Figur permanent im Übergang – auf Wanderschaft, vertrieben, in der Eisenbahn, immer in Bewegung, suchend, ohne Ziel. Nichts sichert ihnen Beständigkeit oder vermag zumindest eine Illusion von Beständigkeit zu vermitteln.

Hardy schrieb seine Romane am Ende der Viktorianischen Epoche aus einem Zeitgefühl heraus, als die Wissenschaften (Biologie, Geologie, Archäologie, Anthropologie, Geschichte) bisher unerforschte Horizonte der Vergangenheit eröffneten und den Menschen in ein unüberschaubares Zeitkontinuum stellten. Fotografie und später Film bedeuteten nicht nur technologische sondern auch ästhetische Neuerungen in der Bewältigung – oder Verdrängung – der eigenen Zeitlichkeit. Der museale Verortungs- und Erlebnisboom der Jahrtausendwende mag als (post-)moderne Spielart desselben Verdrängungstriebs gedeutet werden. Er mag aber auch als Herausforderung zum schöpferischen Umgang mit der Gegenwart gedeutet werden – als Verantwortung, die sich im Öffentlichen wie im Persönlichen mit konkreten Aufgaben verbindet: sei es mit der Errichtung von Mahnmalen und dem Gedenken an die Opfer von politischer oder religiöser Gewalt, sei es mit der Fürsorge für gebrechliche Menschen und der Bewältigung alltäglicher Veränderungen.

Vielleicht ist es der ‚Luxus der Erinnerung', um Hans Neuenfels' Worte zu gebrauchen, – so wie der Traum, die Vision oder andere nicht real existente Gebilde – der es vermag, das Wagnis Leben ins Schöpferische umzuwandeln. Das Erinnerte selbst bietet keinen Schutzwall gegen die Vergänglichkeit der Gegenwart. Vielmehr sind es die Aufgaben und Rollen, die wir darin jeweils erfüllen – als Freund, Sohn oder Tochter, Elternteil, Geschwister, Lehrer oder Wegbegleiter – die uns hoffen lassen, dass unser Sein mehr sein könnte als eine bloß zufällige Aneinanderreihung zufälliger Ereignisse oder Begegnungen, wie das Hardy in seinen Romanen und Gedichten darstellt. Das gilt auch für die Gedanken-Spuren einer gemeinsamen Flusswanderung entlang der Salzach an einem späten Herbstnachmittag auf dem Rückweg zur Abendsitzung der *Museal Turn*-Tagung.

Transferleistungen

Transfer and Translation

Crister S. Garrett (Leipzig)*
Britain's Place in the Transatlantic Space: Cultural Studies, International Politics, and Narrative Choices

For Joachim, the personification of decency, internationalism, and the spirit of generosity in teaching and scholarship. He has taught me that modesty in a scholar allows one to remain open to new ideas and complexity, allowing for one's own thinking to evolve. That is often easier said than done, but Joachim embodies how such a liberal spirit should inform the life of a scholar. He has especially brought it to bear in his work on cultural studies, where his insights and thoughtfulness have opened new spaces for scholars to explore the meaning of the cultural, and to better understand the politics of the choices that we make as scholars and citizens.

Opening Observations

Joachim Schwend has dedicated a good part of his scholarly career to reflecting on the relationship between cultural studies, international politics, and policy choice. His larger political vision for a European humanism (cf. Schwend 1996: 125) emerges from his findings on the nature of identity and their relationship to the political construction of regional, national, and even indeed so-called supranational identities like Europe. Such constructs involve choice, important for Schwend (and for this author), and thus the negotiation of priorities, or in a fuller sense, the political. Ultimately, Schwend wants to open new spaces for dynamic and different relationships with which the *demos* can become empowered to undertake new forms of identity governance or *kratie*. Such a de-

---

* Crister S. Garrett is professor for American cultural history at Leipzig University. After earning his PhD in contemporary history and politics at the University of California, Los Angeles, he taught at the Monterey Institute of International Studies in California and at the University of Wisconsin-Madison. He came to Leipzig in 2003 as the first holder of the Fulbright Chair for American Studies. He is particularly interested in the interplay between cultural studies and international politics with a focus on contemporary transatlantic relations.

mocratization of identity construction can encourage a European humanism with which to infuse international politics and policy choice more fundamentally.

Joachim Schwend has argued that cultural studies can provide the knowledge and intellectual tools with which scholars, students, and societies can pursue such narrative choice. As he observes, "Kulturstudien sollen uns die Welt, die eigene wie die fremde, verständlich machen, Zusammenhänge und Zeichensysteme erklären" (Schwend 1997: 266). Schwend continues in the same essay entitled, "Kultur, Kulturwissenschaft und Translation", that indeed, "Der Bereich der Kultur [...] regelt [...] die Interaktionen und Interdependenzen zwischen Menschen, was uns wieder zum Dolmetsch im Sinne von Dedecius bringt." (ibid.: 268) Cultural studies thus complicates passive assumptions, contextualizes certainties, and adds contingency to core concepts such as nation, state, and national identity. In essence, cultural studies encourages and creates choice, political choice, and thereby democratic spaces for new policies. Schwend's analysis of the construction of "Silicon Saxony", for example, underscores how societies and their leaders (political, economic, or cultural) can and do position their international relations with their policy choices along a type of 'glocal'-scaling. (cf. Schwend 2009)

It speaks for British society and its liberal traditions that the construction of its international relations is currently undergoing such a competitive and contested process. Indeed, its 'awkward relationship' with the European Union and its 'special relationship' with the United States are (once again) in a state of 'crisis', causing national elites and broader publics to debate energetically the future of 'Britain's role in the world'. Whether engaging Brussels or encountering Washington DC, London practices international politics and pursues national interests in the context of where the British people want to place the country between North America and Europe. Britain in this sense is at the center of the influences, institutions, values, and issues that compel the United States and Europe to interact, to influence each other, to compete, in what one can term an evolving transatlantic space.

Crisis, Choice, and Politics
Britain's two most important international relationships – with the EU and the US – were born in weakness. The 'special relationship' with the United States emerged, as is well known, at a moment of geopolitical and military challenge, when the British empire could no longer sustain itself, and Winston Churchill needed a narrative to bind the former colony to the former mother country's future fate. Franklin D. Roosevelt saw the need, but with a circumspect eye. And the 'awkward relationship' with the European Union (the European Community at the time) emerged, as is also well known, at a moment of economic challenge, when Britain's famed industrial and trading prowess of yesteryear struggled to support the Beveridge and Bevan vision for a fairer society. Europe saw the need (especially after de Gaulle was out of office), but remained wary of British intentions for the Community. Both relationships in short have been a steady reminder for Britain, and especially a Churchillian England, that it has been witness to its long-term relative global decline in terms of power (military, economic, political) and prestige (influence).

Naturally, one can narrate these two relationships with a notably different frame. Joining the European Community in 1973 provided Great Britain with the opportunity to shift the country's identity to a more European, less 'isolated', space where it could enhance its power and prestige with new markets and political mechanisms. And engaging energetically in an Anglo-American alliance in global affairs provided Great Britain enhanced power and prestige as it became the closest confidante to the world's dominant superpower (Athens playing to Rome à la Macmillan). Paris and Bonn looked on with envy as London enjoyed a refurbished status as a global actor. Both relationships, in short, underscored a Great Britain able to adapt agilely to evolving twentieth-century geopolitical realities that certainly involved the fading of nineteenth-century primacy (Pax Britannica) and the arrival of a new global order (Pax Americana), but simultaneously meant that Great Britain would have a confident and constructive role in it.

As Joachim Schwend has repeatedly stressed in his scholarship, which narrative one chooses for informing identities and political choices depends importantly on the perceived relative benefits of the opportunities-at-hand. British identity can carry decidedly different meaning for someone sitting in London, Edinburgh, Cardiff, or at one time, Dublin. (cf. Schwend 2002) Or as Ernest Bevin was wont to say as a Labour leader and Foreign Secretary, global power and prestige can have decidedly different meanings for the working class and high society. Relationships pursued are contingent upon choice, and just as importantly, how such choices are seen to aide in achieving basic goals, such as British interests, in short, national interests. And therein lies the rub, of course. To pursue British interests, one must have a reasonable sense of what is British. Is it a formalist, i.e., a functional state? Is it a notion of nation, i.e., a recognizable identity, an identifiable culture? Is it a nation-state, i.e., an interplay between institutions, culture, and interests that frames agendas for politics and policy 'nationally' and 'internationally'? Citing George Orwell, Schwend (2002: 208) underscores that for the nations of Wales and Scotland, a *sine qua non* binding element for these identities is insisting on what they are not, namely, English. In the Churchillian and Thatcherian tradition, British identity and interests *sans* England is but a formality, a state function, an administrative unit, in short, an impossibility. Schwend rightfully sees the ongoing debate about "Britishness" as an opportunity to rethink whole concepts of *leitkultur*, center and periphery, indeed the very notion of the nation.

For Schwend, such fluidity of identity provides political opportunity. An elegant and available model for less 'hierarchical imposition' and greater 'horizontal integration' is a Europe of Regions. (cf. Schwend 2002: 217) Regionalism, per his analysis about the process and nature of identity construction, can be "understood as a realm of the mind, as a conglomeration of beliefs and ideas, can be seen as a strong antidote to nationalism." (Schwend 1996: 117) And as such, "[r]egional diversity in a larger unit than the nation-state and without the borders between nation-states is what a Europe of Regions can offer." (ibid.) Joachim Schwend admires the writings and arguments of William Penn, especially his treatise, "Toward the Present and Future Peace of Europe" (1693). For Schwend, Penn's European House and his Europe of Regions are importantly about toleration for the other. As he (1996: 122) writes gently, for "William Penn, the wise old Quaker whose ideas appear relevant even 300 years after they were first expressed [...,] [t]olerance is the word, education and the willingness to look for compromise."

Competing Dreams

Schwend's appeal reflects a generous spirit. It underscores the power of the 'European Dream' that speaks to populations globally (cf. Rifkin 2005). So much dynamic change requires however a confident spirit, too. And in the context of the ongoing financial crisis and longer term trends in or besetting Great Britain, one reasonably asks to what extent the noted British calm and confidence, as the cliché goes, reigns unmistakably in the United Kingdom. After all, the fastest growing political movement in Britain today is the UK Independence Party; interestingly, it is primarily an English phenomenon. And five years into the economic crisis, the British economy remains, despite signs of fragile recovery, stubbornly anemic. There are few indications that stagnant wages among the less-skilled, manual, or service workers will do anything but continue to decline in terms of real purchasing power (a trend for the last decade at least). (cf. O'Connor 2013)

Capturing how a *zeitgeist* of insecurity pervades the middle of British politics is the éclat caused by the publication of David Goodhart's *The British Dream* (2013). Goodhart has been a journalist for over a decade at the *Financial Times* and has written for *The Guardian*, *The Independent*, and for *The Times*. He is currently head of the left-liberal think tank Demos in London. As with the so-called 'American Dream', Goodhart wants to offer his country a positive, an optimistic narrative to serve as an underpinning for a national social-contract moving forward. To get there, however, he provides a controversial, even confrontational analysis about contemporary Britain. He argues that it is high time to have a national debate about Britishness, especially when it comes to immigration and the fair expectation among current citizens that arrivals fully integrate into British society (to be assessed by an 'integration index'). *The Observer* has taken Goodhart sharply to task, maintaining that his argument is "just the stale suspicion of foreigners dressed up in intellectual clothing and given a slight twist to the left." (Birrell 2013) *The Daily Telegraph* on the other side of the aisle announced that Goodhart's "volume will come to be regarded as one of the most important contributions to political debate in the early 21st century. He demolishes the myths created by the liberal elite about immigration, exposes the lies and contradictions, and suggests a way forward." (Oborne 2013)

Perhaps most telling about how Goodhart's thesis has found a resonance in the center of British politics is a review of *The British Dream* by Labour MP Jon Cruddas, a member of Ed Miliband's Shadow Cabinet serving as Labour Party Policy Coordinator. Writing in the *New Statesman*, he argues about Labour policies on culture, identity, and nation:

> Immigration is as much about those who have lived in these islands for generations as it is about those newly arrived. As Ed Miliband has said, we have to create together a common life around the shared language of English and a willingness to work and obey the laws of the country. It is out of these social bonds that shared ideas of the common good can be built. When people are secure in their culture and identity, they are open to others. […] Labour's "one-nation" politics is less about a society of many cultures and more about creating a common life that allows us to find unity in our differences. (Cruddas 2013)

As for how Goodhart's book contributes to the national debate and narrative on culture, identity, and policy, Cruddas concludes:

> *The British Dream* is an important contribution to any durable 'one nation' politics. The country is heading for some pretty turbulent times and the left must contest these spaces, not vacate them to the right and the politics of loss and demonisation. Goodhart has occupied them longer than many and his work is evolving into something of real substance. I hope the book will be widely read. (Cruddas 2013)

Meanwhile, Conservative Prime Minister David Cameron has announced a new Immigration Bill that is meant to get 'tough on immigration'. While it will be debated vigorously, it has been carefully placed in the current center of a British politics that Labour has helped shape and by which the party itself has been informed.

Awkward Relationships
The 'Britishness debate' is of course a classic case of what is 'us' and what is 'foreign' or 'other'. Intellectually we may well understand to what extent this is an artificial and constructed exercise. But politically and in terms of public spaces – where *Verfassungspatriotismus* ultimately becomes embedded, or not – the debate is very real, with profound consequences at stake. Cruddas alludes to these in admonishing his party and fellow citizens not to abdicate space to more radical voices. Immigration is perhaps the most immediate example for British politics of how democratic voices can shift public debates about diversity and openness. But arguably as central for the future well-being of the UK is its relationship with the EU, an "awkward relationship" (George 1998) from the very beginning. The praiseworthy or notorious *acquis communautaire*, the basic concept underscoring that the EU is not just a trading zone (à la NAFTA) but a political and social union, has always provided the rub for many British and especially English voices. It provided the context for one of the iconic moments during the Thatcher era when she thundered in the House of Commons in 1990 at the possibility of a greater extension of EC influence in British life, "No, no, no!"[1] It was this staunchness (stubbornness) and the 'budget rebate' in 1984 that she succeeded in securing for Britain that has set the political standard in Britain for how national leaders should 'handle Europe'. Tony Blair had to acknowledge this legacy while seeking to pursue the country's fundamental economic and other interests uniquely served by the EU. And David Cameron struggles a quarter century later with the narrative that Thatcher hammered into the British political lexicon. His party is so divided over the issue of British membership in the EU, and indeed so is the entire

---

[1] This piece of political theater can be viewed on YouTube at http://www.youtube.com/watch?v=Tetk_ayO1x4 (18 August 2013).

country, that Cameron has promised by 2017 a 'straight up' (a yes-or-no) referendum for the country on whether Britain should remain a member of the EU.

Both Blair and Cameron understand just how fundamental the EU has become for British well-being, and power. Over half of British exports go to European Union member states, and trade with the EU accounts directly for millions of British jobs. (cf. Cohen 2013) EU laws and guidelines have become woven into daily British life fundamentally. Indeed, a House of Commons report concludes that the "British Government estimates that around 50% of UK legislation with a significant economic impact originates from EU legislation." (House of Commons Library 2010: 1) No longer a global power, perhaps no longer a great power, Great Britain profits from its position within the EU in terms of global reach. President Obama said so concretely during a joint press conference with Cameron in May, 2013, observing that "I think the UK's participation in the EU is an expression of its influence and its role in the world, as well as obviously a very important economic partnership." (Transcript, Obama-Cameron Press Conference, 13 May 2013)

Special Relationships
The American president was thus choosing the positive narrative on British membership in the EU outlined earlier in this essay. By doing so he was in part trying to soothe over the diplomatic éclat caused earlier in the year when the U.S. Assistant Secretary of State Philip Gordon had stated clearly and strongly that "[w]e value a strong UK voice in a strong European Union," especially since "[w]e have a growing relationship with the EU as an institution, which has an increasing voice in the world, and we want to see a strong British voice in that EU. That is in America's interests. We welcome an outward-looking EU with Britain in it." ("Obama administration warns Britain to stay in the European Union" 2013) This was seen as a highly unusual American intrusion into British domestic affairs. Indeed it was just that, with the Obama administration knowing full well that Cameron was struggling to stay ahead of rising public discontent with British membership in the EU. Cameron's effort to

shape British views on the EU culminated in his major speech "Britain and the EU" on 23 January 2013 where he announced the aforementioned in/out referendum to be held at the latest by 2017 (and assuming he wins reelection in 2015).[2] The impact of the Obama administration efforts is questionable to say the least, but their position is clear and consistent with past American administrations: An active and confident Britain in the EU is seen as encouraging a Europe that is open, liberal, not afraid of unfolding globalization, and active in global security politics. Political elites in London are well aware that when Washington DC looks to Europe, it sees a cautious Berlin, an insecure Paris, and a kindred London. That provides political opportunity for Britain on the world stage, in short, influence if not power. This assumes to a large degree, however, Britain's continuing EU membership and its current place in the transatlantic space.

America's relative lack of options in Europe has always been an important element of the 'special relationship' (coined by Winston Churchill for the first time on 16 February 1944). For most of the Cold War, a Gaullist France and a cautious West Germany meant Britain was by default the most robust and reliable presence in European affairs for the United States. By varying degrees of conviction – George W. Bush had a bust of Winston Churchill in the Oval Office; Barack Obama had it removed and replaced by a bust of Martin Luther King – American presidents have relied on a long tradition of Anglo-American cooperation in foreign affairs to pursue mutual interests. From using the British navy to stop slave ships in the nineteenth century as part of the abolition movement to Tony Blair arguing forcefully for military force in former Yugoslavia, the UK has a long tradition of integrating morality into foreign policy logics, as does the United States. It was in particular this 'special relationship' to which Obama turned in the effort to build international support for possible military action against the Assad regime in Syria after its use of chemical weapons against civilians.

---

[2] The full 37-minute speech and national coverage of it can be found at the BBC at http://www.bbc.co.uk/news/uk-politics-21170265 (17 August 2013).

David Cameron himself had been arguing longer and more forcefully than Obama that the international community must act, with military force if necessary, to stop the widespread civilian killing taking place in Syria. But on 29 August 2013, in a contentious and stunning vote, Prime Minister David Cameron could not muster a majority in parliament for Britain joining the United States in a possible military strike against the Assad regime. *The Sun* promptly published a large front-page 'Death Notice' for the 'special relationship', writing, "Beloved offspring of Winston Churchill and Franklin D. Roosevelt. Dearly loved by Ronald Reagan, Margaret Thatcher, Bill Clinton, Tony Blair and George W. Bush" (it went on to add naughtily, "Funeral to be held at The French Embassy […] No flowers please". *The Sun*, 31 August 2013).[3] Ed Miliband felt compelled the next day to explain his opposition, writing in *The Guardian*: "I believe the special relationship should and will endure. Our shared history, values and institutions require nothing less. And there is no solution to most of the problems of the world, whether it is the Middle East peace process, climate change or Syria, which does not go through the United States." (Miliband 2013) And a Conservative member of parliament saw the need to explain the party revolt against the Prime Minister in *The Wall Street Journal*. (Davis 2013)

Many reasons have been offered for the historic parliamentary vote not to support a possible military strike in Syria: Britain is a country exhausted from war after Iraq and Afghanistan, or 10 Downing Street did not prepare the vote properly. But infusing the entire national debate was a feeling that Britain should no longer be 'an American poodle', i.e., automatically support any initiative by the U.S. As already concluded in a House of Commons report dedicated to the 'special relationship' in 2010:

> The perception that the British Government was a subservient 'poodle' to the U.S. Administration leading up to the period of the invasion of Iraq and its aftermath is widespread both among the British public and overseas […] This perception, whatever its

---

[3] Cf. http://www.thesun.co.uk/sol/homepage/news/politics/5107363/France-takes-Britains-place-as-Americas-closest-ally.html (18 March 2014).

relation to reality, is deeply damaging to the reputation and interests of the U.K. (House of Commons 2010: Conclusions and Recommendations, #20)

After the Syria vote, one could almost discern a palpable relief that Britain had 'stood up' to the Americans, or as *The Daily Express* put it, "Britain will no longer be seen as anyone's 'poodle'" (2013).

Choosing Narratives, Reconstructing Relationships
The British debates about EU membership and the Anglo-American alliance are thus importantly about a growing feeling that somehow outside powers are 'imposing' their agendas on the United Kingdom, i.e., the country is no longer in control, that it is losing choice, if not voice. Such a public perception also fuels the current British debate on immigration, that somehow the country is being 'overrun', and that 'Britishness' is no longer secure. These sentiments need to be taken seriously, and are by both elites and broader publics in Great Britain, as Jon Cruddas reminds of with his articulation of Labour's 'one nation' policy. 'Splendid isolation' is obviously no longer an option. Indeed, Britain's standing in the world is contingent upon finding a confident narrative that integrates Europe, the United States and its unique history into a robust, agency-driven strategy for an articulate and strong voice in the evolving transatlantic space and beyond in global politics.

Politics and policy in open societies involve the democratic competition for voter preferences between different narratives, be these 'The European Dream', 'The British Dream', or 'The American Dream'. These 'grand narratives' involve an optimistic, forward-looking story for why citizens should commit to a country or continent, to a certain construction of identity. Or as Barack Obama states often when referring to the American Declaration of Independence, a measure by which to judge where a country stands in terms of proffered ideals and values. As Britain struggles with its place in the transatlantic space, it is undertaking a fundamental debate about how to define its independence so that it can embrace new forms of integration on what it sees as 'its own terms'.

Joachim Schwend is the first to admit that creating such a political space is replete with challenges, but that politicians and citizens possess the agency and choice to do so. It begins by translating our past and present in such a fashion as to allow inclusive and inspiring narratives (what the British historian Timothy Garton Ash (2013), when writing about Germany, calls the "poetry" of politics). Cultural studies as practiced by such scholars as Joachim Schwend allows students to become much better translators of cultures and thus countries and their full range of complexities. These are the initial and indispensable tools and steps toward a better understanding of international politics and thus possible policy choices. In this sense, Joachim Schwend has spent a career empowering students and fellow scholars to be better translators of culture, and thus better participants in democratic politics. This represents one of his lasting and substantial contributions to building a more open and inclusive definition of the United Kingdom, of Europe, and indeed of the transatlantic space.

Sources

Ash, Timothy Garton (2013), "The New German Question", *The New York Review of Books* 60/13, http://www.ny-books.com/articles/archives/2013/aug/15/new-german-question/?pagination=false (24 February 2014).

Birrell, Ian (2013), "The British Dream by David Goodhart; The Diversity Illusion by Ed West – Review", *The Observer*, 14 April, http://www.theguardian.com/books/2013/apr/14/british-dream-david-goodhart-review (24 February 2014).

"Britain will no longer be seen as anyone's poodle", (2013), *Daily Express*, 31 August, http://www.express.co.uk/comment/expresscomment/425849/Britain-will-no-longer-be-seen-as-anyone-s-poodle (24 February 2014).

Cohen, Roger (2013), "Britain's Brussels Syndrome", *The New York Times*, 22 August, http://www.nytimes.com/2013/08/23/opinion/cohen-britains-brussels-syndrome.html (24 February 2014).

Cruddas, Jon (2013), "Reviewed: The British Dream – Successes and Failures of Postwar Immigration by David Goodhart", *New Statesman*, 25 April, http://www.newstatesman.com/books/2013/04/reviewed-british-dream-successes-and-failures-post-war-immigration-david-goodhart (24 February 2014).

Davis, David (2013), "Why I Voted Against Syria Intervention", *The Wall Street Journal*, 1 September, http://online.wsj.com/news/articles/SB10001424127887324432404579048461976397956 (24 February 2014).

George, Stephen (1998), *An Awkward Partner: Britain in the European Community* (Third Edition), Oxford: Oxford University Press.

Goodhart, David (2013), *The British Dream: Successes and Failures of Post-war Immigration*. London: Atlantic Books.

House of Commons Library (2010), "How much legislation comes from Europe?", Research Paper 10/62, 13 October.

House of Commons. Foreign Affairs Committee (2010), "6th Report. Global Security: UK-US Relations", 18 March.

Miliband, Ed (2013), "I believe Britain can still make a difference in Syria", *The Guardian*, 30 August, http://www.theguardian.com/commentisfree/2013/aug/30/britain-still-difference-syria (24 February 2014).

"Obama administration warns Britain to stay in the European Union" (2013), *The Independent*, 9 January, http://www.independent.co.uk/news/uk/home-news/obama-administration-warns-britain-to-stay-in-the-european-union-8444789.html (24 February 2014).

Oborne, Peter (2013), "The British Dream by David Goodhart and The Diversity Illusion by Ed West: review", *The Telegraph*, 15 April, http://www.telegraph.co.uk/culture/books/bookreviews/9986465/The-British-Dream-by-David-Goodhart-and-The-Diversity-Illusion-by-Ed-West-review.html (24 February 2014).

O'Connor, Sarah (2013), "UK trade: one-way traffic", *Financial Times*, 21 August, http://www.ft.com/cms/s/2/a10a649a-098f-11e3-ad07-00144feabdc0.html#axzz2uFUFA5zq (24 February 2014).

Rifkin, Jeremy (2005), *The European Dream: How Europe's Vision of the Future Is Quietly Eclipsing the American Dream*, New York: Tarcher Books.

Schwend, Joachim (1996), "The Nation-State or a Europe of Regions? Some Utopian Ideas about the End of a Paradigm and Possibilities for a New Approach in Ireland", in Horst W. Drescher & Susanne Hagemann, eds., *Scotland to Slovenia*, Frankfurt/Main: Peter Lang, 113-140.

Schwend, Joachim (1997), "Kultur, Kulturwissenschaft und Translation", in Horst W. Drescher, ed., *Transfer: Übersetzen – Dolmetschen – Interkulturalität* (FTSK 23), Frankfurt/Main: Peter Lang, 263-278.

Schwend, Joachim (2002), "Das Vereinigte Königreich im Wandel – Globalisierung und Europäische Integration. Eine kulturwissenschaftliche Textbewertung", in Christian Todenhagen, ed., *Text – Text Structure – Text Type: Festschrift für Wolfgang Thiele*, Tübingen: Stauffenburg Verlag, 207-220.

Schwend, Joachim (2009), "Silicon Saxony: New Life in an Old Country", in Laura Rorato & Anna Saunders, eds., *The Essence and the Margin: National Identities and Collective Memories in Contemporary European Culture*, Amsterdam: Rodopi, 199-216.

"Transcript: Joint Obama, Cameron Press Conference. Washington, DC. 13 May 2013" (2013), *The Wall Street Journal,* 13 May, http://blogs.wsj.com/washwire/2013/05/13/transcript-joint-obama-cameron-press-conference/ (24 February 2014).

Klaus Stolz (Chemnitz)*
The Americanisation of British Democracy?

The following article is the revised version of a presentation I once gave in the presence of Jochen Schwend. Of the many times that our pathways have intersected this occasion is the most memorable for me, as it turned out to be a critical juncture in my professional career. Congratulations, Jochen, on accomplishing such a successful career in British Cultural Studies and thanks for playing your part in my conversion to this field.

Introduction

Modern societies are currently undergoing profound change. Relevant long-term social and cultural developments are analysed in different academic disciplines, from different perspectives, using different concepts. The most frequently used term to describe what is going on is clearly globalisation. This term has been criticised for many things, among others for being too vague in its meaning. A more telling, and perhaps a more relevant concept for the study of British and American society and culture is the notion of Americanisation. In contrast to the rather unspecified term globalisation, Americanisation at least gives us some idea of where this change is supposed to be coming from and/or in which direction it is going. And indeed, Americanisation seems to depict an everyday phenomenon: having your coffee at Starbucks or your burger at McDonalds, listening to American pop music, watching the Simpsons or a Hollywood movie, but also using the products of the likes of Microsoft, IBM, Google in your work place – all this could be the daily routine of anybody in the western world. So is there really a process at work that makes modern societies converge to just one

---

* Klaus Stolz is a political scientist and Professor of British and American Studies at Chemnitz University of Technology. His research interests include British politics (especially territorial politics), regions and regionalism in Europe, political professionalisation and political careers. He has recently published *Towards a Regional Political Class? Professional Politicians and Regional Institutions in Catalonia and Scotland* (Manchester University Press 2010) and, as editor (together with Jens Borchert), *Moving through the Labyrinth: Political Careers in Multi-level Systems* (special Issue for *Regional and Federal Studies*, May 2011).

model? Or in the words of Joachim Schwend (2004: 113): "Does that mean that Americanisation is advancing, that we will end up in a unified global culture [...]?"

In this article I will look at the Americanisation of British democracy. As a political scientist by training, this is clearly the aspect of the Americanisation process that is closest to my personal expertise. Yet, while here I am concentrating on the political aspect, surely this analysis could and should be replicated for other areas (such as the cultural or the economic sphere). Furthermore, politics itself should not be understood as a sealed-off, completely self-referential system. On the contrary, it is strongly embedded in social and cultural practices. This means that even changes in the political system will have to be explained – at least partly – with reference to developments in the social and cultural sphere and will also have repercussions for these spheres. Any analysis of the Americanisation process – even if it concentrates on democracy – should thus go beyond the narrow institutional focus of political science by integrating sociological and cultural perspectives. The article is divided into four parts. After this brief introduction, I will specify the Americanisation hypothesis with regard to British democracy. What is meant by this term? What kinds of changes are inflicted upon British democracy? And what are the causes of this process? Then, I will confront this hypothesis with empirical evidence. In doing so, I will reject this claim and I will also give reasons why I think there is no wholesale Americanisation of British politics and British political culture. Finally, I will return to the wider Americanisation debate drawing some general conclusions from my observations about the change (or the lack of change) in British politics.

British Democracy and the Americanisation Hypothesis
British parliamentary democracy is the oldest in the world. It has developed over centuries adapting to changes in a flexible way and thus avoiding any major break in its set-up. This long-term quality has made the Westminster model a core element of British identity. It has been seen as a cultural accomplishment, an achievement of British civilization even. Consequently it has been exported to British colonies and dominions. Despite this colonial link with

Britain, however, American democracy has developed quite separately. In fact, according to the American political scientist Erwin Hargrove (2001: 49), the American and the British model of democracy can be seen as "mirror opposites". At the heart of this opposition lies their respective system of government. Britain is the mother of the parliamentary system of government, whereas the US was the first democracy to employ a presidential system. This may look like a mere institutional difference, yet in fact it refers to a fundamentally different concept of democracy. The British system is based on the fusion of the executive and the legislative branch of government. Ideally, the British voter casts his/her vote for a party according to its electoral manifesto. The majority party then has the mandate to govern and it can do so with few institutional restrictions. There is a single line of representation and thus a single line of accountability. This mandate theory is based on political parties as the central intermediaries between citizens and their government. This is called the doctrine of 'responsible party government'. By contrast, in the US, the president is elected separately and as an individual. He (and so far there have only been male presidents) has a personal mandate to govern, and he has his own personal infrastructure in place to do so. As an elected head of state, he maintains a direct relationship with the citizens which is not mediated by parties or any other organisations. However, his power is restricted by other institutions, the Congress, the states, and the courts that can also claim to represent the people. While the British system is unitary with respect to the location of sovereignty, US democracy is based on checks and balances and multiple sources of authority.

Given these fundamental differences, how come people are speaking of the Americanisation of British democracy? What is meant by this term and where does it come from? The *special relationship* between the two nations has meant that America has always been an important point of reference and comparison in Britain. However, until recently the term Americanisation – at least in politics – has remained limited in scope to specific actors (New Labour), to specific policies (economic, foreign policy), or to specific points in time. However, recently a school of scholars has claimed that what we are witnessing at the moment is a much more profound and substantial development of British democracy. The British political scientist Michael Foley (2000: 25) has depicted a "systemic shift" in British democracy as presidential politics is "altering the structure and conduct of British political life" (ibid.: 25-26). For him, the comparison with the United States presidency is "not only helpful, but essential, in comprehending the shifting properties of the British premiership" (ibid.: 24). Thus, the presidentialisation thesis is the most advanced and most encompassing thesis of Americanisation. But what exactly is it that has changed in British democracy? According to Foley and others (such as Allen 2001) who are putting this argument forward, the British system of parliamentary democracy is increasingly functioning like a presidential system. Just like in presidential systems, and especially in the US, elections are becoming heavily personalised contests between the top candidates. Following this logic, once elected the British prime minister is seen to be increasingly engaged in a direct relationship with the public. He is using new forms of mass communication and he is also building up his own personal power resources (staff and organisational infrastructure). A new politics of personal leadership is developing in English-speaking democracies (cf. Campbell 1998: 29-34). All this is happening at the expense of traditional modes of governing in the UK via the Cabinet, the party and parliament.

The description of such a radical break with tradition, of course, begs the question, of how all these alien patterns of behaviour are supposed to have been creeping into British politics? Here the answer is two-fold: The first line of argument emphasises America as a role model. Tony Blair and New Labour, for example, borrowed heavily from Bill Clinton and his New Democrats. They even went so far as to employ political advisers and campaign specialists directly from the US (cf. Plasser & Plasser 2002: 73). However, this does not explain why these new campaigning and leadership techniques were needed in the first place, or why they were suddenly seen to be helpful and appropriate in the British context. The second line of argument thus emphasises long-term social and cultural factors to explain this change. For Foley and some of his colleagues, the presidentialisation of British democracy is caused by structural changes rather than by contingent political circumstances. This is not Americanisation by imitation, but Americanisation as a result of parallel social and cultural developments. The most frequently mentioned developments in this respect are (1) the decline of class and ideological conflict and (2) the changing structure of mass communication – changes extensively discussed both in political sociology and cultural studies (cf. Evans 1993, Dalton 1996, Swanson & Mancini 1996, Esser & Pfetsch 2004). The first of these arguments refers to a fundamental change in the social structure: the erosion of class division and of the ideological conflict that comes with this division. The argument is straightforward: When social group identities and fixed ideological positions no longer dictate voting behaviour, factors such as the personal qualities of leaders or of prospective leaders become increasingly more important. This, of course, strengthens their personal mandate, and thus their autonomy in government. The second argument has a clear cultural dimension to it. The growing role of the electronic media, most notably TV, is changing the structure of mass communication in all democracies. It demands a reduction of complexity and a concentration on symbols and personality. This strong personalisation in the coverage of the political process naturally offers leaders (and in particular the head of government) new opportunities to monopolise political communication, again strengthening him in relation to group actors (parties etc.). Together with a number of other changes, these developments are seen to be strengthening the autonomy of heads of governments from their parliamentary and party base, and thus they are seen to move the working mode of traditional parliamentary systems towards what we already know from the presidential system of the United States.

Empirical Evidence

So far, I have presented Americanisation as a hypothesis. I am now going to look for empirical evidence for the supposed changes in British democracy in order to see whether they really merit the name of Americanisation. I will look at the personalisation of elections as well as at the prime minister's newly gained resources and autonomy vis-à-vis the rest of the government, vis-à-vis Parliament and vis-à-vis his party. Finally, I will give some explanations for the persistence of the British pathway to democracy (despite all changes).

The personalisation of the electoral process is a centre stone of the Americanisation hypothesis. And indeed, in many respects the empirical evidence is quite convincing. Studies of electoral campaigning in Britain have shown over and over again the centrality of the top candidate in both the Labour and the Conservative parties' campaigns. Similarly media analysts have shown the growing dominance of party leaders in the media coverage. What is much more disputed, though, is whether leaders and their personality have any effect on the actual voting behaviour. In their comprehensive statistical analyses of British elections, the most authoritative experts have repeatedly come to the astonishing and counter-intuitive conclusion: "Leadership effects may well matter, but not very much and not very often." (Bartle & Crewe 2002: 93) The general belief in such an effect is based on the distorting effect of retrospective judgements: "Winners look good. Losers look bad. But their winning or losing seldom has anything to do with their looks." (ibid.: 95)

Let us turn to the second aspect, to the prime minister's relationship with the rest of the government. Attention is often drawn to the growing number of personal advisers to the prime minister, to the *de facto* organisation of a Prime Ministerial department to set policy agendas, to the 'creeping bilateralism' in the relationship between the prime minister and his departmental ministers, at the expense of Cabinet, which is meeting both less frequently and for shorter periods of time. All these tendencies supposedly started in the 1980s with Margaret Thatcher but clearly accelerated under the Blair government. Again, these observations are not wrong, but we have to put them into perspective. Firstly, the prime minister's personal resources (in terms of staff and organisational power) may have grown, but they still represent only a tiny percentage of the personal resources of the US president, and also only a tiny percentage of the administrative resources of a departmental minister. Secondly, whereas the Cabinet as a collective body may have lost in influence, the power of individual Cabinet members has not. This is particularly true for the current coalition government, where the Conservative Prime Minister David Cameron cannot set his own political agenda without considering the personal as well as party political concerns of his Liberal Deputy Prime Minister Nick Clegg. If coalition government were to become a more permanent feature of the British government (and the likelihood of coalitions has certainly increased) a central plank of the Americanisation hypothesis – the convergence towards a unipersonal executive – is certainly beginning to crack. Yet even a look at the most presidential premiership of recent times – that of Tony Blair – can remind us of the immense significance of individual cabinet ministers: in Blair's government the premier's chancellor and rival Gordon Brown had taken over responsibility for almost all of the social, economic and financial policy making.

Finally, I would again argue that the domination of party leaders (in particular the PM) and the use of plebiscitary strategies to circumvent parliament and party are heavily overstated. Recent prime ministers may have addressed the British public more directly and they have certainly forced some policies on their reluctant parties (just think of Margaret Thatcher and Tony Blair). Yet, they have hardly ever mobilised the public against intra-party rivals, because often these policies were also highly unpopular with the general public (think of Iraq, or the poll tax). They were 'conviction politicians' rather than 'plebiscitary demagogues' using the presidential strategy of 'going public'. Furthermore, despite their autocratic image, in many instances they had to make important concessions to their parliamentary party to get their bills through parliament. Nevertheless, since the early 1970s the share of party rebels voting against their own government has increased (cf. Cowley & Norton 1999, Cowley 2002). And last but not least, both Margaret Thatcher and Tony Blair suffered the typical fate of parliamentary leaders: They had to go, because they had lost support in their respective parliamentary parties. At the current moment, Prime Minister David Cameron has a tough time accommodating not only his coalition partner but also the Eurosceptic faction in his own party over his position towards European integration. Whether he is doomed to experience a similar, unpresidential end is still to be seen.

Taking all three aspects together, I would thus argue that the empirical basis for the presidentialisation thesis and therefore for the notion of a wholesale Americanisation of British democracy is rather weak. British democracy remains deeply rooted in parties and even the most popular (and some would say populist) prime minister in recent history remained strongly connected to his parliamentary party. This is not to say that there has been no change, but this change is distinctively British and thus follows a parliamentary path. But how can we explain the persistence of this distinctively British path? Well, the old institutionalist school of political science would answer this question simply by referring to the formal institutional rules of the parliamentary system. But institutional rules can be changed and they can be broken. So a more sophisticated explanation would have to understand political institutions as historically shaped and re-shaped and as embedded in social structures and cultural practices. In Britain, the concept of social class may have lost its all-determining meaning, yet it has not been eroded to a point where it is just one of many social distinctions in a highly segmented society (as in the US). Instead, there is still a clear correlation between the less well-off and the Labour Party and between the more affluent parts of society and the Conservatives. And even where social change has broken the material base of this correlation, party loyalties often endure. This becomes clear at the constituency level, where in certain areas of Glasgow, Manchester or Birmingham the old saying that the Labour party could nominate a donkey and it would still win the seat, has not yet lost its ring of truth.

Furthermore, even though party leaders and top candidates are at the forefront of political campaigning, even though they are monopolising political communication in the mass media, British voters are not necessarily making a strong distinction between the top candidate and the party. The party is given a mandate in order to implement a political programme or at least because it represents an alternative approach or an alternative camp. The top candidate has to give a face to this alternative, but he or she is not voted for because of his or her personal merits. When Tony Blair got elected for the first time in 1997, he got elected because he was the leader of a reformed Labour Party and because he stood against a discredited clique of Conservatives, who were no longer trusted. At his last election in 2005 he even got elected in spite of his personality. The most recent – and perhaps most convincing – confirmation of this argument is the current prospect of Labour's return to No. 10 led by a largely unpopular Ed Miliband.

The concept of 'responsible party government' and the 'mandate theory' are deeply ingrained in British political culture. There is a deep-seated scepticism of the British public against the use and abuse of individual power and an enduring belief in parties as the intermediaries between citizens and government. This is not only influencing voters' behaviour, it also has a strong impact on how politicians govern. Clearly, there have been prime ministers who cultivated a rather presidential style (like Tony Blair). But as George Jones (1991: 134) once said, "[T]he office of prime minister is like a piece of elastic; it can be stretched to accommodate an active interventionist prime minister [...] but it can also contract [...]". And indeed, the two most presidential figures of recent British history – Thatcher and Blair – have been replaced by the two most unpresidential successors, John Major and Gordon Brown. The current premier David Cameron is not only circumscribed by a coalition government, he has also reduced the prerogatives of the prime minister by culling his power to dissolve parliament. After the elastic has been stretched too far, the parliamentary system is striking back.

General Lessons

As stated above, I have looked at the alleged Americanisation of British democracy as just one aspect/component of a much wider debate. So what general lessons are to be learnt from this analysis? First of all, I think what has become clear is that Americanisation is a term almost as vague as globalisation. If we do not specify exactly what it means, it remains nothing but a catchword. So when we talk about Americanisation we should make clear what we actually mean. Are we talking about America actively exporting its culture, its political doctrines and its economic model? Or is Americanisation seen to be the product of processes of borrowing and institutional learning by lesser developed countries who look up to America as a role model? Are we talking about convergence into just one particular model or about parallel developments, where similar structural changes are pushing western societies into the same direction, while at the same time they still manage to stick to their national pathways?

In my analysis of British democracy, I have exemplified why I think that theories of convergence do not stand the test of empirical reality. Even in a situation where we had direct borrowing from the American role model (Blair – Clinton) plus common structural changes (referred to above), their concrete impact has still been filtered by historically developed mechanisms of adaptation to change. These mechanisms comprise social, cultural and political structures, norms and values that are unlikely to change in just a few years' time.

With my analysis of British politics I have merely touched upon one aspect of the much purported Americanisation process. In other sections of society things might look different. However, it is my contention that if we look deep enough we will find similar mechanisms at work in many other spheres. One frequently cited example of Americanisation is the development of sports, and in particular football in England. And indeed, in the last couple of decades English football clubs have been dramatically increasing their revenues from sponsorship, merchandising and the sale of broadcasting rights. Basically they have become business organisations that are even quoted on the stock exchange. Thus, they can be seen to be following an American model of commercialisation of sports. However, English football is still administered in a completely different legal, social but also cultural context. Its strong social roots, its specific fan culture and the long history of community attachment to specific clubs clearly prevent these clubs from becoming *mere* business organisations. Profit maximisation might be a concern, but utility maximisation (winning competitions) is still at the heart of English club football. Bearing in mind its remaining significance for social and cultural life, English football is still a long way from becoming Americanised in any meaningful sense of the word.

Thus, despite their *special relationship*, despite strong influence from the US, and despite being exposed to common structural changes, British and American politics, society and culture have remained highly distinctive. Perhaps this is a good thing. At least it provides a rich field for comparative investigations by scholars of British and American Social and Cultural Studies.

Sources

Allen, Graham (2001), *The Last Prime Minister*, London: Graham Allen.

Bartle, John & Ivor Crewe (2002), "The Impact of Party Leaders in Britain", in Anthony King, ed., *Leaders' Personalities and the Outcomes of Democratic Elections*, Oxford: Oxford University Press, 71-95.

Campbell, Colin (1998), *The US Presidency in Crisis: A Comparative Perspective*, New York: Oxford University Press.

Cowley, Philip & Philip Norton (1999), "Rebels and Rebellions. Conservative MPs in the 1992 Parliament", *British Journal of Politics and International Relations*, 1/1, 84-105.

Cowley, Philip (2002), *Revolts and Rebellions. Parliamentary Voting under Blair*, London: Politico's.

Dalton, Russell J. (1996), "Political Cleavages, Issues, and Electoral Change", in Lawrence LeDuc, Richard G. Niemi & Pippa Norris, eds., *Comparing Democracies: Elections and Voting in Global Perspective*, Thousand Oaks, CA: Sage, 319-342.

Esser, Frank & Barbara Pfetsch, eds. (2004), *Comparing Political Communication: Theories, Cases, and Challenges*, Cambridge: Cambridge University Press.

Evans, Geoffrey (1993), "The Decline of Class Divisions in Britain? Class and Ideological Preferences in the 1960s and the 1980s", *The British Journal of Sociology*, 44/3, 449-471.

Foley, Michael (1993), *The Rise of the British Presidency*, Manchester: Manchester University Press.

Foley, Michael (2000), *The British Presidency*, Manchester: Manchester University Press.

Hargrove, Erwin (2001), "The Presidency and the Prime Ministership as Institutions: An American Perspective", *British Journal of Politics and International Relations*, 3, 49-70.

Jones, George (1991), "Presidentialization in a Parliamentary System", in Colin Campbell & Margaret Jane Wyszomirsk, eds., *Executive Leadership in Anglo-American Systems*, Pittsburgh, PA: University of Pittsburgh Press, 111-138.

Plasser, Fritz & Gunda Plasser (2002), *Global Political Campaigning. A Worldwide Analysis of Campaign Professionals and their Practises*, Westport: Praeger.

Schwend, Joachim (2004), "Editorial", *Journal for the Study of British Cultures*, 11/2, 111-116.

Swanson, David L. & Paolo Mancini, eds. (1996), *Politics, Media and Modern Democracy: An International Study in Electoral Campaigning and their Consequences*, London: Praeger.

Clausdirk Pollner (Leipzig/Aachen)*
"The Twits? They're Just Eejits!"
Matthew Fitt Translates Roald Dahl into Scots

The author of the following wee essay has known the honouree for a time longer than we both care to remember. If I recollect correctly, we first met at the memorable Scottish Conference (Medieval and Renaissance Language and Literature), held in the late seventies of the last century at the University of Mainz-Germersheim, then Jochen's home turf. Memorable not so much for the brilliance of the speakers – that goes without saying – but for the splendid fact that bang in the middle of the Conference Dinner at a local yachting club a blazing row in the kitchen led to the chef storming out. Prof. Jack Aitken was about the last guest to be given a proper hot meal – for the rest of us (the majority!) it was strictly sandwich time...

Jochen has always been interested in the construction (de-construction?) of personal/national/political/historical/contemporary identities. One important way of expressing identity is language. Matthew Fitt manages to turn a very 'English' story into a very 'Scottish' one, by his use of Older Scots words (some going back to the Middle Ages), modern Scots slang terms, idioms that are unique to Scots, and cultural 'icons' such as food items.

In 2006, a small Edinburgh-based imprint published a Scots version of Roald Dahl's much-loved *The Twits* ([1]1980). The imprint is, rather charmingly, called Itchy Coo; it is devoted exclusively to books in Scots for young readers – prose and poetry, plays and picturebooks. It was founded in 2001/2002 by two friends, both of them writers who are deeply committed to the Scots language and to improving its overall social and academic status: Matthew Fitt and

---

* PhD degree and *Habilitation* at Aachen University. Then, after a mercifully brief period of unemployment, Guest-Professorships at, inter alia, the universities of Essen, Paderborn, Trento (I) and Vienna. From 1990 C2-Professor at the University of Osnabrück / Campus Vechta. Between 1993 and 2011 Professor of "Varieties of English World-wide" at the English Department of the University of Leipzig – a rather wonderful experience, at least for C.P. Now retired – another experience: but somewhat underwhelming.

James Robertson. *Itchy coo* is defined by *The Essential Scots Dictionary* (2004; *ESD*) as "anything causing a tickling, e.g. the prickly seeds of dog-rose put by children down each other's backs." But since, of course, *coo* is Scots for *cow* as well, the imprint's logo is a jumpy, tickled black-and-white cow. Itchy Coo started publishing in August 2002; rumours in 2011 (and indeed a brief statement by Fitt and Robertson on their website) about its imminent demise were somewhat premature. 2012 and 2013 saw the Itchy Coo publications of Robertson's translations into Scots of *The Gruffalo* and *The Gruffalo's Child* as well as the first ever Scots version of an *Asterix* volume: *Asterix and the Picts*, translated by Fitt as *Asterix and the Pechts*. What Fitt and Robertson did bring to an end in 2011 were the education, outreach and strategic liaison elements of the Itchy Coo project. Printed publications in Scots are – apart from Itchy Coo's activities – few and far between. There are two Edinburgh-based publishers that have some books in Scots in their back-list and current production, namely Luath Press and Waverley Books, the latter specializing in Graphic Novels (including some R.L. Stevenson adaptations). *One* Itchy Coo book deserves to be singled out: the 2002 publication of the history of the Scottish parliament by James Robertson, aimed at adult readers and, say, secondary school students. It shows brilliantly – contrary to all notorious gainsayers and sceptics – that Scots is of course perfectly equipped to be used for academic and expository prose!

Since its heyday in the late Middle Ages and early Renaissance, the Scots language has been in a precarious situation, particularly after the two blows of 1603 and 1707 – the Union of Crowns and Union of Parliaments respectively. What used to be Scotland's national tongue ("The King's Scots") is now seen by many as just a 'funny', mainly working-class variety of 'proper' (!) English and is more or less ignored by officialdom and the media – compared to Scottish Gaelic, which is widely seen as a 'proper' (again!!) language in its own right and not just a poor relative of English. It does not have to be pointed out at great length that funding for all things Gaelic seems to be much more easily forthcoming than funding for all things Scots (or should that have been "for no things Scots"?)

Itchy Coo's back-list includes Matthew Fitt's translation of *The Twits* as *The Eejits* (2006; *idiots* in Scots pronunciation). Since both versions, Dahl's original and Fitt's translation, carry the same illustrations by Quentin Blake that have to be in their specific places, Fitt's individual paragraphs, chapters and the whole book have to be exactly the same length as Dahl's – which is not a particularly difficult achievement, because the one linguistic level where English and Scots differ least is that of syntax, as opposed to all other language levels: sounds, grammar, wordstock, where differences can be considerable.

Translating literary texts tends to be tricky. Julian Barnes, in his latest collection of essays (2012), quotes the Spanish/English translator John Rutherford as saying, tongue-firmly-in-cheek: "Translation is a strange business, which sensible people no doubt avoid." (150) Matthew Fitt is, one thinks, very sensible – and yet he translates, and translates well. And he does more: he 'transposes', 'transliterates'. He turns an English text into a Scottish one by – blindingly obvious, this – using Scots. But then he goes beyond this: he turns a story set in England (albeit in an unnamed location) into one set in Scotland (ditto), namely by changing English cultural items into Scottish ones.

A possible taxonomy of Fitt's lexical material might look like this: (1) Traditional / Older Scots words; (2) Newer Scots words, say from the 18th, 19th and early 20th centuries; (3) Modern Scots slang and informal items; (4) Word-play instances of the *argy-bargy* kind, and alliterations; and (5) Cultural Scotticisms. It is particularly the latter that give *The Eejits* a very distinctive Scottish flavour. Before we look at (5) in some detail, just two examples each of categories (1) to (4): Older / Traditional Scots: e.g. Dahl's *to know* is *ken* right through Fitt's version, *every* is *ilka*, etc. Newer lexical items: *A lot* is *clossach* (this is incidentally one of the very few cases where Fitt does not follow the spelling option chosen by *ESD*, namely *closhach*), *great* is *gallus* etc. Slang and informal Scots: Dahl's *face* is *coupon*, *nitwit* is *bawheid* etc. Where Dahl has *cut and trimmed*, Fitt makes use of alliteration: *snippet and sneddit*, *gravy* becomes *broon bree* (where *bree* on its own *is* gravy, and that is usually *brown, broon* ...) But it is in category (5) where Fitt's text becomes truly Scottified – by the use of cultural Scottish items and idiomatic phrases.

In Dahl, the Twits eat *beef stew*; they do not in Fitt, where they partake of *potted heid* (*Pocket Scots Dictionary* (2002); *PSD*: "a dish made of meat from the head or skin of a cow or pig, boiled, shredded and served cold in a jelly made from the stock." Yuk!), they have *ice cream* as dessert in Dahl, but *cream crowdie* (or *cranachan* in Gaelic) in Fitt (*PSD*: "a dish made by mixing toasted oatmeal into whipped cream, sometimes adding fruit or other flavouring." Yum!) *Spinach* is rendered as *cauld kail* (presumably something like *coleslaw*), *minced chicken liver* becomes *chappit chicken herts* (and note the alliteration).

Dahl's three instances of *What on earth...* are in Fitt given as *Whit in the name...* followed by three different items: *...o Auld Nick's breeks*, *...o Beelzebub's bunnet* and *...o Jack Tamson's troosers*; this is in each case an item of Scottish clothing. *Celebrating* becomes *haein a ceilidh*, *every Tom, Dick and Harry*, the riff-raff in England, are turned into *every Tam, Jock and Jimmy*, the riff-raff in Scotland. *He'll stew us alive*: *He'll turn us into stovies* (*PSD*: "dish of stewed potatoes, onions etc, sometimes with small pieces of meat etc". Oh well!).

When Dahl introduces, somewhat incongruously, an Australian marsupial: *I watch you like a wombat*, Fitt has, somewhat more fittingly, *I watch ye like a hoolet*, i.e. the Old Scots / Middle Scots word for *owl*. Dahl's *screwdrivers* are Scottified into *dirks* (*ESD*: "a short dagger worn in the belt by Highlanders, now as part of the Highland dress"). *You old goat* becomes *Ye auld neep* (*ESD*: "a turnip; *neep-heid*: a stupid person"; and this is of course a reference to the preferred accompaniment of the national dish haggis: turnip). Dahl's somewhat tame *oh dear me, no* is more slangily Scottified into *help me boab* (*ESD*: *help ma bob* "exclamation of astonishment and exasperation").

In the old days is rendered, obviously, as *auld lang syne*. *Never mind why* is really not translated at all but transposed into *Dinna ask glaikit* ('stupid') *questions*. A similar example of transposing is *Get on with it*: *Shift yer bahookies* (*ESD*: "[often to children]: the behind, backside, bottom"). *Bahookie*, like *coupon* (see above), is incidentally an entry in Simpson's (2004) little dictionary of Scots slang words.

We have mostly been talking about the Scottification of an English text by means of adding a distinct Scottish flavour via the use of cultural Scotticisms. But Fitt goes that one step further. He relocates not just the novel's language but the story and plot itself. Dahl's *But these were English birds* becomes *thae birds were Scottish*. And finally: Dahl's *Here in England?* Oh no: *Here in Scotland!* The Eejits have gloriously made it to Caledonia.

Sources

Barnes, Julian (2012), *Through the Window. Seventeen Essays (and one Short Story)*, London: Vintage.

Dahl, Roald (2007), *The Twits* (¹1980), London: Penguin.

Dahl, Roald, (2006), *The Eejits*, transl. Matthew Fitt, Edinburgh: Itchy Coo.

The Essential Scots Dictionary (¹1996; repr. 2004), Edinburgh: Edinburgh University Press. (*ESD*)

Pocket Scots Dictionary (¹1988; repr. 2002), Edinburgh: Edinburgh University Press. (*PSD*)

Simpson, Scott (2004), *Shut Yer Pus. The Wee Book of Scots Slang*, Edinburgh: Black and White.

Thomas Kühn (Dresden)*
„Popular Culture" –
Kulturkontakt und die Übersetzung eines Terminus

Ein deutscher Kulturkontakt ist die Ursache des folgenden Beitrags: Es ist der zwischen dem Schwaben Schwend und dem Badener Kühn, der einjährige enge Kontakt der Kollegen Schwend und Kühn in Leipzig und schließlich der langjährige zwischen den Kollegen an den mitunter freundschaftlich rivalisierenden Universitäten Leipzig und Dresden. Dass ein gelernter Übersetzer die Übertragung eines Terminus als eine Frage des Kulturkontakts versteht, dürfte für Jochen Schwend eine Selbstverständlichkeit sein. Umso mehr trifft dies im Falle der Personalunion des Übersetzers und Kulturwissenschaftlers (als unprofessoraler Cultural Studies-Professor) zu. Jochen Schwend ist dieser Beitrag gewidmet.

Schon eine kritische Gegenüberstellung des Begriffs „Kulturkontakt" mit dem englischen „cultures in contact" deutet an, dass bei einer sprachlichen Kontaktnahme auch naheliegende Begriffe aus vermeintlich eng verwandten Kulturen unterschiedliche Assoziationen wecken und zum Teil divergierende semantische Bezugsfelder aufrufen. Dies gilt auch und besonders für die in den heutigen Kulturwissenschaften zentrale Vokabel „popular culture", deren Übersetzung vom Englischen ins Deutsche als terminologisches Kulturkontaktproblem im Folgenden näher untersucht werden soll. Dabei steht nicht die Frage im Vordergrund, was *popular culture* ist, welche divergierenden oder ähnlichen Praxen und Formen im deutschen und britischen Kontext zu finden sind, oder

---

* Nach Studium und Promotion an der Universität Freiburg arbeitete Thomas Kühn an der TU Berlin, weiteren deutschen Universitäten, darunter Leipzig, und der University of Sussex. Er war zudem Lehrer an einem Gymnasium. Seit 2004 ist er Professor für Großbritannienstudien an der TU Dresden. Nach Anfängen als Literaturwissenschaftler wandte er sich in der Forschung seit den 1990er Jahren zunehmend kulturwissenschaftlichen Fragen zu, darunter den englischen Universitäten als Institution und Universitätsromanen, der „Two Cultures"-Kontroverse, medialen Fragen von Ritualisierungen im öffentlichen Leben sowie zeitgenössischen Debatten in Historienfilmen. Zurzeit arbeitet er über mediale Aspekte populärer Kultur.

wie sich die jeweiligen wissenschaftlichen Bezugsdisziplinen mit Phänomenen von *popular culture* befassen. Es soll vielmehr primär darum gehen zu bedenken, was geschieht, wenn „popular culture" ins Deutsche überführt wird, wobei der verhandelte Begriff nicht von disziplinären Aspekten zu trennen ist. Ziel dieses Beitrags ist es, mit Hilfe begriffshistorischer Überlegungen zu einem Verständnis dessen zu gelangen, was „popular culture" bzw. seine Übertragungen ins Deutsche als vor allem in der jüngeren Vergangenheit gebräuchliche Vokabel kennzeichnet und dies als eine Frage des Kulturkontakts zu formulieren. Zunächst soll die Begriffsentwicklung von „popular culture" vorgestellt, danach die Übertragung ins Deutsche diskutiert werden, und beides wird mit disziplinären Implikationen verbunden. Denn wie häufig spielen auch im vorliegenden Fall Auseinandersetzungen um Termini bei der Entstehung und im Selbstverständnis von Disziplinen eine wichtige Rolle.

Dass bei der Übertragung des britischen „popular culture" ins Deutsche Probleme auszumachen sind, illustrieren zwei Beispiele. In einer Umfrage unter Kollegen, Studierenden, Freunden und Bekannten mit recht unterschiedlichem Bildungshintergrund – dies als erstes, recht impressionistisches Beispiel – bat ich um eine möglichst spontane und kurze Übertragung von „popular culture" ins Deutsche. Das Ergebnis war fast immer ein Zögern, ehe ein vorsichtiges und relativiertes „populäre Kultur", „Populärkultur" oder „Popkultur" genannt wurde. Häufig wurde eine kurze oder klare Antwort als unmöglich bezeichnet. Erst auf Nachfrage wurde dann mitunter bestätigt, dass „Volk" durchaus bei der Überlegung mitspielte, letztlich aber verworfen wurde, weil es entweder Assoziationen an unsympathische Derivate wie „Volksmusik" hervorriefe oder mit der in der Zeit des Nationalsozialismus reichlich missbrauchten Vokabel in Verbindung gebracht wurde. Der vollen Ausnutzung des Übersetzungsspektrums – inklusive des nie genannten „Alltagskultur" – wurde mit Skepsis und einer gewissen Unsicherheit begegnet; unbefangen waren die Reaktionen in aller Regel nicht, was auch an der fragenden Person hängen mag. Ähnliche Probleme mit einer einfachen Übersetzung – dies als zweites Beispiel – heben verschiedene deutsche Publikationen hervor (cf. Hecken 2006 und 2009, Hügel 2003, Maase *et al.* 2011).

„Popular" und „Popular Culture" im Englischen

In Bezug auf den Begriff „popular culture" nimmt Berndt Ostendorf (2001: 341) aus amerikanistischer Perspektive an, eine amerikanische *popular culture* sei als demokratischer Gegenbegriff zu einer das Populäre als volkstümlich, das einfache Volk verachtenden britischen Tradition zu verstehen. Morag Shiach (2005) dagegen beschreibt eine deutlich differenziertere terminologische Entwicklung von „the popular" und mithin „popular culture". So wird der von Ostendorf als Zeuge aufgerufene Dr. Johnson bei Shiach als nur eine Stimme eingebettet in eine Entwicklung vom 16. bis ins späte 20. Jahrhundert, die „popular" als äußerst vielschichtige und häufig umstrittene, von diversen (kultur)politischen Überzeugungen instrumentalisierte Vokabel erscheinen lässt. Mit Hilfe des *Oxford English Dictionary* deutet Shiach „popular" zunächst als Rechtsbegriff mit einer frühen Nennung aus dem Jahr 1579 als „equation of the interests of the people with the interests of the state" (ibid.: 56). Dies sei zugleich als Versuch zu sehen, die Allgemeingültigkeit des Begriffs „the people" in Übereinklang zu bringen mit der Absicht, dem Volk seine Grenzen gegenüber der politischen Macht aufzuzeigen (ibid.: 57). Zudem werde „popular" auf eine soziale Schicht bezogen und bezeichne die Eigenschaften des niederen Volks, des Pöbels (ibid.). Die beiden skizzierten Bedeutungen fänden ihre abgewandelte Fortsetzung bis über die Mitte des 20. Jahrhunderts hinaus. Sie bezeichneten einerseits das Volkstümliche, Beliebte als Ausdruck des Geistes eines Volks und andererseits verwiesen sie darauf, dass Waren der Industriegesellschaften allgemein und der Kulturindustrie im Besonderen als massenhaft Reproduziertes „popular" und somit von – allenfalls – geringem Wert seien. Sie seien, von der Kulturindustrie erzeugt, den sozial niederen, gewöhnlichen, ignoranten Schichten aufoktroyiert und würden von diesen stumpf konsumiert.[1] Shiach konstatiert zudem in der Verwendung von „popular" eine Distanznahme eines – in der Regel intellektuellen – Beschreibenden, der „popular" als das Andere fasst und bei Bedarf zurückweisen kann. Damit werde „popular" zum Antonym eines dominanten Dis-

---

[1] Diese Bedeutung von „popular culture" ist von der Kritischen Theorie Adornos und Horkheimers geprägt.

kurses. Darüber hinaus sieht Shiach vor allem im 20. Jahrhundert eine eher positive Indienstnahme und zugleich politisierte Bedeutung von „popular", wie sie etwa in Bezeichnungen wie „popular front" aufscheint. Diese Entwicklung führe zu einer Umdeutung bzw. Bedeutungserweiterung des Begriffs.[2] Beim Blick in neuere Wörterbücher der letzten 10 bis 20 Jahre kommt Shiach zu dem Befund, dass der Bezug zu „the people" durch den auf „the general public", also die Allgemeinheit, Öffentlichkeit ersetzt und somit seines kontroversen, spannungsreichen Potenzials weitgehend beraubt worden sei. Dies sei als Versuch einer Entpolitisierung des Begriffs zu deuten, als Entleerung des Bedeutungsspektrums eines Diskurses weg von der Auseinandersetzung um gesellschaftliche Macht und hin zu einer Individualisierung (cf. ibid.: 60). An diesem Punkt kommt der zweite Terminus des Kompositums ins Spiel und die Bezugsdisziplin Cultural Studies, ohne die die Geschichte von „popular culture" der letzten 50 Jahre im englischen Sprachraum kaum vorstellbar ist.

In der Einleitung zu dem vierbändigen Quellenband *Popular Culture* erweist sich Michael Pickering in der Verwendung des Terminus „popular culture" als typischer Vertreter der British Cultural Studies:

> All we can say, perhaps, is that 'the people' is not a category that precedes cultural forms and practices. Rather, it is a product of cultural forms and practices, and so dependent on representation, with either popular culture producing the people, or with popular culture and the people always existing in a contingent, transactional relationship. (Pickering 2010: xxxi)

Der Begriff selbst wird durch Pickering nicht klar definiert sondern eher vage gehalten. Gleichwohl wird der Anspruch sichtbar, *popular culture* als Repräsentation von „the people" zu fassen, auch wenn nicht deutlich wird, wer „the people" sind. In terminologischer Hinsicht macht Pickering darauf aufmerksam, dass „popular cul-

---

[2] Shiach beschränkt diese politisierte Bedeutung des Begriffs auf das 20. Jahrhundert. Aber auch schon spätestens im zweiten Drittel des 19. Jahrhunderts ist diese Verwendung verbreitet, etwa wenn das in der *People's Charter* deutlich werdende Selbstbewusstsein, für „the people" zu sprechen, sie zu repräsentieren, als „popular" im oben beschriebenen Sinn zu verstehen ist.

ture" als historisch und politisch umstrittener Begriff positive Konnotationen aufweist. In diesem Zusammenhang verwirft Pickering den Begriff „mass culture" als Synonym zu „popular culture", denn dieser sei eine ausschließlich negativ konnotierte Vokabel der Massengesellschaft, der Warenwelt und Kulturindustrie (cf. ibid.: xxi). In diesem Punkt ist er vom Kulturindustriebegriff der Kritischen Theorie der Frankfurter Schule beeinflusst und deutet ihn ohne Kenntnis des Deutschen zu einseitig. Denn wie Thomas Hecken (2009: 196) ausführt, ist „populäre Kultur" noch in den 50er Jahren weitgehend ungebräuchlich. Zudem werde die Verwendung von „Massenkultur" unter deutschen Intellektuellen quer durch das politische Spektrum allgemein abgelehnt als Gefahr, der Einzelne werde zur „irrationalen, unmoralischen Masse zusammengeballt" (ibid.: 197). In jüngerer Zeit schreibt Kaspar Maase (2003: 48-55) „popular" und Massenkultur einen eingeschränkt synonymen Charakter zu. Im Selbstverständnis der britischen Cultural Studies hingegen gilt es die *popular culture* zwar kritisch zu untersuchen; vor allem aber soll sie gegenüber der *high culture* aufgewertet, zumindest jedoch gleichrangig neben sie gestellt werden; die hegemoniale Macht der *high culture* solle, so nicht nur Pickering, gebrochen werden. „Popular culture" sei zwar ohne den Gegenbegriff „high culture" einerseits kaum vorstellbar, andererseits seien paradoxerweise die fundamentalen Differenzen obsolet geworden (Pickering 2010: xxi). Dieser Widerspruch bleibt weitgehend unaufgelöst und verweist auf das politische Programm der Cultural Studies, das Pickering wiederum sehr vage und widersprüchlich skizziert:

> If the movement from lived experience to object of criticism has generally paralleled a movement from immersion in popular culture to distancing from it of some kind, those who study popular culture may well be involved with it, though equally they may not. (ibid.: xxxi)

Pickering stellt sich, soviel wird trotz seiner Vorsicht deutlich, in guter Cultural-Studies-Tradition auf die Seite des engagierten Einlassens auf die *popular culture*. Dazu benötigt er die Hochkultur als das Andere. Zugleich hilft ihm das Festhalten am Begriff „popular" gegen „mass culture", eine andere Spaltung zumindest terminologisch zu verhindern, die im Gefolge der Industrialisierung und der Entwicklung einer Massengesellschaft seit der Mitte des 19. Jahrhunderts zwischen der Massengesellschaft und der Vorstellung von „the people" entstanden sei, eine Trennung „between an idealised 'folk' or 'genuine' popular culture and the artificial, inauthentic and debased forms of commodified 'mass' culture" (ibid.: xxi; cf. Hecken 2009: 59). Insgesamt präsentiert Pickering ein verallgemeinerbares Begriffs- und Bedeutungsprofil, das sowohl auf den Gebrauch des Terminus „popular culture" als auch auf seine in den letzten Jahrzehnten international sehr erfolgreiche Bezugswissenschaft Cultural Studies angewendet werden kann.

Popular Culture, Volkskultur – die deutsche Spezifik

Aleida Assmann verdeutlicht aus der Perspektive einer deutschen Anglistin in fast programmatischer Weise den spannungsreichen terminologischen und davon abzuleitenden wissenschaftsdisziplinären Unterschied zwischen dem Englischen und Deutschen,

> dass es in den Cultural Studies vorrangig um die Abschaffung des elitären Begriffs von Hochkultur und einen neuen Zugang zur Popkultur, sowie um eine Neuordnung des literarischen Kanons geht, an dem soziale und kulturelle Minderheiten verstärkte Rechte der Teilhabe einklagen. Die Cultural Studies verstehen Kultur als einen Kampfplatz der Wertungen, Umwertungen und Identitätspolitik, auf dem sie selbst agieren. Demgegenüber bleibt für die Kulturwissenschaften Kultur primär ein Forschungsgegenstand. Ihr primäres Anliegen ist es, diesen Forschungsgegenstand zu kontextualisieren, d.h. die kanonisierten (und damit automatisch entkontextualisierten) Texte und Artefakte in jene größeren kulturellen Zusammenhänge zurückzubetten, in denen sie entstanden sind. [...] Der wichtigste Unterschied zwischen Cultural Studies und Kulturwissenschaften besteht wohl darin, dass letztere ausschließlich in akademischen Institutionen verankert sind, während erstere gleichzeitig Teil einer sozialen Bewegung und kulturellen Praxis sind. (Assmann 2006: 25)[3]

In der Beschäftigung mit *popular culture* als Gegenstand kommt der soeben formulierte Unterschied besonders klar zum Ausdruck.

---

[3] Die englische Fassung von 2012 trägt den Titel *Introduction to Cultural Studies*. In der zitierten Passage verwendet Assmann jedoch den deutschen Begriff „Kulturwissenschaften" (cf. Assmann 2012: 27-28).

Popular culture wird in der deutschen Tradition zum Gegenstand wissenschaftlicher Untersuchung, während sie in der britischen Tradition darüber hinaus zugleich Gegenstand der Untersuchung wie Grund eines (politischen) Engagements ist, das die Hochkultur nivellieren will, um die *popular culture* in emanzipatorischer Absicht auf die gleiche Stufe zu stellen. Ästhetische Ansätze finden sich in diesem Zusammenhang, so Hans-Otto Hügel (2003: 16) zu Recht, eher selten.

Für Deutschland und den deutschsprachigen Raum lässt sich die Schwierigkeit einer einfachen Übertragung von „popular culture" in wissenschaftsdisziplinärer Sicht nicht zuletzt aus der (mangelnden) Übertragbarkeit der Begriffe erklären, die auch – vor allem in den letzten 50 Jahren – mit der Verschiebung des Terminus im Englischen sowie seiner Hochkonjunktur als zentralem Terminus der Cultural Studies zusammenhängen (cf. Hecken 2009: 58-59). Dass „popular culture" mittlerweile in maßgeblichen deutschsprachigen Publikationen mit „populäre Kultur", „Populärkultur" oder abgekürzt „Popkultur" übersetzt wird, zeigt, dass der Begriff in Deutschland Fuß gefasst hat. Belege dafür sind etwa das von Hans-Otto Hügel herausgegebene *Handbuch Populäre Kultur* (2003), Bücher von Thomas Hecken mit Titeln wie *Populäre Kultur* (2006), *Theorien der Populärkultur* (2007a) oder der soziologische Band *Unterhaltungswissenschaft: Populärkultur im Diskurs der Cultural Studies* (2008). Immer wieder jedoch wird auch, vor allem von Hecken und Hügel aber auch von Maase (1997), auf die Begriffsgeschichte eingegangen, die eine einfache Übersetzung wenig sinnvoll erscheinen lässt. Dies hängt mit „Volk" als einer Übertragungsmöglichkeit von „popular" zusammen, um die es im Folgenden gehen wird.

Hat die Verwendung von „populär" als Übertragung von „popular" im Deutschen heutzutage Konjunktur, so kann ähnliches von dem verwandten Terminus „Volk" und seinen Derivaten nicht gesagt werden. So zeigt sich ein wesentlicher Unterschied zwischen dem Englischen und dem Deutschen in der deutlich prominenteren – und zugleich problematischeren – Verwendung des Substantivs „Volk" und seiner Derivate, die spätestens mit dem Idealismus von der Wende des 18. zum 19. Jahrhundert durch Johann Gottfried

Herder einsetzt. Zwar ist im Englischen ebenfalls das germanische „folk" gebräuchlich, ohne dass jedoch eine dem Deutschen vergleichbare zwiespältige Entwicklung zu beobachten ist.[4] Durch die weite Verwendung von „Volk" gibt es im Deutschen für die *popular culture* demnach zwei gängige Termini: den aus dem Lateinischen stammenden Begriff „populär" und das aus dem Germanischen abgeleitete „Volk". Dabei ist die Übersetzung von „popular culture" mit „Volkskultur" zumindest dann keineswegs von der Hand zu weisen, wenn sie auf den deutschen Idealismus, insbesondere eben auf Herder, zurückgeführt wird, dem „Volk" als Abgrenzungsbegriff zu „Pöbel" dient (cf. Hecken 2007b: 199). Mit dem Aufkommen der industriellen Revolution in Deutschland und den damit verbundenen großen sozialen und regionalen Verschiebungen vor allem ab dem späten 19. und frühen 20. Jahrhundert wird eine stabil und homogen gedachte Volkskultur zunehmend als Gegenbegriff zur Verstädterung, zur Entwicklung zur Massengesellschaft und zur Instabilität der zunehmenden materiellen wie geistigen Mobilität konstruiert. Zugleich wird dies im Deutschland des frühen 20. Jahrhunderts kulturpolitisch nationalistisch vereinnahmt, um schließlich von den Nationalsozialisten fortgeführt und rassistisch existentialisiert zu werden (cf. Göttsch 2003: 87). Eine Übersetzung von „popular culture" in „Volkskultur" ist nach dem Zweiten Weltkrieg damit äußerst problematisch. Hermann Pauls *Deutsches Wörterbuch* (1992: 998) zeigt das sehr weit gefasste, widersprüchliche und durch die Nazis kompromittierte Bedeutungsspektrum auf. Demnach reicht „Volk" von dem rein deskriptiven „Menschenmenge" in positiver wie negativer Konnotation (z.B. „Pöbel") über „eine durch gemeinsame Kultur und Geschichte verbundene Menschengruppe", einschließlich der „Abgrenzung von den höheren Schichten", einem „aufwertend auf das Ursprüngliche, Bodenständige bezogen" – hier kommt die Herdersche Bedeutung zum Tragen – bis zum „auf das regierte Gemeinwesen bezogen" (ibid.: 998-999). Hinzu kommen von „Volk" abgeleitete Adjektive wie „volkseigen", „volkstümlich" und

---

[4] So verwenden etwa F.R. Leavis und Denys Thompson in der Beschreibung der „organic community" immer wieder das Wort „folk" (cf. Leavis & Thompson 1933: 1) als eine Vokabel mit historisch fast utopischen Implikationen, über die der deutsche Gebrauch weit hinausgeht.

„völkisch". Letzteres wird schon bei Fichte national gedacht und schließlich von den Nationalsozialisten mit einer deutlich rassistischen und antisemitischen Bedeutung versehen (ibid.: 999). Wie Paul schärft auch der *Duden* den Blick auf historische Probleme kaum und lässt etwa unter „3b) Gruppe, Sorte von Menschen" positive wie negative Wertungen zu (*Duden* 1999: 4338). Damit sind zwar die Möglichkeiten des Begriffs als Übersetzung von „popular" genannt; die Problematik der Möglichkeit des Deutschen, für „popular" sowohl „Volk" wie „populär" zu verwenden ist jedoch noch nicht hinreichend geklärt. Weitet man den Blick von den Wörterbucheintragungen in Richtung terminologische Implikationen in der Wissenschaft und einer damit verbundenen Disziplinenbildung, dann tritt die Problematik noch deutlicher zu Tage.

So historisiert Silke Göttsch „Volkskultur" in Bezug auf die Wissenschaft und bezeichnet sie „als eine spezifische Lebensform der Frühen Neuzeit" (2003: 83). Zugleich räumt sie ein, dass eine wissenschaftsterminologische Beschränkung keineswegs ausreicht, denn „Volkskultur" sei darüber hinaus auch eine „vor- und außerwissenschaftliche Vorstellung von der Lebenswelt, der Kultur bestimmter Bevölkerungsschichten" (ibid.). In einem solchen Zusammenhang werde „Volkskultur" zur Kompensationsvokabel für die Defizite der modernen Gesellschaft und darüber hinaus zu einer begrifflichen Ermöglichung der – rückwärts gewandten – Kompensation für eine Kulturtechnik, die keineswegs auf die Moderne beschränkt sei. Wichtig sind hier die Äußerungsformen der „Volkskultur" als konstruierte Ensembles von räumlichen, sozialen und temporalen Gegensätzen, bei denen die „Volkskultur" gegenüber der Kulturindustrie das stabile Andere, etwa in Gestalt von ‚ewigen' unberührten Landschaften, bäuerlichen trachtentragenden und Volksmusik spielenden Gemeinschaften, repräsentiert. Damit wird „Volkskultur" zwar nicht als Kandidatin für „popular culture" ausgeschlossen, sie verkümmert jedoch zu einer reduzierten Teilmenge. Zugleich wird in der Beschreibung von Göttsch das Problem dessen deutlich, der das Andere beschreibt. Denn es gelingt ihr nur unzureichend, spezifische Aspekte der deutschen Volkskultur neutral zu beschreiben, ohne sie zumindest indirekt in ihrem Wert als durch die Maschinerie der Kulturindustrie „folkloristisch" vermarktet zu mindern. In dieser Hinsicht scheint Göttschs Artikel typisch für eine akademisch-kritische Auseinandersetzung mit der beschriebenen Art von Volkskultur zu sein. Abgesehen von der Kontamination durch die Nationalsozialisten, kann oder will Göttsch nämlich ein wie auch immer zu fassendes widerständiges Potenzial einer so beschriebenen Volkskultur nicht erkennen. Die vor allem unter dem Einfluss der Cultural Studies eingeforderten Gramscischen subversiven Eigenschaften für *popular culture* können (oder sollen) hier nicht erbracht werden; somit kann die Nobilitierung von Volkskultur zur *popular culture* nicht erfolgen.

Der Begriff „Volk" hat weiterhin eine spezifisch deutsche disziplinäre Komponente, die sie deutlich von den britischen Cultural Studies abhebt. Mag „Volkskultur" durch die Nationalsozialisten zum reichlich beschädigten Terminus geworden sein, so stellte sich eine begriffliche Konsequenz in Bezug auf die Benennung der Disziplin, die sich mit *popular culture* beschäftigte, unmittelbar nach dem Zweiten Weltkrieg keineswegs ein. „Volkskunde" als Wissenschaft, die die „Wechselbeziehung zwischen Volk und Volkskultur" (Göttsch 2003: 83) untersucht, war lange nach dem Zweiten Weltkrieg bis in die jüngere Vergangenheit der gängige Begriff und ist immer noch Bestandteil des Namens vieler Institute.[5] Nicht nur die verstärkte Aufarbeitung des Erbes der Nazizeit seit den 1960er Jahren führte zu einer allmählichen (Namens-)Änderung der Disziplin, sondern auch das Aufkommen der Jugendkultur ab den späten 50er Jahren und die Studentenproteste am Ende der 60er Jahre hatten einen erheblichen Anteil. Besonders hervorzuheben ist dabei im deutschsprachigen Raum die Rolle von Hermann Bausinger, der zunächst in *Volkskultur in der technischen Welt* (1961) für eine neue Volkskunde unter alter Bezeichnung plädierte, ehe unter seiner Federführung in Tübingen das volkskundliche Institut in „Ludwig

---

[5] Die Benennungen einschlägiger Institute an deutschen Universitäten zeigen dies. Manche Namen wurden geändert, wie in Freiburg, wo die ehemalige Volkskunde seit dem Jahr 2003 unter „Europäische Ethnologie" firmiert. Andernorts wurde „Volkskunde" zum Teil erst jüngst ergänzt, wie an der Universität Bonn, wo eine Namensänderung in „Kulturanthropologie/Volkskunde" im Jahr 2006 erfolgte. Auch an anderen Universitäten kam es zu Namenserweiterungen wie in Jena, wo es ein Fach „Volkskunde/Kulturgeschichte" gibt.

Uhland Institut für empirische Kulturforschung" umbenannt wurde (cf. Herz 1992: 1-3).

Wichtig ist in diesem Zusammenhang der Unterschied zu den sich mit *popular culture* befassenden Cultural Studies britischer Prägung. Diese entwickelten sich als akademisch unterstützte Emanzipations- und Selbstermächtigungsbewegung aus der Überzeugung, dass – etwa bei Richard Hoggart – die Kultur der unteren Schichten der Bevölkerung durch das (kulturpolitische) Establishment nicht anerkannt wird. In Deutschland hingegen galt es hauptsächlich, das Erbe des Nationalsozialismus zu überwinden und eine damit häufig verbundene disziplinäre – oft germanistisch geprägte – Ausrichtung, die die terminologische Verwendung von „Volkskultur" bis heute schwierig macht. Zudem kommen durch die Hinwendung zu Phänomenen der – keineswegs klar definierten – Alltagswelt, durch die Beschäftigung mit der aufkommenden Jugendkultur und den Massenmedien und vor allem im Hinblick auf die Rolle der Unterhaltung seit den späten 50er und 60er Jahren neue Untersuchungsfelder hinzu, durch die sich „Populärkultur" auch als deutscher Terminus allmählich durchsetzt. In einem solchen Zusammenhang wäre, nicht zuletzt durch das idealistische Erbe, „Volkskultur" ein unbrauchbarer Begriff, impliziert dieser doch eine homogene Kultur, die gerade durch die Entprivilegierung des Hochkulturbegriffs und eine Pluralisierung der Forschungsgegenstände als obsolet angesehen wird.

Populärkultur, Popkultur?
Unter Berücksichtigung der obigen Ausführungen komme ich nun zur Diskussion von „populär". Über die zwei Bedeutungen „bekannt und beliebt", „leichtverständlich" und davon abgeleiteten Substantiven sowie dem Verb „popularisieren" hinaus vermeldet Paul nichts (cf. Paul 1992: 659-660). Im *Duden* wiederum ist die Anzahl der von „popularis" abzuleitenden Vokabeln bedeutend höher als im Falle von Volk. Sie reichen von „Popfan" als „begeisterter Anhänger der Popmusik" und „Popfarbe" über „Popliteratur" mit der Erklärung

Techniken und Elemente der Trivial- und Gebrauchsliteratur benutzende Richtung der modernen Literatur, die provozierend exzentrische, obszöne, unsinnige od. primitive, bes. auch der Konsumwelt entnommene Inhalte bevorzugt. (*Duden* 1999: 2969)

bis hin zu „Populismus" (ibid.: 2969-2970). Für das Lemma „Pop" ist der zitierte Eintrag bezeichnend, denn er beschreibt aus deutlich hochkultureller Perspektive Phänomene der *popular culture*. Literarische Entwicklungen der letzten zehn bis fünfzehn Jahre würden laut Wyss (2004: 21) häufig aus der Sicht eines hochkulturellen ‚intellektuellen Beobachters' als das – negativ bewertete – Andere begriffen und damit ihr Ziel verfehlen. Am Beispiel der Entwicklungen in der Literatur wird zudem deutlich, wie sehr sich in den letzten Jahren Elemente der *popular culture*, hier wäre nun tatsächlich von „Populärkultur" zu sprechen, mit denen der Hochkultur vermischt haben. Die meisten Eintragungen im *Duden* beziehen sich indes weniger auf die Literatur als auf die Musik – auch als Lebensform. Auch hier zeigen sich durchaus Spannungen, etwa darin, wie der Begriff „Volksmusik" vermieden und, etwas ungeschickt aber durchaus gerechtfertigt, „Folklore" verwendet wird, wie das Beispiel „Popmusik" als „[m]assenhaft verbreitete populäre Musik bzw. Unterhaltungsmusik unterschiedlicher Stilrichtungen (wie Schlager, Musical, Folklore, Funk u.a.)" zeigt (*Duden* 1999: 2969).

In Bezug auf „populär" nennt der *Duden* zwei Grundbedeutungen: Zum einen bedeutet es „beim Volk, bei der großen Masse, bei sehr vielen bekannt und beliebt, volkstümlich" oder „beim Volk, bei der Masse Anklang, Beifall und Zustimmung findend", zum anderen „gemeinverständlich, volksnah" (*Duden* 1999: 2969). Dass „Volk", „Masse", „sehr viele" präzisiert werden sollte, ist nicht Aufgabe des Wörterbuchs, sondern derer, die Teil einer „Populärkultur" sind oder derer, die sich mit „populärer Kultur", „Volkskultur", „Massenkultur" oder der „Kultur der sehr vielen" befassen. Als Gegenbegriff zu „Masse", den sehr vielen, bietet sich „Elite" und die Hochkultur als die der wenigen an. Zugleich ist damit wiederum die Bemerkung von Shiach relevant, die „popular" als Beschreibung des Anderen durch – hochkulturelle? – Intellektuelle fasste (Shiach 2005: 60). Kaspar Maase trifft in diesem Zusammenhang eine Unterscheidung in „populär" und „popular", wobei er den Begriff

„popular" für Phänomene verwendet, die er den Unterschichten zuordnet; „populär' meint breite Beliebtheit quer durch die Klassen" (Maase 1997: 23). Hier ist Maases historische Sichtweise zu berücksichtigen; schließlich schreibt er eine Geschichte der Massenkultur von der Mitte des 19. Jahrhundert bis ins Jahr 1970. Unter Berücksichtigung neuerer, vor allem medialer und theoretischer Entwicklungen, erhielt „populär" weitgehend den Vorrang gegenüber dem von Maase vorgeschlagenen „popular".

„Popkultur" als Kultur, die etwa die weiter oben genannten Phänomene und Praxen beinhaltet, wird doppelt verwendet: zum einen als Abkürzung für „popular culture". Zum anderen hat „Popkultur" eine spezifische Bedeutung als Epochenbegriff ab dem Ende der 50er Jahre (cf. Wyss 2004: 22). In diesem Sinn bezeichnet „Popkultur" eine ästhetische, zunächst aus den bildenden Künsten stammende und diese schon zu Beginn überschreitende Entwicklung, die vom Begriff der „PopArt" abgeleitet ist. Dazu schreibt Beat Wyss (ibid.: 31): „Popkunst erzielt zum ersten Mal ganz unangestrengt und auf der Höhe der technischen Verfahren eine Synthese zwischen den neuen Medien, künstlerischem Anspruch und allgemeiner Akzeptanz". In der Bildenden Kunst verbraucht sich die Provokation gegen die dominante Hochkultur der 60er Jahre allmählich, während in der Musik die Verflechtung mit den Massenmedien bis heute Bestand hat (cf. ibid.: 21). Wird in der Popkultur das „subversive Potential gegen die etablierte Kultur und ihre Vertreter gerichtet" (Grasskamp 2004: 41-42), so ist dies keineswegs klassenspezifisch oder sozial determiniert zu sehen und steht in Spannung zur Theorie der *popular culture* à la Cultural Studies. Eine terminologische Überlagerung der zur „pop culture" verkürzten *popular culture* trifft auf das Englische ebenso zu wie auf das Deutsche. Aus Gründen der begrifflichen Trennschärfe sollte demzufolge eher von „populärer Kultur" oder „Populärkultur" als von „Popkultur" die Rede sein, eine Begrifflichkeit, die sich weitgehend durchgesetzt hat, ohne dass „Popkultur" gänzlich verschwunden wäre.

Zusammenfassend lässt sich die Übersetzungsfrage des Terminus „popular culture" vom Englischen ins Deutsche als Kulturkontaktproblem fassen. Schon die Geschichte im Englischen kennzeichnet den Begriff als vielschichtig, zum Teil umstritten und politisch durchaus umkämpft. Diese Vielschichtigkeit tritt vor allem im Zuge der Entwicklung der Cultural Studies seit den 60er Jahren zu Tage, die die *popular culture* zum einen positiv gegen eine Hochkultur, die sie als hegemonial bekämpfen, absetzen, und zum anderen die *popular culture* in Auseinandersetzung mit der Massenkultur und Analysen der Kritischen Theorie zwar kritisch aber keineswegs negativ als Untersuchungsgegenstand wahrzunehmen beginnen. Insofern ist die Geschichte des Terminus als ‚innerenglischer' Kulturkontakt zu begreifen. Zum englisch-deutschen Kulturkontakt wird die Übersetzung dadurch, dass die Cultural Studies mitsamt ihrer Begrifflichkeit als erfolgreiches Modell auch in Deutschland rezipiert werden, darunter an zentraler Stelle *popular culture*. Produktive Reibungen entstehen, indem diese Entwicklung auf eine eigenständige deutsche Terminologie trifft, die neben „populär" auch mit „Volk" operiert, und die ihrerseits auf eine reiche, keineswegs unumstrittene Geschichte zurückblickt. Zur Terminologie kommt eine damit verbundene akademisch-disziplinäre Tradition von Kulturwissenschaften und Volkskunde, die bis in die jüngere Vergangenheit eine komplexe Auseinandersetzung mit dem Begriff „popular culture" führt. Erst in den letzten Jahren scheint es möglich, die inhaltlichen und disziplinären Implikationen von „Populärkultur" als Übersetzung von „popular culture" unter Beibehaltung der Differenzen gelassener zu betrachten. Dies als bereicherndes Phänomen eines – nicht nur akademischen – Kulturkontakts zu begreifen, wollten die gemachten Überlegungen helfen.

Quellen

Assmann, Aleida (2006), *Einführung in die Kulturwissenschaft. Grundbegriffe, Themen, Fragestellungen*, Berlin: Erich Schmidt Verlag.

Assmann, Aleida (2012), *Introduction to Cultural Studies. Topics, Concepts, Issues*, Berlin: Erich Schmidt Verlag.

Digitales Wörterbuch der Deutschen Sprache (n.d.), http://www.dwds.de/ (4. Oktober 2013).

Duden. Das große Wörterbuch der deutschen Sprache, 10 Bd. (1999), Mannheim: Dudenverlag.

Göttsch, Silke (2003), „Volkskultur", in Hans-Otto Hügel, Hrsg., *Handbuch Populäre Kultur*, Stuttgart: Metzler, 83-89.

Grasskamp, Walter (2004), „Einleitung. ‚Pop ist ekelig'", in Walter Grasskamp, Michaela Krützen & Stephan Schmitt, Hrsg., *Was ist Pop? Zehn Versuche*, Frankfurt/Main: Fischer, 9-19.

Hecken, Thomas (2006), *Populäre Kultur. Mit einem Anhang ‚Girl und Popkultur'*, Bochum: Posth.

Hecken, Thomas (2007a), *Theorien der Populärkultur. Dreißig Positionen von Schiller bis zu den Cultural Studies*, Bielefeld: Transcript.

Hecken, Thomas (2007b), „Der deutsche Begriff ‚populäre Kultur'", *Archiv für Begriffsgeschichte*, 49, 195-204.

Hecken, Thomas (2009), *Pop. Geschichte eines Konzepts 1955-2009*, Bielefeld: Transcript.

Herz, Dieter (1992), „Den Alltag dechiffrieren", http://www.zeit.de/1992/28/den-alltag-dechiffrieren/seite-1-3 (4. Oktober 2013).

Hügel, Hans-Otto (2003), „Einführung", in Hans-Otto Hügel, Hrsg., *Handbuch Populäre Kultur*, Stuttgart: Metzler, 1-22.

Leavis, Frank Raymond & Denys Thompson (1933), *Culture and Environment: The Training of Critical Awareness*, London: Chatto & Windus.

Maase, Kaspar (1997), *Grenzenloses Vergnügen. Der Aufstieg der Massenkultur 1850-1970*, Frankfurt/Main: Fischer.

Maase, Kaspar (2003), „Massenkultur", in Hans-Otto Hügel, Hrsg., *Handbuch Populäre Kultur*, Stuttgart: Metzler, 48-56.

Maase, Kaspar, Anke Heesen & Brigitta Schmidt-Lauber, Hrsg. (2011), *Das Recht der Gewöhnlichkeit. Über populäre Kultur,* Tübingen: Tübinger Vereinigung für Volkskunde.

Ostendorf, Berndt (2001), „Why Is American Popular Culture so Popular? A View from Europe", *Amerikastudien / American Studies*, 46/3, 339-366.

Paul, Hermann (1992), *Deutsches Wörterbuch*, Tübingen: Max Niemeyer.

Pickering, Michael (2010), „Editor's Introduction. Studying Popular Culture", in Michael Pickering, Hrsg., *Popular Culture. Vol.1. Historical Perspectives on Popular Culture*, London: Sage, xxi-xxvi.

Shiach, Morag (2005), „The Popular", in Raiford Guins & Omayra Zaragoza Cruz, Hrsg., *Popular Culture. A Reader*, London: Sage, 55-63.

Strehle, Samuel & Sacha Szabo, Hrsg. (2008), *Unterhaltungswissenschaft. Populärkultur im Diskurs der Cultural Studies*, Marburg: Tectum.

Wyss, Beat (2004), „Pop zwischen Regionalismus und Globalität", in Walter Grasskamp, Michaela Krützen & Stephan Schmitt, Hrsg., *Was ist Pop? Zehn Versuche*, Frankfurt/Main: Fischer, 21-41.

Anne Koenen (Leipzig)*
Dachshund Revisited, or: Excesses of Consumerism

To Ronja (and Thommie and Annie and Lisa)

When did you last see a poodle or a dachshund in the streets and parks of Leipzig? Among your family and friends, who, when deciding to include a pet in the family, goes for a poodle or a dachshund?

I have to confess that when I first met Jochen twenty years ago (I was not yet an animal lover back then) and learnt of his love for his dachshund, I was impressed that he had obviously not given in to the reigning opinion of academic circles, which associated dachshunds with a well-ordered, conservative, even bourgeois life. Not chic at all. The only personal memory I myself had of that breed of dog was of a dachshund who had been the darling of an ex-boyfriend's parents and who obsessively cared for my shins whenever possible. Hearing Jochen talk about his pet made me utterly forget the breed, and the individual dog emerged: Ronja.

Since then, I've definitely changed into an animal lover (my poison, so to speak, is cats), and – co-incidentally – have met more dachshunds, and have joined Jochen in his affection for that breed (one teckel in France, Thommie, does not really count for this German story because in the French countryside, dachshunds are not out, but decidedly in; and, sadly, since writing the first version of this tribute to Jochen and Ronja, Thommie has died – thus breaking his

---

* Anne Koenen is professor of American Literature at Leipzig University. She was president of the German Association for American Studies from 1999-2002. Her research has focused on African American literature, popular culture, and the fantastic, and her publications include monographs on Black women's literature, the fantastic in women's literature, as well as an interview with Toni Morrison and numerous articles. Her current research project is in the context of animal studies, on zoo architecture as focalisation of a culture's attitudes towards animals.

owner's heart). One dachshund story got me thinking. Friends of mine who had mourned the death of their sheep-dog went to the local animal shelter to look for and maybe adopt another dog (one! if at all). They left the shelter with two dogs, the sisters Anna and Lisa, mini-dachshunds whom they had immediately fallen in love with. Wherever these friends have gone with their mini-dachshunds, people are beside themselves with delight, the minis look/ed excessively cute, and they have a charming disposition. I can testify to that; once both of them squirmed on my lap, trying to lick my face while enthusiastically wagging their tails; I was utterly in bliss. Also, in addition to cuteness, the mini-dachshunds are convenient in logistical terms (they easily fit into bags, for example). In the animal shelter as well, everybody who saw them had been enthusiastic.

And yet: these two cuties (still puppies in the beginning) had lingered in the shelter for more than half a year because none of the people who found them adorable felt that they were ideal dogs for them; again and again, they were not picked to leave the shelter and join a family. Why? Well, dachshunds are not in fashion, and much as we'd like to think that people choose their pets according to criteria like mutual attraction and suitability (like Jochen, obviously), the reality is less appealing. People select dogs according to socio-cultural stereotypes/norms rather than individual standards. Animal shelters regularly complain that black dogs and black cats will have to stay longer (or forever) than animals with lighter fur. People have a prejudice against dark animals (for somebody who's spent decades researching racism, this rejection of blackness is utterly disturbing). Dogs have become fashion items or even fads. If a movie stars Dalmatians, that's the breed many people want to own then.

Research in consumerism, for example by Jochen, has convincingly suggested that we use consumption to establish identity.[1] From choosing outfits and listening to music to selecting food and buying

---

[1] For example see Joachim Schwend & Dietmar Böhnke, eds. (2004), "Consumption and Consumer Cultures", *Journal for the Study of British Cultures*, 11/2.

a car, we are not (only) driven by what orthodox left-wing theorists like Adorno would acknowledge as real needs, but by the desire to send messages about ourselves, actually, to be that construction. This, of course, results, as other research has suggested, in a paradox: a troubling conformity coexisting with an intense need to signal one's individuality. Amusing (or irritating, depending on one's perspective) evidence are the annual statistics about names that parents choose for their newborns. There are waves of unusual names – people who back in the seventies would have felt psychologically challenged if they had been christened Marie or Sophie now insist on naming their newborn girl Marie or Sophie –, waves that of course are impacted by class (the lower classes tend to copy media celebrities – remember Kevin? –, the higher classes yearn to demonstrate their superior taste by resorting to tradition etc.), as Bourdieu has convincingly argued. Needless to say, the individual at the time of choosing is utterly convinced of his/her 'authentic' taste, which they deem to be utterly individualistic. Just think of all those people who chose their bathroom tiles in the 1980s: remember these Mexican-art-inspired tiles with patterns in earthy colors with orange-turquoise? They did find them beautiful, and nobody could have talked them out of it. When we look at older photographs of ourselves (preferably, for us in Jochen's age bracket: pictures from the 1970s), we are embarrassed by the obvious lack of taste and the obvious slavish adherence to fashion, but at the time we thought we were dressing smartly, and that these neon colors were not just beautiful, but anti-establishment as well (and flattering).

Yet the faddish relationship to the construction of identity (more orthodox leftists talk about consumer fetishes and commodification) does not stop here, with things and signs, but – unfortunately – includes living beings as well. I do not want to go into the selection of a mate or human love object here – although the sociological observation that men choose down, while women choose up suggests that supposedly real love indeed follows clear patterns of self-interest and socio-cultural stereotypes – how many male mail-carriers you know are married with women thirty years their junior? How many women you know have a relationship with a man who is significantly shorter? What I am interested in is an area where faddish selection is less frightening than selecting a trendy lover, but frightening enough: selecting a trendy pet.

We've known the symptoms for some time. Suddenly, it seemed, there was not a single poodle or dachshund in all of Leipzig, while wave after wave of other breeds populated the parks and pooped on the sidewalks: Labrador and Golden retrievers, then beagles, then King Charles spaniels and sheepdogs. Never mind that people in the city usually don't have sheep, never mind that summers in the era of global warming get uncomfortably sweltering even for people, let alone huskies in Leipzig: people must have a sheep-dog, they must have a husky. They don't want to be associated with being straight (dachshund), or effeminate and stilted (poodle), they'd rather come across as adventurous (Alaskan trail!) and invest in the elaborate and communicative training of a different species (that sheep-dog will recognize twenty commands!). At the same time, the media are full of reports about sick puppies (and worried and broke owners), puppies that have become the merchandise of criminal animal-traders who see pets only as a source of profit (other animals, like pigs and chickens, have suffered that fate for quite some time). So, if beagles are in demand, they'll be bred in large numbers, regardless of health concerns, and be sold in markets; there was a mini scandal in Germany when, a year ago, a store that specializes in pet accessories actually began to sell puppies and kittens and display them for window shoppers; non-mammals like lizards and birds have already been sold in stores for a long time.

The rules of fashion apply also to the role of the avant-garde. If you want to be ahead of the cohort, it becomes a challenge (and mandatory) to identify the right moment when retrievers are on the way out and beagles on the way in, when 'Marie' is on the way out and 'Mia' is on the way in. Be the first in your peer group to re-introduce the poodle! But only if the moment is right, only if your choice is interpreted as a gesture of self-assertion and flagrant violation of conformity, and cannot (not ever!) be misconstrued as not being hip (if 'hip' is still the word). I myself have fantasized about stunning friends (and, alas, my cats) by adopting a poodle, who – by the way – belongs to one of the most intelligent, sociable and least allergenic breeds (they don't shed). The poodle is more of a challenge than the dachshund, because there are still quite a few dachshund lovers in the country, and dachshunds have never disappeared from the bestseller list of most frequent/popular breeds in Germany. The poodle, by comparison, has become invisible, maybe also a victim of gendered stereotypes and discrimination; just remember the Jacob sisters and their poodles, and you know what I mean. They (poodles, but the same applies to the sisters) seem to project an aura of pink perm, a stilted artificiality that is at odds with the Zeitgeist.

Observations on the objectification of pets are far from original; animal shelters and experts regularly (i.e. always before Christmas) warn of getting a pet on a whim or impulse, of checking which breed will fit the owners' needs and life-style (for example, I myself rarely follow the Alaskan trail nor do I corral sheep). The consequences of people not listening to such advice are blatant in animal shelters, where rejected animals end, pets that did not fit the families' needs or that turned out to be more demanding (of time, attention, love, money, space) than initially expected.

Let me get moral in concluding: We need to choose our animal companions on a more solid basis than fashion and fads. Here's to Jochen, and here's to Ronja! Cheers!

Kulturhund Ronja, das tierische *alter ego* von Joachim Schwend